Political Ideas in Eighteenth-Century Ireland

IN THIS SERIES

Hiram Morgan (ed.), *Political Ideology in Ireland, 1541-1641* (Four Courts Press, 1999)

Jane H. Ohlmeyer (ed.), *Political Thought in Seventeenth-Century Ireland* (Cambridge University Press, 2000)

S.J. Connolly (ed.), *Political Ideas in Eighteenth-Century Ireland* (Four Courts Press, 2000)

Political Ideas in Eighteenth-Century Ireland

S.J. Connolly
EDITOR

FOUR COURTS PRESS

Set in 10.5 on 12.5 point Bembo for
FOUR COURTS PRESS LTD
Fumbally Lane, Dublin 8, Ireland
e-mail: info@four-courts-press.ie
and in North America
FOUR COURTS PRESS
c/o ISBS, 5804 N.E. Hassalo Street, Portland, OR 97213.

© Four Courts Press and the various authors 2000

A catalogue record for this title
is available from the British Library.

ISBN 1–85182–556–8

All rights reserved. No part of this publication may be reproduced, stored in or introduced into a retrieval system, or transmitted, in any form or by any means (electronic, mechanical, photocopying, recording or otherwise), without the prior written permission of both the copyright owner and the publisher of this book.

Printed in England
by MPG Books, Bodmin, Cornwall

Contents

Preface 7

Abbreviations 9

S.J. Connolly
1 Introduction: varieties of Irish political thought 11

S.J Connolly
2 The Glorious Revolution in Irish Protestant political thinking 27

Jacqueline Hill
3 Corporatist ideology and practice in Ireland, 1660-1800 64

Robert Mahony
4 Protestant dependence and consumption in Swift's Irish writings 83

Patrick Kelly
5 The politics of political economy in mid-eighteenth-century Ireland 105

S.J. Connolly
6 Precedent and principle: the patriots and their critics 130

Ian McBride
7 The harp without the crown: nationalism and republicanism in the 1790s 159

James Kelly
8 Conservative Protestant political thought in late eighteenth-century Ireland 185

J.G.A. Pocock
9 Protestant Ireland: the view from a distance 221

Notes on contributors 231

Index 233

Preface

The essays in this volume are based on the papers delivered at a series of seminars held at the Folger Institute, Washington D.C., in May-June 1998, under the auspices of the Centre for the History of British Political Thought. Two previous sets of seminars had dealt with Irish political thought in earlier periods; these are being published in Hiram Morgan (ed.), *Political Ideology in Ireland, 1541–1641* (Dublin 1999) and Jane H. Ohlmeyer (ed.), *Political Thought in Seventeenth-Century Ireland* (Cambridge 2000). The rationale for thus extending the concerns of the Centre to include Ireland, and some of the problems this might be seen to involve, are discussed in Professor Pocock's paper below.

Thanks are due to Professor John Pocock, who first suggested the project; to the Folger Institute and to its executive director, Kathleen Lynch, for commissioning and supporting the seminar series; and to Dr Peter Smyth and Ms Janet McIver of the Northern Ireland Bureau in Washington, and Mr Michael Moloney of the Irish Embassy, for their hospitality during the proceedings. I should also like to thank Ms Kelleen Zubick of the Folger, who provided such admirable administrative support throughout. The attendance at the seminar of Dr James Kelly and Dr Patrick Kelly was made possible by a grant from the Cultural Relations Committee of the Department of Foreign Affairs, Dublin.

An essential contribution to the success of the seminar was made by the participants, who subjected every paper to friendly but searching scrutiny during our twice weekly sessions. They were

> Frank T. Boyle, Fordham University; Scott Cummings, Boston College; Christopher Fox, Notre Dame; David Green, Catholic University; Sean Moore, Duke University; Leigh Partington, Emory University; James Patterson, Fordham University; Hans Pawlisch, Pentagon; Linda Levy Peck, George Washington University; James Smyth, Notre Dame; and Iain Valentine, George Washington University.

All of the contributors benefitted greatly from their perceptive, constructive and, where necessary, sceptical criticism.

S.J. Connolly
January 2000

Abbreviations

The following abbreviations have been used throughout:

BL	British Library
HMC	Historical Manuscripts Commission
NLI	National Library of Ireland
PRONI	Public Record Office of Northern Ireland
PRO(L)	Public Record Office, London
Swift Corr.	*The Correspondence of Jonathan Swift*, ed. Harold Williams (Oxford, 1963-5)
Swift, *Prose Works*	*The Prose Works of Jonathan Swift*, ed. Herbert Davis (Oxford, 1939-68)
TCD	Trinity College, Dublin

Introduction: varieties of Irish political thought

S.J. CONNOLLY

I

'... there were in Ireland a number of people endowed with vigorous and ingenious minds, and their views on social and political topics are not devoid of interest.'[1] In these modest terms R.B. McDowell, writing in 1944, introduced what was to remain for almost fifty years the only book-length study of eighteenth-century Irish political thought. His assessment, particularly for a first book by a young academic, was remarkably low key. Yet his caution was, at the time, understandable. Eighteenth-century Ireland produced a varied and extensive political literature. Much of this, however, was rooted in specific Irish controversies, with little theoretical originality or depth. Of the two writers who might be regarded as leading candidates for a canon of classic authors, one, Jonathan Swift, specialized in polemic and satire rather than theoretical analysis; the other, Edmund Burke, was for long discussed as writing within a British rather than an Irish context.

Half a century later a great deal has changed. An increased concern with context as well as content has meant that Burke, as well as other authors such as John Toland and Francis Hutcheson, have been reassessed with a new regard for their Irish background.[2] More generally, discussion of political thought has

---

1 R.B. McDowell, *Irish Public Opinion 1750-1800* (London 1944), p. 10. The next book to deal specifically with eighteenth-century Irish political writing was Neil Longley York, *Neither Kingdom nor Colony: The Irish Quest for Constitutional Rights 1698-1800* (Washington D.C. 1994). 2 The overriding influence of Burke's Irish background on every aspect of his thought provides the central theme of C.C. O'Brien, *The Great Melody: A Thematic Biography and Commented Anthology of Edmund Burke* (London 1992). The alternative view, that Burke was a metropolitan author whose concern with Ireland faded once he had moved to England, is trenchantly restated by R.B. McDowell in David Dickson, Daire Keogh and Kevin Whelan (eds), *The United Irishmen: Republicanism, Radicalism and Rebellion* (Dublin 1993). For Toland see Philip McGuinness, 'John Toland and eighteenth-century Irish republicanism', *Irish Studies Review*, 19 (1997); Philip McGuinness, Alan Harrison and Richard Kearney (eds), *John Toland's Christianity Not Mysterious* (Dublin 1997). For Hutcheson see Ian McBride, 'The school of virtue: Francis Hutcheson, Irish Presbyterianism and the Scottish Enlightenment' in D.G. Boyce, Robert Eccleshall and Vincent Geoghegan (eds), *Political Thought in Ireland since the Seventeenth Century* (London 1993).

expanded from the examination of a canon of outstanding thinkers to a broader concern with the symbols, languages and conceptual frameworks through which politics was discussed. Within this wider context, Irish political thought in the eighteenth century takes on a new potential interest. This is all the more so given the growing concern in recent years with the study of political and cultural relationships in the British Atlantic world as a whole. In this perspective, England, Scotland, Ireland and North America appear as separate but closely related in terms of both political structures and ideological heritage; to study Irish political writing is to examine the development and character in that particular theatre of ideas and debates current in all parts of the first British empire. Indeed it could be argued that in Ireland political doctrines central to the British Atlantic world as a whole were subjected to a series of particularly revealing tests, as fundamental principles of authority and legitimacy had to be applied to the anomalous case of a separate but dependent kingdom, and as cherished notions of civil liberty and consent had to be upheld in a society in which religious disabilities barred a majority rather than just a small minority from public life. There are also direct influences – for example, the role of Molyneux and Hutcheson in the American colonies – that assume a new importance in this context.

The problems and possibilities thus becoming visible provide the background to the present volume. The essays it contains look in detail at selected aspects of the political thought of the period: the immediate and long-term influence of the Revolution of 1688, the economic and constitutional debates of the 1720s and 1730s, the defence of sectional and corporate liberties, the recurring motifs of patriot and anti-patriot writing, and the emergence in the last decades of the century of new or redefined radical and conservative ideologies. The present chapter, by way of introduction, offers a brief overview of some of the main traditions of political thinking that can be detected in eighteenth-century Ireland, and of the influences that helped to shape them.

II

In 1769 an anonymous author addressed a public letter to William Fitzgerald, marquis of Kildare and heir to the dukedom of Leinster. The ostensible aim was to instruct the young nobleman, descendant of 'champions of liberty and true patriotism', in the duties of his new role as the recently elected member of parliament for the prestigious open constituency of Dublin. Fitzgerald's first task, it was suggested, would be to prepare himself for public life by a course of suitable reading. As well as acquiring a knowledge of history, 'which is the study of mankind', the young nobleman would have to work through the original sources from which his country's laws were derived: 'the civil law of the

Romans which (we may say) is the law of the world; the law of nature and nations, and the feudal law'. To this end he was advised to read a range of works: Justinian's Institutes and Cicero's Offices, Grotius, Pufendorf, Montesquieu and Burlamaqui, as well as leading treatises on feudal law and tenures and the work of a range of current authors on trade and commerce. He was also to study a treatise on the workings of parliament, and the journals of the House of Commons itself.[3]

All this represented a formidable assignment for the young nobleman. Almost certainly what was intended was the expression of an ideal rather than a realistic prescription. Yet even taken on this basis the recommendations remain of interest for the light they throw on the political culture of mid-eighteenth-century Ireland. In particular they reveal two things: the elevated self-image of that culture, and the diversity of influences that went into its making. The day-to-day political affairs of Hanoverian Ireland, it has long been recognized, revolved around the pursuit of patronage and influence, and the exercise and defence of privilege. But there was also another level at which public life was conceived of as defined and governed by fundamental principles. These principles, moreover, were seen as part of a complex heritage, in which elements from the classical world and the medieval past combined with the work of more recent thinkers and writers.

One feature of the young Kildare's imagined reading list that should be particularly emphasized is its European character. It is true that one of the authors recommended for the apprentice statesman's instruction was the Baron de Montesquieu (1689-1755), whose most celebrated work, *De l'Esprit des Lois* (1748), took as its model of what government should be an idealized version of the constitution of Hanoverian Britain. However the other three non-classical authors mentioned, the Dutch Hugo Grotius (1583-1645), the German Samuel von Pufendorf (1632-94) and the Swiss Jean-Jacques Burlamaqui (1694-1748), were all part of a much broader European tradition of political writing, whose concern was not with any particular set of political institutions but with a wider concept of natural law, seen as applying both to the conduct of individual governments and to international relations. Nor was their inclusion a personal enthusiasm or affectation of the anonymous pamphleteer. The authors he cited were in fact standard authorities in Irish political writing. William King, in his apologia for the Revolution in 1691, cited Grotius on arbitrary government. So too did William Molyneux, in his defence of Irish parliamentary rights in 1698. Robert Molesworth, speaking in 1720 against the claim of the British parliament to legislate for Ireland, cited Grotius and Pufendorf. Francis Hutcheson edited one of Pufendorf's texts. Much later in the century William Steel

---

[3] *Advice to a Newly-Elected Member of Parliament: Inscribed to the Right Hon. William Fitzgerald, Commonly Called Marquess of Kildare* (Dublin 1769), pp. 3-6.

Dickson, the Ulster Presbyterian radical of the 1780s and 1790s, attributed his political awakening to his reading in Locke, Montesquieu and Pufendorf.[4]

The continued attention thus paid to leading Continental political theorists can be linked to a second striking feature of Irish political writing: the willingness of a variety of authors, in the first half of the century at least, to place their analysis of domestic political developments in a wider European context. Robert Molesworth, the Irish nobleman whose name was to become synonymous with the concept of the real Whig or commonwealthman, made his first major contribution to political writing with an account of the overthrow of representative institutions in Denmark.[5] His other best known work was his translation of a classic of sixteenth-century French constitutionalism, Francois Hottman's *Franco-Gallia*, intended by Molesworth to give what were now 'the only possessors of true liberty in the world' an account of 'the ancient free state of above three parts in four of all Europe'.[6] For Molesworth, as these comments indicate, the parliamentary monarchy of Great Britain and Ireland was a survival of the system of 'Gothic' liberty which had once been general throughout Europe, but had now almost everywhere been overthrown by the rise of absolute monarchy. Other authors took a similar view. Molyneux, for example, placed his defence of the legislative autonomy of the Irish parliament partly in the context of the 'noble Gothick constitution ... once so universal all over Europe' but now in decline.[7] For Henry Brooke, writing in 1745, the inhabitants of Great Britain and Ireland were 'now the only remaining heirs of liberty upon earth'.[8] Jonathan Swift, characteristically, took a more gloomy view still. 'We see the Gothic system of limited monarchy is extinguished in all the nations of Europe,' he told an English correspondent in 1737. 'It is utterly extirpated in this wretched kingdom, and yours must be the next.'[9]

This sense of constituting the last home of a retreating liberty was inevitably strongest in the early eighteenth century, when memories of what was interpreted as James II's attempt to make himself an absolute monarch on the French model were still sharp and when the long term prospects of the Revolution settlement remained unclear. After 1714, as the stability of the Hanoverian state seemed increasingly assured, and as Great Britain advanced to world power status, the obsession with threatened Gothic liberties gradually gave way to a

---

4 William King, *The State of the Protestants of Ireland under the Late King James's Government* (London 1692), p. 2; William Molyneux, *The Case of Ireland Stated*, ed. J.G. Simms (Dublin 1977), p. 119; HMC, *Various Collections*, vol. 8 (1913), p. 283; McBride, 'School of virtue', 79; McDowell, *Public Opinion*, p. 41. **5** Robert Molesworth, *An Account of Denmark as it was in the Year 1692* (London 1694). **6** *Franco-Gallia: or, An Account of the Ancient Free State of France and Most Other Parts of Europe before the Loss of their Liberties* (London 1711), pp. i-ii. **7** Molyneux, *Case of Ireland*, p. 132. See below, pp. 137. **8** Henry Brooke, *The Farmer's Letter to the Protestants of Ireland* (Cork 1745), Letter 6, p. 5. **9** Swift to William Pulteney, 8 March 1735 (*Swift Corr.* vol. 4, p. 303).

more confident image of the British constitution as a uniquely superior, even providential, set of arrangements. 'No scheme of human invention', Charles Lucas proclaimed in 1747, 'ever formed such a constitution as ours.'[10] Philip Skelton, two years earlier, contrasted the arbitrary government of France and Spain with conditions in Great Britain and Ireland, where 'the lowest and poorest subject ... is at the defiance of the king, so long as he conforms himself to the laws'.[11] By the second half of the century defensive pessimism had wholly given way to chauvinistic celebration. In visiting France, Henry Grattan was assured by a friend in 1771, 'you are conscious what every son of freedom is who has long resided in England – that he can meet no government so well adapted to the dignity of human nature, but indeed in every other its violation'. Even the Swiss enjoyed 'less political and less civil freedom'.[12] In this sense it can be suggested that the eighteenth century saw a significant narrowing in both the geographical and the conceptual basis of Irish political thinking, at least until the century's closing decades, when new influences from America and France began to make themselves felt.

The exalted notion of British constitutional liberties that thus came to be central to Irish as well as English thinking rested primarily on the doctrine of the ancient constitution: the image of an effective balance of monarchy, aristocracy and representative government, and of a body of legal principles, rules and procedures evolved through the practice of centuries, and preserved and perfected in recurrent struggles against the attempted encroachments of tyranny. Charles Lucas, for example, illustrated his notion of parliamentary rights with examples drawn from the reigns of Richard II, Henry VII and Henry VIII. Indeed he traced the tradition of liberty further back, to the Anglo-Saxon past, recalling how Alfred the Great had hanged 44 dishonest judges, and presenting judicial corruption as a 'badge of the Norman conquest'.[13] Henry Brooke, likewise, wrote of liberties preserved 'through a thousand dangers, diseases, recoveries, lapses, revolutions, the ambitions of princes, the struggles of patriots, the toils of the wise, and the blood of the valiant'.[14]

This centuries-old struggle for liberty had culminated in the Revolution of 1688. The centrality of the Revolution in the political culture of both English and Irish Protestants is often taken for granted. However, Patrick Kelly has already demonstrated that the work of the supposed spokesman of the Revolu-

---

10 Charles Lucas, *The Complaints of Dublin, Humbly Offered to his Excellency, William, Earl of Harrington* (no place, 1747), p. 3. 11 'The Chevalier's hopes' in *The Complete Works of the Late Rev. Philip Skelton*, ed. Robert Lynam (London 1824), vol. 5, pp. 306-7. 12 Henry Grattan jr., *Memoirs of the Life and Times of the Rt. Hon. Henry Grattan* (London 1839), vol. 1, pp. 249-50. 13 Charles Lucas, *A Letter to the Citizens of Dublin*, 3rd edn (Dublin 1749), p. 3; Lucas, *Complaints of Dublin*, pp. 18, 20-1; [Lucas], *A Second Letter to the Citizens of Dublin* (Dublin 1749), pp. 16, 18-25. 14 Brooke, *Farmer's Letter,* Letter 6, p. 5.

tion, John Locke, played relatively little part in Irish political debate before the last two decades of the eighteenth century.[15] In other respects too, it is argued below that the idea of the Revolution as a uniquely significant event, rather than as just the latest in a long series of struggles in defence of the ancient constitution, developed rather more gradually than is often assumed. Irish Protestants in the immediate aftermath of the Revolution welcomed their deliverance from Catholic ascendancy, but were for the most part cautious in their assessment of its constitutional significance. In particular Irish Tories, like their English counterparts, resisted all attempts to explain what had taken place in terms of constitutional innovation. Their Whig opponents, on the other hand, were anxious to define 'Revolution Principles' in a manner that would express their commitment to the future as well as the past defence of the Protestant succession; but they were also constrained by the fear of seeming to endorse resistance to legitimate authority. After 1714, with the succession issue resolved and Toryism in disarray, supporters of the now dominant Whig establishment felt more able to offer an explicit defence of the Revolution as having established a new and effective balance of power. Critics of that establishment, like Lucas, could likewise appeal from time to time to 1688 as a precedent for resistance to a government that sought to overstep the limits of its authority. But even at this point references back to the Revolution and its aftermath remained for the most part sporadic, unsystematic and often superficial. It was only in the last quarter of the eighteenth century, in fact, that members of the patriot opposition made appeals to an idealized version of 1688 a prominent feature of their rhetoric. In doing so they gave the event precisely that significance, as a precedent for future action, which the majority of their fathers and grandfathers, whether Whig or Tory, had been reluctant to contemplate. Not for the last time in Irish history an episode which in reality had been characterized by hedged bets and deep uncertainties was transformed in historical memory into a moment of heroic self-definition.[16]

The relevance of this celebration of British liberty, whether derived from the ancient constitution or from the Revolution, rested on the assumption that the principles concerned extended to Ireland as well as England. At the beginning of the eighteenth century Irish Protestants most frequently thought of themselves as Englishmen living in Ireland. Their claim to British constitutional liberties could thus be seen as a hereditary entitlement, carried with them to their new homeland. By the mid-eighteenth century this sense of a separate ethnic identity within Ireland was in decline. One consequence was that appeals

---

[15] Patrick Kelly, 'Perceptions of Locke in eighteenth-century Ireland', *Proceedings of the Royal Irish Academy*, Sect. C, 89 (1989), 17-35.   [16] See below, pp. 57-61. For a somewhat different chronology see below, p. 188, where James Kelly follows Gerard McCoy in seeing a sense of the particular importance of 1688 as gaining ground from the 1730s onwards.

to the inherited rights of Englishmen gave way to a looser claim to share in the liberties of other subjects of the British crown. However, there was also a wholly separate strand of argument, recurring throughout patriot writing from the 1690s to the 1780s, which focused instead on the specific liberties of the kingdom of Ireland. Henry II and his successors, it was claimed, had offered the people of Ireland, in exchange for their submission to the English crown, the same civil liberties as Englishmen, including the right to live under laws made by their own parliament. Medieval precedents were then ransacked and twisted to support the claim that these liberties had been consistently upheld from the twelfth to the seventeenth century.[17]

These different lines of argument were rarely developed, or their implications probed, in any depth. Molyneux, for example, offered what became the classic exposition of the constitutional bargain supposedly concluded between the English crown and the Gaelic chiefs of twelfth-century Ireland. But he also hedged his bets by claiming that the majority of the island's current inhabitants were in any case descendants of the English conquerors rather than of the Gaelic population of that time.[18] This general lack of precision leaves open the question of the ideas of national identity that informed Irish political argument. Traditionally the eighteenth century has been seen as the great age of Protestant patriotism, sometimes described, rather tendentiously, as 'colonial nationalism'.[19] More recent work, however, has cautioned against a teleological search through the varied political and constitutional conflicts of the late seventeenth and early eighteenth centuries for the origins of a clear cut patriot tradition. In particular James Smyth has emphasized the extent to which Irish Protestants in the 1690s and early 1700s based their political arguments primarily on a claim to the rights of Englishmen. This continuing reliance on an English identity was reflected in the apparent willingness of many to accept a legislative union with England, rather than the strengthening of an Irish parliament, as a means of achieving the goal of representative government. If the emphasis eventually shifted to the defence of Irish rights then this was, in Smyth's words, because Protestants had 'their Irishness thrust upon them' by a British government and public that remained indifferent to their appeals to common citizenship.[20] Patrick McNally, likewise, has argued against taking too much at face value contemporary accounts of a clearly defined conflict between 'English' and 'Irish' interests in early Hanoverian Ireland.[21]

17 See below, ch. 6. 18 See below, p. 137. 19 J.G. Simms, *Colonial Nationalism 1698-1776: Molyneux's 'The Case of Ireland ... Stated'* (Cork 1976); 'Introduction' to J.G. Simms, *War and Politics in Ireland 1649-1730*, ed. D.W. Hayton and Gerard O'Brien (London 1986), pp. xiii-xiv; W.E. Vaughan (ed.), *New History of Ireland*, vol. 4: *Eighteenth-Century Ireland 1691-1800* (Oxford 1986), ch. 5, 8. 20 James Smyth, '"Like amphibious animals": Irish Protestants, ancient Britons 1691-1707', *Historical Journal*, 36 (1993), 785-97; idem, 'Anglo-Irish unionist discourse c.1656-1707: from Harrington to Fletcher', *Bullán*, 2 (1995), 17-34. 21 See

If Smyth and McNally emphasize the limits of Protestant patriotism, two other accounts go further, to redefine its basic character. Joep Leerssen suggests that the growing concern with the defence of Irish constitutional rights evident from the 1690s should be compared, not with the nationalism of a later era, but with the endless tussles over local and sectional liberties that were generated by the multiple and overlapping jurisdictions characteristic of *ancien régime* Europe. In this interpretation the proper parallel for the politics of Molyneux, Swift or Grattan is to be found in such contemporary episodes as the struggles of the *parlements* of regional France to defend provincial customs and exemptions from the encroachments of the crown, or the efforts of Dutch patriots to preserve provincial autonomy against the pretensions of the house of Orange.[22] Jacqueline Hill, in a major study of Dublin politics and in a chapter in the present volume, argues forcefully for a recognition of the importance throughout the eighteenth century and beyond of what she defines as corporatism, a political language explicitly concerned with the defence of sectional and exclusive liberties within the framework of a society of hierarchy and privilege.[23] Such an analysis, among other things, makes it easier to understand what is otherwise one of the most puzzling aspects of Irish patriotism, the willingness of Protestants like Lucas to combine a passionate defence of Irish liberties with a determination to uphold the exclusion from any share in those liberties of the Catholic majority.

A further political language contributing to Irish political debate was that of civic humanism or classical republicanism. The significance of this tradition, originating in the city states of Renaissance Italy then carried forward and developed in seventeenth- and eighteenth-century England and subsequently in America, has long been a commonplace of the history of political ideas.[24] More recently its importance has been recognized by historians of eighteenth-century Ireland, for whom the concept of an Atlantic republican tradition provides both a longer term background to the sudden emergence of democratic republicanism in the 1790s, and a means of placing Ireland in a recognizable international context. Republicanism in this eighteenth-century sense was not necessarily incompatible with limited monarchy. It was concerned less with the promotion of any one form of government than with the values of active citizenship, civic virtue and opposition to tyranny. Its most notable Irish manifestation has been identified as the loose circle of 'real Whigs' or 'commonwealthmen' whose central figure was Molesworth and

---

below, pp. 131-2. **22** J. Th. Leerssen, 'Anglo-Irish patriotism in its European context: notes towards a reassessment', *Eighteenth-Century Ireland*, 3 (1988), 7-24. **23** J.R. Hill, *From Patriots to Unionists: Dublin Civic Politics and Irish Protestant Patriotism 1660-1840* (Oxford 1997). **24** The classic survey is J.G.A Pocock, *The Machiavellian Moment: Florentine Political Thought and the Atlantic Republican Tradition* (Princeton 1975).

whose most celebrated member, in retrospect at least, was the polymathic John Toland.[25]

Civic humanism, in Ireland as elsewhere, drew on a variety of sources. A comment by Lucas' most prolific critic, and an indirect reference by a patriot opponent of Archbishop Stone, suggest that for most people, at both ends of the political spectrum, the name of Machiavelli was primarily a term of abuse.[26] On the other hand Henry Maxwell, in 1704, commenced his argument in support of a union between Ireland and Great Britain in terms that seem directly to echo certain parts of the *Discourses*, citing the precedent of ancient Rome to discuss the ways in which conquered or annexed territories could be maintained without threatening the preservation of freedom in the conquering state itself.[27] Bishop Berkeley denouncing the corruption revealed by the South Sea Bubble scandal, also quoted Machiavelli, this time with acknowledgement.[28] More commonly, however, the republican tradition was approached through the more accessible work of its seventeenth-century English exponents. James Harrington, in particular, has been identified as a direct influence on Toland, who edited his writings, and also on Francis Hutcheson. Swift, wearing his old Whig rather than his Tory hat, boasted of his familiarity with the work of 'Colonel [Algernon] Sidney, and other dangerous authors'.[29] Conservative writers fixed gleefully on the apparent link between eighteenth-century radicalism and a past history of regicide and revolution. An attack on the Patriot Club of Antrim in 1756, for example, mockingly commended to them the examples of Lucius Brutus, 'who sacrificed his own sons for liberty', and of Andrew Marvell, before concluding with a reference to 'Cromwell's grim ghost'.[30]

The influence of the republican tradition can also be detected in the recurrence throughout the eighteenth century of a characteristic theme, the glorification of the armed citizen and the denigration of standing armies. Maxwell's argument for a union, already mentioned, depended partly on the proposition that an annexed territory that was not admitted to equal political rights could be maintained only by the maintenance of a permanent military establishment, which would inevitably become the instrument for subverting constitutional lib-

---

[25] Caroline Robbins, *The Eighteenth-Century Commonwealthman* (Cambridge, Mass. 1959). [26] Anthony Litten, *The Cork Surgeon's Antidote ... Number II* (Dublin 1749), p. 5; *A Few Words More of Advice to the Friends of Ireland on the Present Crisis* (Dublin 1755), p. 21. [27] [Henry Maxwell], *An Essay upon an Union of Ireland with England* (Dublin 1704), pp. 4-8. [28] Patrick Kelly, '"Industry and virtue versus luxury and corruption": Berkeley, Walpole and the South Sea Bubble crisis', *Eighteenth-Century Ireland*, 7 (1992), 57-74. [29] Swift, 'A Letter to Lord Viscount Molesworth' in *The Drapier's Letters and Other Works 1724-5*, ed. Herbert Davis (Oxford 1941), p. 86. For Swift's concept of himself as a 'real Whig' see James Downie, *Jonathan Swift, Political Writer* (London 1984), pp. 37-41, 259-60. [30] *Advice to the Patriot Club of the County of Antrim on the Present State of Affairs in Ireland* (Dublin 1756), p. 14.

erties in the home country. Molesworth, setting out the principles of a true whig in 1721, accepted that an army had to be maintained until the Hanoverian succession was secured; once this was achieved, however, 'no such thing as a mercenary soldier should subsist in England'.[31] Swift, likewise, saw standing armies as 'only servants hired by the master of the family for keeping his own children in slavery'.[32] These, of course, were general statements of principle, framed with an eye as much on English as on Irish debate. But the ideal of the citizen soldier also appeared in applied form in a specifically Irish context. Opposition spokesmen in the period between the Hanoverian accession and the American war sporadically attacked the failure of the government to maintain the Protestant militia.[33] Grattan, in praising the achievements of the Volunteers, made free use of the concepts of the citizen soldier and the people armed.[34] Recent studies have also identified the attempts of plebeian Protestants to reassert their exclusive right to bear arms, interpreted as a badge of full citizenship, as one cause of the sectarian violence that began in south Ulster from around 1784.[35]

Each of these traditions, British constitutionalism, corporatism and civic humanism, provides a connecting thread linking a variety of political debates, from the immediate post-Revolution period through to the conflicts of the 1790s. At the same time it is important to draw attention to discontinuity as well as continuity. The focus on specifically British liberties, as already mentioned, replaced an earlier, more outward looking perspective. The special status of 1688, and of its putative spokesman Locke, emerged as a clear theme only in the later decades of the century. Corporatism, likewise, does much to place the patriotism of early and mid-Hanoverian Ireland in context. But there are also new developments, in the last decades of the eighteenth century, that fit less comfortably into that framework. In particular there is the growing tendency of patriot spokesmen, falling into a conceptual trap of their own making, to frame their demands in terms of absolute sovereignty rather than of the mixed and overlapping jurisdictions characteristic of a corporatist regime.[36] There is also the willingness of some, though by no means all, Irish Protestants to link their political aspirations to an imaginative identification with the Gaelic past in ways that come much closer to the traditional notion of patriotism as an early phase in the development of a fully-fledged Irish nationalism.[37] In the case

---

31 Robert Molesworth, *Franco-Gallia, or an Account of the Ancient Free State of France and Most Other Parts of Europe Before the Loss of their Liberties*, 2nd edn (London 1721), p. xxv. **32** Swift to Pope, 10 Jan. 1721 (*Swift Corr.* vol. 2, p. 372). **33** Jim O'Donovan, 'The militia in Munster 1715-78' in Gerard O'Brien (ed.), *Parliament, Politics and People: Essays in Eighteenth-Century Irish History* (Dublin 1989), pp. 40-1. **34** *The Speeches of the Right Hon. Henry Grattan*, ed. Daniel Owen Madden (Dublin 1874), pp. 67-8, 73-4. **35** D.W. Miller, 'The Armagh Troubles 1784-95' in Samuel Clark and J.S. Donnelly (eds), *Irish Peasants: Violence and Political Unrest 1780-1914* (Manchester 1983). **36** Below, pp. 155-8. **37** Norman Vance, 'Celts, Carthaginians and

of civic humanism, likewise, we need to note a major change in the thrust of opposition politics in the second half of the eighteenth century, as calls for measures to reduce corruption in public life were supplanted by proposals to improve the mechanics of parliamentary elections, and a concern with the maintenance of constitutional checks and balances gave way to a more specific emphasis on the effective representation of the people.[38] All of these changes were accelerated, from the mid-1770s onwards, by the impact of the American and French revolutions, which provided opponents of the political order both with new ideas and with a new sense of what was politically possible.[39] Meanwhile, as James Kelly demonstrates in the final chapter below, the same combination of internal and external developments provoked an equally radical redefinition of conservative political principles.

III

So far our concern has been with the political thinking of the Anglican elite. To conclude, we must look briefly at the other two main ethnic and religious groups within Ireland.

Where Ulster Presbyterians are concerned the last twenty years or so have seen two major shifts in interpretation. The celebrated radicalism of Presbyterian Ulster in the era of the American and French revolutions, culminating in the rising of Antrim and Down in 1798, was traditionally linked to the influence of the Scottish Enlightenment. The same broad cultural and intellectual influences that produced the rise among Irish Presbyterians of a 'New Light' tradition of liberal theological speculation were also assumed to have contributed to a growing commitment to rational political reform, and to a new willingness to transcend traditional religious animosities by joining with Catholics in an attempt to create a secular democratic republic. This whole tradition of explanation was severely shaken in 1978, when David Miller demonstrated that there was in fact no correlation among Ulster Presbyterians between support for the United Irish movement and adherence to 'New Light' theology. Active Presbyterian radicals in the 1790s were in fact just as likely to belong to the 'Old Light' tradition and to interpret political events at home and abroad within a conservative theological framework, in which the fall of the French monarchy was seen less as a triumph for the values of secular rationality than as the overthrow of anti-Christ (in the form of Popish absolutism)

---

constitutions: Anglo-Irish literary relations 1780-1820', *Irish Historical Studies*, 22 (1981), 216-38. **38** James Kelly, 'Parliamentary reform in Irish politics 1760-90' in Dickson et al. (eds), *The United Irishmen*, pp. 74-5. **39** The relationship between the radicalism of the 1790s and earlier ideologies of opposition is a central theme of Ian McBride's paper below.

and as a signal to begin the construction of a covenanted society.[40] More recently, however, Ian McBride has partially rehabilitated the traditional view. While recognizing the complex sub-divisions of Ulster Presbyterian culture, and paying due attention to religious as well as secular elements, he has nevertheless argued that one distinctive strand in eighteenth-century Irish radical thought was indeed a creative fusion of Whig constitutional doctrine, Enlightenment philosophy, and a Presbyterian tradition of opposition to the pretensions of the confessional state.[41]

McBride's analysis, drawing on a sophisticated and nuanced vision of the interaction of ideas, culture and practical politics, firmly re-establishes the notion of a Presbyterian radical tradition. The origins of this tradition can be traced back to the forthright defence of the principles of the Revolution, combined with a vigorous critique of the claims of the established church, offered by a range of writers in the early eighteenth century. It continues in the work of slightly later figures such as James Arbuckle and John Smith, in the work of Hutcheson, and in the open support shown by many for the revolt of the American colonists. In the 1780s and 1790s it became a central force in the politics of Ireland as a whole, as Presbyterian Ulster provided the original and strongest power base first for the Volunteer movement and then for the United Irishmen. Having said all this, however, it might be useful to add two minor caveats. The first is the extent to which many of the central figures in this tradition were linked together, not just by ideological affinities, but by a network of personal and family connections, possibly further reinforced by a shared involvement in freemasonry. At times, in consequence, it becomes difficult to draw the line between 'Presbyterian radicalism' and the activities of a particular clique within the Presbyterian world.[42] The second is the number of key figures in this chain of influence and connection who made their careers, like Arbuckle, Smith, Hutcheson and Thomas Drennan, outside the tight, self-contained world of Presbyterian Ulster. The radical potential of the culture in which they had been brought up, in other words, seems often to have been most fully realized in conjunction with wider political and intellectual influences.

Catholic political writing in this period was by comparison limited, both thematically and in overall volume. Two texts which have been analyzed in

---

[40] D.W. Miller, 'Presbyterianism and "modernisation" in Ulster', *Past & Present*, 80 (1978), 66-90. [41] Ian McBride, *Scripture Politics: Ulster Presbyterianism and Irish Radicalism in the Late Eighteenth Century* (Oxford 1998); idem, 'William Drennan and the dissenting tradition' in Dickson et al. (eds), *The United Irishmen*; idem, 'The school of virtue'; idem, '"When Ulster joined Ireland": anti-popery, Presbyterian radicalism and Irish republicanism in the 1790s', *Past & Present*, 157 (1997), 63-93. See also Peter Tesch, 'Presbyterian radicalism' in Dickson et al. (eds), *The United Irishmen*. [42] This theme is developed in detail in A.T.Q. Stewart, *A Deeper Silence: The Hidden Roots of the United Irish Movement* (London 1993).

some detail are the anonymous 'A Light to the Blind', composed, apparently by a member of the Old English Plunkett family, in 1702-3 with additions up to 1714, and the history of Ireland published between 1758 and 1762 by the émigré priest James MacGeoghegan. Both remained firmly within the limits of traditional dynastic and theological assumptions. 'A Light to the Blind' offered a primarily religious interpretation of the events of 1688-91, identifying rebellion against lawful authority with Protestantism, and appealing to the Catholic powers of Europe to support the cause of the Stuarts.[43] MacGeoghegan provided a more clearly articulated theory of hereditary monarchical right, but combined this somewhat awkwardly with an Irish patriotism, leading him to lament the poor treatment Ireland has received under the Stuarts while continuing to assert their dynastic claim to the throne.[44] During the early and mid-eighteenth century the Catholic clergy and a section of the laity also engaged in an intense, divisive, but almost wholly inward-looking debate concerning the terms on which it might or might not be permissible to seek to improve their position under the Hanoverian dynasty by offering a declaration or oath of allegiance. What proved to be the insuperable obstacle was not, significantly, the necessity of renouncing the claim of the exiled Stuarts to the Irish and British thrones. Instead it was the inability of those involved to formulate a definition of the pope's temporal authority that would allay Protestant doubts about the capacity of a Catholic to be a loyal subject while at the same time being acceptable to theological opinion at home and on the Continent.[45]

The difficulty which even the more pragmatic Catholic authors had in moving beyond these traditional religious and political frames of reference is evident in the pamphlet on Catholic rights written in 1724 by the Dublin priest Cornelius Nary. Nary defended the refusal of Catholic priests to take the oath of abjuration, which declared that the Pretender had no right whatever to the thrones of Great Britain and Ireland. He was, however, willing to swear a full and binding oath of allegiance to George I, 'which the law of nature and the common practice of all nations allows me to take with a safe conscience to any prince who conquers me and the country of which I am a member'. The central argument, for submission to *de facto* authority, was one also advanced by some more conservative-minded Protestant defenders of the Revolution. But Nary's insistence on conquest, and his rider that such a conqueror was entitled to allegiance 'though he be never so great a tyrant or usurper, even to the tsar of Muscovy or the great Turk', undermined the conciliatory purpose of his

---

43 Patrick Kelly, '"A light to the blind": the voice of the dispossessed elite in the generation after the defeat at Limerick', *Irish Historical Studies*, 24 (1985), 431-62. **44** Vincent Geoghegan, 'A Jacobite History: The Abbé Geoghegan's *History of Ireland*', *Eighteenth-Century Ireland*, 6 (1991), 37-55. **45** Patrick Fagan, *Divided Loyalties: The Question of the Oath for Irish Catholics in the Eighteenth Century* (Dublin 1997).

pamphlet, and in so doing revealed his own continued reservations concerning the basis of Hanoverian rule.[46]

In the second half of the eighteenth century, with Jacobitism no longer a realistic political option, both clergy and laity became more willing to seek accommodation with the ruling dynasty, although the issue of allegiance was not finally laid to rest until 1778, when the provisions of a significant measure of Catholic relief were restricted to those who had taken an oath provided four years earlier. The most important Catholic political writers of this crucial period of transition, John Curry and Charles O'Conor, generally avoided discussion of abstract political issues. Curry concentrated on attempts to combat exaggerated Protestant accounts of the massacre of Protestant settlers during the initial stages of the rising of 1641. O'Conor is best remembered for his writings on early history, where he sought to establish pre-Christian Gaelic Ireland as conforming to the Enlightenment definition of a civilized, literate society. At the same time both authors, and especially O'Conor, have also been seen as having played an important part in recasting the Catholic case for a relaxation of the penal laws in the language of orthodox Whig constitutionalism.[47]

A final expression of a specifically Catholic political outlook is provided in the pastoral addresses and other statements, urging their hearers to remain loyal and obedient to government, which were issued by a number of bishops in response to the growth of popular disaffection and conspiracy during the 1790s. The majority of these, however, avoided any discussion of general political principles. Instead most bishops confined themselves to straightforward moral exhortation, emphasizing the religious duty of obedience to temporal authorities and the sinfulness of rebellion. A few added a reminder of the gratitude due for recent reversals of the penal laws, combined with dire warnings that disloyalty might provoke a return of religious persecution. The exception was William Coppinger, bishop of Cloyne and Ross, who added an explicit rejection of French-inspired egalitarianism, insisting instead on the necessity of hierarchy and inequality for the proper functioning of society. 'How can there be cultivation where there are no tillers? And where shall you find tillers if all become gentlemen?'[48]

A more substantial work of political reflection provoked by the developing crisis of the 1790s was the lengthy pastoral letter, *On the Duties of Christian*

---

[46] Cornelius Nary, 'The case of the Roman Catholics of Ireland, humbly represented to both houses of parliament 1724', in Hugh Reily, *The Impartial History of Ireland* (Limerick n.d.), p. 130. It is not clear whether Nary's pamphlet was actually published as a separate work. [47] The most recent survey is C.D.A. Leighton, *Catholicism in a Protestant Kingdom: A Study of the Irish Ancien Régime* (Dublin 1994). [48] P.F. Moran (ed.), *Spicilegium Ossoriense*, vol. 3 (Dublin 1884), pp. 591-2. For a fuller discussion see S.J. Connolly, *Priests and People in Pre-Famine Ireland 1780-1845* (Dublin 1982; repr. Dublin 2000), pp. 220-4.

Citizens, published in 1793 by John Thomas Troy, archbishop of Dublin. Troy wrote for two purposes: to counter the growing revolutionary movement with a firm statement of the duty of obedience to established government, but also to repudiate the recent accusations of Richard Woodward, Church of Ireland bishop of Cloyne, that Catholicism naturally favoured tyranny over freedom. His argument, in consequence, steered a careful middle course. On the one hand he cited Bossuet, the seventeenth-century French theorist of divine right, on the duty of submission even to infidel princes, supported by references to the behaviour of the Old Testament prophets, of Jesus, and of the early Christians under persecution.[49] At the same time he also insisted that rulers were subject to both divine and natural law, and presented examples of Catholics active in the cause of liberty in Renaissance Italy and in contemporary Switzerland. In addition Troy offered what was in effect a Catholicized version of the doctrine of the ancient constitution, in which the liberties defined by Alfred the Great and Edward the Confessor had been determinedly preserved throughout the middle ages in an England faithful to the Roman church, until they were subverted by the tyranny of Henry VIII and his successors.[50] This left open the crucial question of how one defined the point at which the duty to defend fundamental liberties took over from the obligation to uphold established authority. However, Troy consciously kept his argument at a practical level, rejecting theories of government as of interest only to 'the speculative reasoner in his closet', and offering instead an endorsement of the British constitution as a middle way between the extremes of anarchy and tyranny.[51] In this sense his pamphlet is of significance less as an original contribution to political argument than as confirmation of the extent to which Irish Catholicism had absorbed the conventional assumptions of British constitutional thought.

IV

The study of eighteenth-century Irish political ideas necessarily involves an examination of the influence and interaction of a range of traditions and influences, some of them old and some of recent development, some an integral part of the culture of the society, others operating as an external influence. It also involves a discussion both of continuity, the transmission of ideas and modes of argument from generation to generation, and of discontinuity, the sudden emergence, most notably in the 1790s, of radically new ways of thinking and responding. To do justice to this complexity it is necessary to look closely at formal political argument, examining the assumptions and principles on which

---

[49] J.T. Troy, *A Pastoral Instruction on the Duties of Christian Citizens*, 2nd edn (Dublin 1793), pp. 10-15. [50] Ibid., pp. 26-8. [51] Ibid., pp. 2-3, 123-4.

it rested, the lines of thought it followed, the conclusions it reached, its loose ends and evasions. At the same time the discussion of ideas can never be wholly divorced from the context in which they occurred: the structure of Irish and British government, with its subtle division of power between centre and periphery, the vested interests jostling for position and influence, the reassessment of received beliefs required or encouraged by rapid economic expansion and cultural change, the influences rippling outwards from the American and French revolutions. The authors of this volume are all concerned to demonstrate that ideas had a significance in the world of politics whose complexity and importance has not always been fully appreciated. None, however, sets out to study ideas in isolation. Instead their concern is with that most revealing and complex of all areas, the interaction between ideas and action, thought and experience.

The Glorious Revolution in Irish Protestant political thinking

S.J. CONNOLLY

I

The English Revolution of 1688 was a confused and hesitant affair. William, prince of Orange, landed on the south coast on 5 November 1688 with the declared object of forcing his father in law, James II, to summon a free parliament. By this means he could be sure of obtaining what was throughout his main aim, which was to ensure that James' three kingdoms did not become allies of France in the impending European war. James' decision in December to abandon his kingdom and take refuge in France, an unpredictable response in a man who had earlier demonstrated stolid courage in battle, made it possible and necessary to consider more far-reaching change in the government of the British state. But the course eventually adopted, the conferring of the crown on James' daughter, Mary, and her husband, William, as joint sovereigns, was by no means predetermined. One recent account suggests that what took place was in effect a bloodless coup, in which William's supporters exploited military, political and popular pressures to ensure that joint monarchy prevailed over such alternatives as a regency or the succession of Mary as her father's sole heir.[1] If so, however, it was a coup concealed behind a screen of deliberate ambiguity. The resolutions of the Convention that declared William and Mary to be joint monarchs were so phrased as to minimize the departure from the principles of hereditary monarchy. The restatement of constitutional principles that came to be known as the Bill of Rights, equally, was at best a partial resolution of the issues that twice in the seventeenth century had plunged all three of the Stuart kingdoms into civil war.[2]

These modern perspectives must be set against almost three centuries of mythology. It is true that the issues that had been evaded or fudged in the set-

---

[1] Robert Beddard, 'The unexpected Whig revolution of 1688' in idem (ed.), *The Revolution of 1688* (Oxford 1992). [2] For some of the issues see T.P. Slaughter, '"Abdicate" and "contract" in the glorious revolution', *Historical Journal*, 24 (1981), 323-37; John Miller, 'The glorious revolution: "contract" and "abdication" reconsidered', *Historical Journal*, 25 (1982), 541-55. For a balanced general discussion see W.A. Speck, *Reluctant Revolutionaries: Englishmen and the Revolution of 1688* (Oxford 1988), pp. 139-65.

tlement of 1688-9 continued for almost three decades to haunt the politics of all three kingdoms, providing the potentially explosive foundations of Britain's first age of party.[3] Within a short time thereafter, however, debate gave way to celebration. What near contemporaries had referred to as 'the late revolution' or 'the late happy revolution' became, from the mid-eighteenth century, 'the Glorious Revolution'.[4] Debate on the precise meaning of the event continued. Supporters of the Hanoverian establishment offered a conservative interpretation of 1688 as the triumphant assertion of constitutional liberties now fully realized in Britain's parliamentary monarchy; its critics appealed to the repudiation of James II as a precedent justifying their continuing opposition to oligarchy. Yet all but a handful of dissidents were agreed that the event remained a central reference point in political debate.[5]

All this relates to England's Revolution. Events in Ireland took a very different course. In England James II's reign saw the admission of the small Catholic minority to religious freedom and to a few positions of influence; in Ireland his accession was followed by the progressive creation of an almost wholly Catholic military and civil administration. Where Englishmen could celebrate a bloodless victory over absolutism, Ireland was the theatre of a prolonged and bloody civil war. Yet despite these contrasts the anguished political debate that accompanied the Revolution extended to Ireland also. Irish Protestants had endured a traumatic reversal of political fortune wholly different from the experience of those they thought of as their kinsmen in Great Britain, and they had far more to gain or lose from the outcome of the conflict that followed. But this did not mean that they could ignore the troubling implications of the removal of a monarch from his throne. And indeed existing work by J.I. McGuire, Robert Eccleshall, David Hayton, Patrick Kelly and Raymond Gillespie has demonstrated both the complexity of their response to the crisis of James II's reign and the intensity of the subsequent debate on the legitimacy of his removal.[6]

---

3 John Kenyon, *Revolution Principles: The Politics of Party 1689-1720* (Cambridge 1977). 4 For the history of the term see L.G. Schwoerer, 'Introduction' to Schwoerer (ed.), *The Revolution of 1688-1689: Changing Perspectives* (Cambridge 1992), pp. 3-4. 5 H.T. Dickinson, *Liberty and Property: Political Ideology in Eighteenth-Century Britain* (London 1977), pp.140-2, 198-9. 6 J.I. McGuire, 'The Church of Ireland and the "glorious revolution" of 1688' in Art Cosgrove and Donal McCartney (eds), *Studies in Irish History* (Dublin 1979), pp.137-49; Robert Eccleshall, 'Anglican political thought in the century after the revolution of 1688' in D.G. Boyce, Robert Eccleshall and Vincent Geoghegan (eds), *Political Thought in Ireland since the Seventeenth Century* (London 1993), pp. 36-72; Raymond Gillespie, 'The Irish Protestants and James II 1688-90', *Irish Historical Studies*, 28 (1992), 124-33; David Hayton, 'The Williamite revolution in Ireland 1688-91' in Jonathan Israel (ed.), *The Anglo-Dutch Moment* (Cambridge 1991); Patrick Kelly, 'Ireland and the glorious revolution: from kingdom to colony' in Beddard (ed.), *The Revolutions of 1688* .

Against this background the present essay tries to do two things. First, it examines some of the major Irish contributions to the contemporary and later debate on the events of 1688-91. Secondly it explores the part played by the Revolution, or a particular image of the Revolution, in the subsequent development of Irish Protestant political thought. In part this requires a discussion of political ideas in their own right: the alternative arguments put forward by those who debated the legitimacy or meaning of the Revolution, the internal coherence of such arguments, the interaction of different lines of thought, and the development of ideas over time. At the same time it is also necessary to consider the wider context: the relationship between the arguments put forward by defenders of the Revolution and the political concerns and responses of Protestant Ireland as a whole, the means by which theoretical differences over the meaning of 1688 became the basis of a short lived but intense party conflict in the years before 1714, and the subsequent transmutation of real political events into slogan and mythology. Only the first approach can allow us to assess the character of Irish Protestant political thinking, in terms of its depth and level of rigour, the theories and values on which it rested, and the self-understanding it promoted. Only the second makes it possible to understand the real but indirect influence of ideas on the world of practical politics.

II

The best known contemporary defences of the Revolution from an Irish Protestant point of view were those published in 1691 by two clergymen of the Church of Ireland, Edward Wetenhall, bishop of Cork and Ross, and William King, just promoted from the deanery of St Patrick's cathedral, Dublin, to the bishopric of Derry. The earlier of the two, Wetenhall's *The Case of the Irish Protestants*, published anonymously in London, was first composed, according to the preface, as a private meditation, intended to satisfy the author's own conscience on the question of how he should respond to the overthrow and replacement of James II. Wetenhall's anxiety in this regard was understandable. He had been closely associated with the Jacobite regime, having been one of only seven bishops to remain in Ireland throughout the crisis of 1688-91, and one of only four who took their seats in the House of Lords of James' Irish parliament.[7] Earlier, in 1686, he had responded to allegations that his preaching against the evils of popery had encouraged hostility to James' government by publishing a collection of sermons under the title *Hexapla Jacobaea*. This set out a starkly unqualified statement of the traditional Anglican teaching on the duty

---

[7] Charles A. Webster, *The Diocese of Cork* (Cork 1920), pp. 285-9.

of unlimited obedience to temporal rulers. Preaching during the rebellion in England of Charles II's illegitimate son, Monmouth, for example, Wetenhall had reminded his hearers of the obedience which Christ and the apostles had paid to 'the unjustest and most tyrannical persons the earth ever bore' and had outlined the classic Anglican doctrine of double or passive obedience: where a command was lawful, the subject was bound to obey actively; where it was unlawful, he or she must refuse, but must then 'meekly and patiently submit thy self to suffer whatever penalty the lawgiver thinks fit to inflict for the breach of his law'. Other sermons outlined the advantages of hereditary over elective monarchy, and reiterated 'the utter unlawfulness of subjects resisting the prince or magistrate whom God has set over them'. The preface to the collection, meanwhile, offered what seemed in the light of subsequent events an alarmingly explicit declaration:

> We of the Church of England avow and protest we will be loyal, should we put in never such circumstances; yea even in the worst circumstances, wherein any adversaries we have could wish us. It is and ever has been our doctrine, it is and ever has been our practice, to be loyal absolutely and without exception.[8]

Against this background it is hardly surprising that Wetenhall should have felt that his subsequent acceptance of the new government of William and Mary required some justification.

The question round which Wetenhall constructed his pamphlet closely reflected his personal dilemma. Did Protestants who now swore allegiance to William and Mary thereby violate the oaths they had formerly taken to James II? Wetenhall offered three arguments to show that these earlier promises of allegiance had ceased to apply. The first was that James' actions had made it unlawful for his Protestant subjects to obey him. He had subjected the crown of his three kingdoms to the power of a foreign potentate, the pope, and he had sought to destroy the Protestant religion. To assist in the former would be treason, to assist in the latter contrary to the law of God.[9] Wetenhall's second argument was that fulfilment of the obligations of the oath had now become impossible. This was partly because James had been defeated, and his kingdom had passed to another by right of conquest: 'God has now put us under the power of the second William the conqueror'. Partly it was because the terms

---

[8] Edward Wetenhall, *Hexapla Jacobaea: A Specimen of Loyalty towards his Present Majesty James the II in Six Pieces by an Irish Protestant Bishop* (Dublin 1686), sermon 3, pp. 34, 16; sermon 5; sermon 6, p. 36; preface. [9] [Edward Wetenhall], *The Case of the Irish Protestants in Relation to Recognizing or Swearing Allegiance to and Praying for King William and Queen Mary Stated and Resolved* (London 1692), pp. 3-5.

of the oath had become contradictory: Protestants were sworn to defend the king, his heirs, and their crown and dignity, yet James himself was subjecting his crown to papal and French domination, and allowing the threatened destruction of the link between Ireland and England.[10] Thirdly, Wetenhall argued, James himself had made it impossible for Protestants to fulfill their oath, first by disarming them, then by allowing his Irish parliament to abolish the existing oath of allegiance and replace it with one which Protestants could not in conscience take, and finally, after the defeat at the Boyne, by releasing his followers from their allegiance and telling them to make the best terms for themselves that they could.[11]

Wetenhall's concern with the obligations imposed by oaths and declarations no doubt reflected his priorities as a conscientious churchmen. But it also had the effect of simplifying his task. The perspective adopted was that of those Protestants, like Wetenhall himself, who had taken no active part in the conflict between William and James, but had only to decide how to respond to the outcome. Towards the end of the pamphlet, indeed, the point was made explicitly: 'God has not vouchsafed to us ... any active part in advancing these princes to their power. He has thought fit to assign us still only a passive lot.'[12] Yet this, as Wetenhall himself clearly recognized, was not enough. There was also the much more awkward issue of those Protestants who had actively contributed to the defeat of James' forces by the Williamites, and in doing so were open to the charge of having betrayed their own doctrine of passive obedience. Here Wetenhall's defence was in part to emphasize the extent to which Irish Protestants had in fact abided by the obligation to obey or submit to punishment. 'Many hundreds of able, lusty and well spirited men have rendered themselves up in a body ... to a few people then in power, whose persons they would have scorned, had they not worn the most plausible character and pretence ... of legal and ordinary authority.'[13] At the same time, however, he also advanced the more radical argument that non-resistance 'has its bounds, and seasons of practice'. For this purpose he distinguished between 'private rules of holy living', and the laws binding whole societies or corporate bodies. 'Who can imagine not resisting evil, turning the other cheek, giving the cloak also, are duties to be preached to, or required of a parliament?'[14] In addition he distinguished between personal injustices, which the subject was obliged to endure, and more public ills, which could justify resistance. Irish Protestants might have felt obliged to sacrifice their own persons and estates. But what was at stake under James II was not individual fortunes, but 'the destruction of the

---

10 Ibid., pp. 5-9. 11 Ibid., pp.11-13. Wetenhall also noted the renewed recognition of James' title by his Irish parliament in May 1689, but argued that this had been rushed through with menaces and at a time when the constitutional position in England was not yet fully understood (ibid., pp.14-16). 12 Ibid., pp. 24-5. 13 Ibid., p. 21. 14 Ibid., p. 22.

whole body of the English Reformation'. Christ's call to take up the cross 'did not command us to destroy our fellow Christians and ruin our posterity'.[15]

All this marked a significant retreat from the doctrine of unvarying obedience which Wetenhall himself had expounded in such uncompromising terms only four years earlier. Double obedience, it now seemed, ceased to apply at some undefined point where the consequences of adhering to it became unreasonably damaging. Indeed a later passage made the appeal to common sense explicit: '… it is as unreasonable as impossible to persuade three kingdoms to give all their throats to be cut'.[16] At a couple of points Wetenhall came close to taking a more radical step still, away from the doctrine of indefeasible monarchical right towards the notion of something more limited and liable to forfeit. Discussing the situation of those who had actually been in arms against their king, he relied mainly on the argument that the commissions granted to the Catholics who commanded the Jacobite forces were invalid because contrary to law, so that resistance to those officers was legitimate. However, he also dismissed the presence of James himself at the head of this army with the comment that by appearing thus he 'could only thereby make himself less a legal king, not them more legal officers'. More explicitly there was the claim that James, by releasing his subjects from their allegiance in the various ways already listed, had thereby 'unkinged himself'.[17] But this raised a new set of problems. If passive obedience had its limits, then it was no longer necessary to appeal to providence as the author of the Revolution, or to quibble over the nature of Jacobite commissions. If a monarch who released his subjects from their obedience could be held to have 'unkinged' himself, equally, both Wetenhall's appeal to providence and his convoluted redefinition of passive obedience were largely beside the point.

These inconsistencies in part reflected a particular style of argument. The task Wetenhall had set himself was not to present a coherent set of political principles, but to establish the legitimacy of a course of action. Like other defenders of the Revolution he thus felt entitled to cite the full range of arguments that might support his case, even if the assumptions on which these rested were not wholly compatible. 'Now if any one of these three be true,' he observed of his arguments regarding the oath of allegiance, 'the obligation thereof to King James is discharged: much more if all.'[18] In practical terms, too, it made sense for an author appealing to the whole body of Irish Protestants to concentrate on those arguments that would command the widest assent. Right at the beginning of his pamphlet Wetenhall had introduced the idea that James, having failed to govern by law, was no longer legally king, but rejected it as too subtle, and too 'odious' in the proof that would be required.[19] At the same time

---

15 Ibid., p. 17. **16** Ibid., p. 23. **17** Ibid., p. 14. **18** Ibid., p. 3. **19** Ibid., p. 5.

there are also grounds for suggesting that Wetenhall's evasions and inconsistencies reflected his own continued uneasiness at what had taken place. A striking passage in his pamphlet conceded that his arguments exempted Protestants only from such obedience as was unlawful or impossible; they were still obliged to hold James' person religiously inviolable, and to include him, at least tacitly, in their prayers.[20] And as late as 1699, when he was transferred to the see of Kilmore, he appears to have had qualms about thus taking the place of the ousted non-juror William Sherlock.[21] Against this background the *Case of the Irish Protestants* must be read, not as a triumphalist celebration of victory, but as reflecting a conservative churchman's struggle to reconcile long held beliefs with political realities never previously imagined.

In this respect the second major defence of the Revolution from an Irish Protestant point of view, William King's *The State of the Protestants of Ireland*, presents what is, at first sight at least, a striking contrast. The difference in approach is evident even in the subtitles of the two works. Where Wetenhall had written of the case of the Irish Protestants 'in relation to recognizing or swearing allegiance to and praying for King William and Queen Mary', King's self-defined task was to present an account 'in which their carriage towards [King James] is justified and the absolute necessity of their endeavouring to be freed from his government and of submitting to their present Majesties is demonstrated'. The shape of the central argument also differed. Wetenhall's definition of the limits of passive obedience had wavered somewhat uncertainly between three separate distinctions – individuals and corporations, public and private ills, reasonable and unreasonable submission. King, by contrast, began with a single, straightforward proposition: that passive obedience could apply only to mischiefs that were particular or tolerable. Where a ruler went beyond mere oppression to seek the actual destruction of his subjects, he abdicated his government of them. In the case of James II, he had packed the army, the courts and the civil administration with men whose beliefs, character and social situation guaranteed that they would murder and despoil Protestants; he had destroyed the commercial wealth of Protestants and initiated the confiscation of their estates; he had dispossessed and persecuted their church; and his government had tolerated or connived at acts of violence and plunder against them. In all of these ways, King argued, James II had sought the ruin of the English and Protestant interest in Ireland, and by doing so had abdicated the government of his Protestant subjects.[22]

On a first reading, then, King's defence of the Revolution was everything that Wetenhall's was not: positive, confident and consistent. This was certainly

---

20 Ibid., pp. 5, 10-11. 21 Richard Mant, *History of the Church of Ireland* (London 1840), vol. 2, p. 55. 22 William King, *The State of the Protestants of Ireland under the Late King James's Government*, 4th edn (London 1692).

how it was seen at the time. *The State of the Protestants of Ireland* went through four editions in its first year, and Bishop Gilbert Burnet called it 'the best book that hath been written for the service of the government ... it is worth all the rest put together, and will do more than all our scribblings for settling the minds of the nation'.[23] This first impression, and the contemporary reactions based on it, need to be kept in mind, for on closer analysis King's arguments rapidly become less compelling. His entire case, in the first place, rests on the proposition that all doctrines concerning the rights of government are annulled at the point where adhering to them would entail the destruction of the governed. Yet from a religious point of view, in which God's purposes might transcend any temporal or earth bound considerations, it is by no means self-evident that this must be so. Secondly, and of greater importance, King's distinction between mere misgovernment and destruction, taken as rigorous argument rather than rhetoric, is open to serious question. Irish Protestants under James II may have faced political and religious oppression and the loss of their wealth. But were they really threatened with extermination? King commented darkly on the likelihood that there had been more arbitrary killings than had so far been discovered. But even if that were the case, would the condition of Irish Protestants have been any worse, for example, than that of early Christians under the Roman empire, to whom St Paul had addressed his exhortation to be subject to higher powers? The non-juror Charles Leslie pitilessly highlighted the exaggerations on which King's case rested. He wrote of the destruction of the Protestant population, but in practice justified resistance to King James' government by citing the taking away of the charter of the city of Derry, and the only partially successful confiscation of arms in Protestant hands. Even if the 'entire' destruction of property were accepted as bringing about the dissolution of government, likewise, that could not be alleged to have occurred while any man in the kingdom had a groat left in his possession. Leslie also drew attention to the wider implications of King's argument that a ruler who sought the destruction of his subjects abdicated his government over them. By that reasoning, criminals condemned to death were no longer subjects, and William III had abdicated his rule over the Catholic Irish, to whom his initial offer of surrender terms had given no security for life or liberty, and whom he had subjected to another religion. Indeed the Scottish episcopalians, whose established church William had actually overthrown, as James had only threatened to do in Ireland, also 'had reason to think themselves free from all obligation to K[ing] W[illiam]'s government'.[24]

Seen as a contribution to the doctrine of passive obedience, then, King's arguments are transparently unconvincing. Where they would have worked far

---

23 Sidney Lee (ed.), *Dictionary of National Biography*, vol. 31 (1892), p. 164. **24** [Charles Leslie] *The Right of Monarchy Asserted, Wherein the Abstract of Dr King's Book, with the Motives for the Reviving it at this Juncture are Fully Considered* (London 1713), pp. 5-8, 25-7, Preface.

better was as part of a frankly secular and contractarian theory of government, in which a ruler who sought the destruction of his subjects self-evidently failed to provide the protection which was the justification for his authority over them. And indeed at one point King came close, not just to a contractarian argument, but to the specific form of that argument developed by John Locke:

> It is property that makes government necessary; and the immediate end of government is to preserve property; when therefore a government, instead of preserving, entirely ruins the property of the subject, that government dissolves itself.[25]

Yet neither this specific proposition relating to property, nor the broader contractarian implications, were developed. Instead King's argument, as he moved forward from his initial, potentially radical premise to the moment at which Irish Protestants had in fact 'endeavoured to be freed' from James II's government, became increasingly evasive. Even after news had reached them of William's landing in England, he insisted, the majority had rejected proposals that they should strike against the Jacobite government by seizing Dublin Castle. The mobilization that subsequently took place at Derry and Enniskillen, likewise, had been initially defensive in character.[26] Elsewhere King briefly took up the argument that the outcome of the struggle, in which Irish Protestants had triumphed over such superior forces, should be seen as the workings of divine rather than human agency.[27] He also acquitted them more directly of responsibility for the outcome by pointing to their constitutional status. Since Ireland was dependent on the English crown, it could not decline to follow its fate 'without apparent ruin to the English interest in it. Now James having abdicated the government of England, and others being actually possessed of the throne, it was the business of the Protestants of Ireland to preserve themselves, rather than dispute the titles of princes ...' Thus they had legitimately acknowledged William and Mary, who were not only in actual possession but were acknowledged as rightfully so 'by those who had best reason to know'.[28]

Despite his subsequent reputation as a Whig champion, then, King's response to the Revolution was in fact a very cautious one, evading the issue of direct resistance to James II in favour of appeals to divine providence and force of circumstances. The contrast with Wetenhall, indeed, is more one of tone than of substance. Once again there is the possibility that King's choice of arguments was influenced by his desire to reconcile as many Protestants as possible to the Williamite regime. But this is at most a part of the story. Other comments by King regarding the basis of the Revolution, made in quite different contexts,

25 King, *State of the Protestants*, p. 109. 26 Ibid., pp. 109-19. 27 Ibid., pp. 120-2. 28 Ibid., p. 120.

follow very much the same cautious lines. In November 1690, for example, he was invited to preach before the Williamite lords justices at a service of thanksgiving for the liberation of Dublin from Jacobite control. The commission might have been seen as an invitation to hail the victory of Protestant arms. But instead King, even more firmly than in *The State of the Protestants*, elevated the role of providence over that of human agency. What had been defeated, he argued, was a conspiracy to make the king of France 'the universal monarch of the west', and to destroy 'the free states of Europe'. This had been accomplished only through a long chain of providential events, from the pope's refusal to back the French to the mysterious collapse of nerve that had led James to abandon England without a fight. Most of all the decision to replace James with William was a triumph, not of constitutional principle, but of divine intervention.

> It was indeed strange we should come to a resolution so soon, especially where the weight of the matter was so great, and the opinion of men so divided, that in a near equality of voices the wisest could not foresee how it would end, till heaven itself determined it. For what else could have brought such different interests and judgements to acquiesce in the conclusion?

All in all, King concluded, "'twas manifestly God, rather than the people, set our king and queen on the throne'.[29]

King's reliance on the idea of the Revolution as the work of God rather than man is confirmed in a fragment of autobiography, probably written after 1710, which acknowledges with surprising frankness the scruples he felt in the uncertain period during and following William's invasion of England. On the one hand he accepted that his oaths of fealty and similar legal subscriptions 'were not instituted with the object of conferring on the king absolute power over the laws or over his subjects or of changing the constitution and form of the state'. He even accepted that a war for the purpose of preventing such an outcome 'might be lawful'. At the same time 'I could scarcely convince myself, whether it might lawfully proceed so far as to absolutely depose the king, which I yet foresaw was certain, if the arms of the Prince of Orange were successful'. Once again his response was 'to commit myself to providence'. Later, as the misdeeds of the Jacobite regime against the constitution and the established church multiplied, 'I doubted no longer but that it was lawful for me and others to accept that deliverance, which providence brought by the prince of Orange ... and to submit myself to him as king and liberator'.[30] This was a final position very little different from that expounded by Wetenhall.

---

[29] William King, *Europe's Deliverance from France and Slavery* (Dublin 1691), pp. 18, 21. [30] 'Quaedam vitae meae insigniora' [Some important events in my life], printed in C.S. King

King's declared position on the legitimacy of the Revolution, in *The State of the Protestants* and elsewhere, is thus consistent in its emphasis on submission to providence and circumstance, as opposed to the active defence of constitutional principles or the exercise of the right of resistance. When these statements of principle are set against the evidence of King's actual behaviour during the crisis of 1688-91, however, new difficulties arise. King insisted in his autobiography that he was never 'the counsellor of any one to take up arms'. Although he had been imprisoned twice by the Jacobite authorities, this was because he had been wrongly blamed for information which others had transmitted to England and Ulster, where it had been imprudently published. But these claims are contradicted by the evidence of James Bonnell, a pious Anglican layman and close friend, who in 1691 reported privately to a cousin in England that King had indeed maintained a secret correspondence with the Williamite forces from within Jacobite-controlled Dublin. At the time he had kept his actions from Bonnell, who was not so 'clear in the point of opposing K[ing] J[ames]', but 'it has made some matter of entertainment since, to tell me what he then did'. King, Bonnell added, 'managed his correspondence so, that though they shrewdly suspected him, they could never find it out; for he never employed fools, and those that carried it, had it always from a third or fourth hand.' He had relaxed these precautions only once, when he sent two messengers directly to London after learning that Schomberg, William's commander in Ulster, was not making proper use of the intelligence sent to him.[31]

Was King, then, guilty of simple bad faith, presenting an account of his conduct that accorded with traditional Anglican teaching, while having in fact acted on very different principles? Certainly, if Bonnell is to be believed, his autobiography told less than the whole truth. Yet there is other evidence to suggest that more was involved than simple hypocrisy. On the contrary King seems to have been genuinely torn beween conflicting impulses. A revealing passage in his autobiography recalled a visit to England during the struggle provoked by attempts to exclude James, then duke of York, from succeeding his brother, Charles II, as king. There King had observed both the opponents of the monarchy, 'republicans ... noted for impiety and vice, no less than for faction', and the royalists, sober and religious men who nevertheless seemed in danger, for the best motives, of surrendering the kingdom to royal absolutism.[32] Later, in 1701, King wrote disapprovingly of the terms of the proposed succession act, telling episcopal colleagues that the restrictions to be imposed on the monarch made him no more than 'a *princeps concilii*' and demonstrated 'to what a pass the

---

(ed.), *A Great Archbishop of Dublin* (London 1906), pp. 22-3. For the date of composition see G.T. Stokes, *Some Worthies of the Irish Church* (London 1900), p. 301, n.2. **31** Bonnell to Revd John Strype, 21 Feb., 24 April 1691 (Cambridge University Library, Strype Correspondence, vol. I, ff 87, 93v). **32** King (ed.), *Great Archbishop*, pp. 19-20.

king has brought the monarchy by a republican ministry'.[33] Such comments suggest that the self-limiting caution of King's justification of the Revolution was genuine, reflecting an instinctive suspicion of any person or group who took the initiative in challenging the existing order. If, in the crisis of 1688-91, he went further than his declared principles warranted, or than he later wished to acknowledge, this revealed only the impossible conflict that arose when those principles appeared to prescribe a submission to popery and absolute power.

In this sense the best summary of King's stand on the Revolution is not *The State of the Protestants*, with its convoluted and sometimes evasive arguments, but a private letter in 1710 to the non-juror Henry Dodwell. Here King dismissed as irrelevant claims that it had been permissable to resist James II's officers because their commissions were invalid or because they had exceeded their authority. If each subject were allowed to form their own judgement in such matters, 'resisters will no more want pretences than for [if?] resistance in case of necessity were declared lawful'. Instead

> they seem to me to act more ingenuously that confess all resistance to be unlawful as it was for David to eat the shew bread, but cruel necessity has no law and therefore when that necessity is real they hope God will forgive them as he did David. I am much mistaken if this has not been and is like to be the general sense of mankind, and endeavours ought to be employed to prevent the disturbance of government on this pretence by condemning resistance generally, as we do telling a lie, the cases being so rare in which we expect pardon if guilty, and the mischief of the abuse so great, that none can with security state them or limit them in a theory so as to prevent the dissolution of peace and society if we once come to exceptions and allow them.[34]

At this point King's attempts to explain the Revolution moved from the realm of political theory into that of theology. His suggestion that the Revolution was a necessary breach of the law which it was better to trust God to pardon than to seek to justify was wholly compatible with the broad theological view which he had by that time developed, emphasising the necessary imperfection both of the created world and of man's knowledge of God.[35] But it would hardly have satisfied his readers in the way that the superficially more confident arguments of the *State of the Protestants* had done two decades earlier.

---

33 King to Thomas Lindsay, bishop of Killaloe, 21 March 1701 (TCD Ms 750/2/2, p. 88). See also King to St George Ashe, bishop of Clogher, 21 March 1701(ibid., p. 87). **34** King to Henry Dodwell, 24 Nov. 1710 (TCD Ms 2531, pp. 226-8). **35** For a brief account of King's theology see David Berman's introduction to *Archbishop King's Sermon on Predestination*, ed. A. Carpenter (Dublin 1976).

III

The pamphlets of King and Wetenhall stand out as the most elaborate defences of the Revolution from an Irish point of view. But that is because both men were deeply troubled by the conflict between the political principles to which they had earlier committed themselves and the political realities of 1688-91, and anxious to justify the actions of themselves and others. For this reason their ideas may usefully be compared with those of two other contemporary authors, neither of whom felt compelled to discuss the Revolution at length, but whose passing comments are for that very reason of potential interest.

The first of these is John Vesey, archbishop of Tuam, in a sermon preached at the opening of the first post-Revolution Irish parliament, in October 1692. Vesey's main purpose was to urge the newly elected members, by means of 'righteous laws and severe executions and good examples', to suppress immorality and irreligion. For this purpose he took his text from the Book of Judges: 'In those days there was no king in Israel; but every man did that which was right in his own eyes'. 'King', Vesey argued, was here being used as a synonym for civil government in general. Such a usage, however, could be taken as an indication that 'if any form of government be of divine right, more than another ... as being a copy from the divine original', it was 'a paternal government in a gentle and well tempered monarchy'. There was of course the fact that the demand of the Jews to Samuel that they should have a king like other nations, rather than a judge, was presented in the Old Testament as a crime for which they had suffered. But their offence had not been in the type of ruler they had preferred, but rather in their rejection of what God had provided for them. Having thus clarified the wider question of the nature of government, Vesey went on to develop his main theme of the 'absolute necessity of civil power, and a due execution of penal laws, for the well governing of any people'.[36]

Vesey was to be a leading Tory in the next reign, and his sermon dextrously combined two classic Tory themes: a defence of monarchy as an institution, along with a reassertion of the religious duty to obey whatever form of temporal government God's providence had appointed. Indeed it is possible that he had chosen his biblical text precisely so as to allow him to reaffirm the continuing validity of these traditional doctrines in the post-Revolution world. But this left the question of how the recent abrupt replacement of one monarch with another was to be explained within such a framework. Vesey's condemnation of the Jews for rejecting God's provision for their government, and his

---

36 John Vesey, *A Sermon Preached before his Excellency the Lord Lieutenant and the Two Houses of Parliament in Christ's Church, Dublin, when they first Met There Together, October 16, 1692* (Dublin 1692), pp. 15, 4-6, 10.

insistence on the need to accept such provision without question, might well have provided the basis for yet another appeal to divine providence. But in fact he opted for a bolder and more positive argument. The period in which 'there was no king in Israel' had clearly represented 'a vacancy in the throne'. As such it had demonstrated how the absence of firm government led inevitably to universal debauchery and disorder.

> If the want of civil government be so great an evil, then it is both the duty and interest of any people, who are fallen into such a circumstance, immediately to apply the proper remedy, by filling the vacant throne by a free election, where they have power so to do; or peaceable submission to those, who have a right without it. And the public necessity of affairs, the *salus ecclesiae & salus populi*, does both require and justify their doing so, as well for God's honour as their country's safety.[37]

This was of course a general prescription, recognizing the possible legitimacy both of hereditary monarchy ('those who have a right') and of other forms of government ('a free election'). Yet it is impossible to imagine that Vesey did not have in mind the events of the preceding four years. Taken in that sense, his remarks remained usefully vague on whether William and Mary had taken the throne by hereditary right or through the will of the English Convention. But what was striking, especially in comparison to the evasions of Wetenhall and King, was Vesey's frank pragmatism. 'The public necessity of affairs' required men to provide themselves with a government as an alternative to anarchy and licentiousness, and the means by which they did so could be guided only by the specific political context.

Vesey's comments may be compared with those of Richard Cox, a County Cork born lawyer who in the reign of Queen Anne was to become a leading member of the Irish Tory party, serving as lord chancellor 1703-7 and later, until his removal in 1714, as chief justice of the Queen's Bench. Cox was one of the Protestants who fled the Catholic dominated Ireland created by James II's viceroy, the earl of Tyrconnell, abandoning his post as recorder of Kinsale in 1687 and withdrawing to England. There he published, in 1689, the first volume of his history of English rule in Ireland, *Hibernia Anglicana*. This covered the period up to 1603, and as such was not required to discuss directly the events of James II's reign. It did, however, include an earlier episode, in 1553, when Protestants in both England and Ireland had accepted as their queen Mary Tudor, a Catholic whose hereditary claim was undermined by the annulment years before of the marriage between her mother, Catherine of Aragon, and Henry VIII. Cox, writing in English exile in a volume to be dedicated to

---

37 Ibid., p. 12.

William and another Mary, can hardly have been blind to the contemporary implications of the issues he discussed. And the terms in which he framed his argument suggest that his mind was in fact focused far more on the events of the past two years than on those of the mid-sixteenth century.

Irish Protestants, Cox argued, had accepted Mary as *de facto* queen because they believed themselves obliged to do so by the laws of God and man. 'It is necessary to add, that the preservation of the community is the end and design of all laws, and that the greatest solecism that can be in the economy of a kingdom, is to suspend the government, though but for a moment.' At first sight, this came closer than any of the other texts so far examined to justifying the Revolution in terms of a theory of government based on the mutual obligations of ruler and ruled. Indeed Cox himself introduced the language of reciprocity:

> For the relation that is between king and subject, protection and allegiance, is reciprocal, and the obligation is mutual, as it is betwixt husband and wife; and therefore whensoever a king totally ceaseth the exercise of his royal office, he is dead in his politic capacity, with which the relation is ... and whether this happens by force or consent, is no more to the purpose, than it is whether a man's first wife was murdered or died of a fever.

Looked at more closely, however, Cox's arguments stop well short of any notion of a contract between a monarch and his subjects. The reciprocity he referred to was on deeply unequal terms. The reason why it had been the duty of Protestants to accept Mary was that 'it was not the duty of the subject to dispute the title of the prince in possession; this were to make the rabble judges of the rights of princes, and to erect a judicature above the legislative power and to introduce an appeal from the parliament to the people'. The argument, in other words, was closer to Hobbes than to Locke, emphasizing the need for authority and order rather than the rights of the subject. Yet if Cox's argument was authoritarian, it was also intensely pragmatic. In particular it explicitly rejected all attempts to oppose notions of divine or hereditary right to the facts of power. The words 'king *de jure*' were 'terms of art ... to signify an imaginary notion'. 'If this were not so, there could be no peace upon earth, since there is not a crown in Europe to which there are not several plausible pretenders, whose claims have many warm and furious abettors.'[38] This clear sighted acceptance of political necessity as the ultimate arbiter makes Cox's arguments, like

---

38 Richard Cox, *Hibernia Anglicana, or The History of Ireland* (London 1689), vol. 1, pp. 296-8. I am grateful to Mr Ian Montgomery who first drew my attention to this passage and its possible significance.

the broadly similar views of Vesey, a valuable corrective to the quasi-theological agonizings of Wetenhall and King.

IV

Although Wetenhall and King were equally concerned to reconcile the events of 1688-9 with traditional principles of non-resistance and passive obedience, both were in practice forced to qualify strict principle by appeals to circumstances. Wetenhall argued that passive obedience had common sense limits; King turned in the end to the overriding force of 'cruel necessity'. This was largely because both men wrote during or in the immediate aftermath of the crisis of James II's reign. As a result they were forced, however unwillingly, to confront the specific details of what they and others had done. By contrast later writers who shared their concern to minimize the dangerous implications of the Revolution were able to benefit from a convenient blurring of awkward historical detail.

This process of expedient partial amnesia may be seen at work as early as 1707. On 30 January in that year Samuel Synge, dean of Kildare, preached a sermon in Christ Church cathedral, Dublin, to mark the anniversary of the execution of Charles I. The feast of King Charles the Martyr had been a prominent feature of the ritual calendar of Restoration Anglicanism. In the aftermath of the Revolution, however, its observance had become something of an embarrassment. Synge confronted the difficulty head on, setting himself the task of demonstrating that there was in fact no contradiction between a total repudiation of the regicide of 1649 and an approving acceptance of the events of 1688. His argument consisted partly of a detailed historical account intended to show that the limited abuses of Charles' reign, for which redress had eventually been promised, could in no way be equated with the arbitrary proceedings, and complete disregard for legitimate protest, experienced under his son. But Synge also maintained that in any case James II had not in fact been deposed as his father had been. Instead he had abdicated, allowing himself to be prevailed on to abandon his kingdom without a government, so that 'their own necessary preservation' had led his people to fill the throne he had left vacant. The resulting constitutional settlement, moreover, had been guided by the principle of hereditary succession. By conferring the throne on 'her who had the next right, together with her husband who, under God, had been their deliverer', the people had 'preserved the succession in the royal family, in such a manner as may be consistent with the safety of the nation, only setting our present most gracious queen one step back from her right of inheritance, but that not without her own consent'.[39] As a summary of the settlement this glided over such

---

[39] Samuel Synge, *The Case of King Charles the First and King James the Second Stated and*

inconvenient details as the by-passing of the son born to James II's queen in June 1688, whose legitimacy had been contested but never fully explored, and the conferring of the crown not just on James' daughter Mary but, in an unprecedented constitutional move, on her husband. More blatantly still the fiction of abdication ignored the fact that in Ireland at least James had quite clearly not surrendered his crown, but had fought a civil war to keep it. Here Synge's argument depended on the silent assimilation, by an Irish clergyman preaching to an Irish audience, of events in his own kingdom to those on the other side of the Irish Sea. Neither set of evasions, it seems safe to say, would have allowed either Wetenhall or King to meet either their own scruples or the allegations made against them by others.

The same convenient blurring of the historical record is evident in the political thinking of the two leading Irish Tory intellectuals of the early eighteenth century, George Berkeley and Jonathan Swift. In the case of Berkeley the importance of the retreat from an engagement with the detail of events is heightened by the two very different contexts in which he discussed the Revolution. The first of these was the series of three sermons on the theme of passive obedience delivered originally to an undergraduate audience at Trinity College and published in 1712.[40] Here Berkeley approached the question of the duties of the subject from an abstract, philosophical standpoint. He began with the proposition that God was perfectly good, and therefore concerned only for the welfare of mankind. It followed that any rule of behaviour that promoted that welfare could be taken to be the will of God. This in turn meant that such a rule constituted one of the laws of nature, a fixed, unalterable standard of behaviour. The next step was to argue that, since a state of anarchy inevitably implied extreme human misery, the obligation of loyalty to established authority came into this category of an unbreakable law. Rebellion and disobedience were thus as much sins as murder, perjury or adultery. At first sight this was a version of the conventional argument that obedience to government was the only means of escaping the evils of unrestrained human violence. What gave it a wholly different character was Berkeley's introduction of the will of God. In his famous theory of matter Berkeley had argued that objects had a permanent existence, independent of human perception, through the presence of the infinite spirit of God. In the same way his identification of what was conducive to human well being with God's will elevated the proposition that one should prefer obedience to anarchy from the status of prudential advice to that of an absolute requirement. Just as God did not suspend the laws of nature even when their operation brought famine, earthquake or other disasters, so the obligation

Compared (Dublin 1707), p. 26. **40** George Berkeley, 'Passive obedience', in A.A. Luce and T.E. Jessop (eds), *The Works of George Berkeley, Bishop of Cloyne* (London 1953), vol. 6, pp.15-46.

to obey continued even when it meant the loss of possessions, liberty, or life itself. It was here that Berkeley parted company with Wetenhall and King. Wetenhall had argued that passive obedience had its practical limits. King had maintained that a ruler who sought to destroy his subjects ceased to govern them. But Berkeley explicitly rejected all such appeals to what King had called 'cruel necessity'. To limit the duty of obedience by the 'law of self preservation', he pointed out, would imply that a man could commit any sin in order to save his life.[41]

Berkeley's three sermons, despite the general and abstract terms in which they were couched, had an obvious relevance to the question of the Revolution. Indeed he made clear in his preface that his main motive for delivering them was the unease he felt at some of the conclusions which his contemporaries were drawing from the events of 1688-9. Specifically he sought to combat what he saw as the dangerous notion that the duty of obedience to government should be limited by the good of society. Not surprisingly his efforts gave rise to charges of Jacobitism. As far as we can tell, however, these were wholly without foundation. In a private letter in October 1709 Berkeley had written a detailed critique of a recently published book by a former English non-juror, endorsing its arguments for swearing allegiance to Queen Anne and criticizing it only for seeming to distinguish between an acceptance of the government established by the overthrow of James II and an acceptance of the Revolution itself.[42] In 1715, during the Jacobite insurrections in England and Scotland, he offered a more public declaration of his loyalties, in an anonymous pamphlet insisting that Tories remained bound by their oaths of allegiance to George I. To those who might cite the earlier breach of similar oaths of allegiance to James II, Berkeley replied with the simple proposition that 'when any person by forfeiture or abdication loseth dominion, he is no longer sovereign'. This was what had happened, 'in the judgement of most men', in the case of James II, but it was clearly not true of George I, who 'legally administers that government to which he came with the joint consent and acclamations of his people'.[43]

The contrast between the apparently uncompromising conclusions of Berkeley's sermons on passive obedience and his declared acceptance of the Revolution settlement has given rise to much discussion.[44] To some extent

---

41 Ibid., pp. 35-6. 42 Berkeley to Percival, 21 Oct. 1709 in Benjamin Rand (ed.), *Berkeley and Percival: The Correspondence of George Berkeley ... and Sir John Percival* (Cambridge 1914), pp. 61-4. 43 'Advice to the Tories who have taken the oath' in Luce and Jessop (eds), *Works*, vol. 6, p. 56. 44 G.P. Conroy, 'George Berkeley and the Jacobite heresy: some comments on Irish Augustan politics', *Albion*, 3 (1971), 82-91, presents the allegation of Jacobitism as Whig propaganda. David Berman, 'The Jacobitism of Berkeley's *Passive Obedience*', *Journal of the History of Ideas*, 47 (1986), 309-19, argues that Berkeley was in fact a Jacobite in 1712, but had

Berkeley, like others in the fraught political climate of the post-Revolution period, simply failed to be consistent. In particular there is a clear contradiction between one passage in *Passive Obedience*, which goes out of its way to reject the proposition that the duty of obedience could in any way be restricted by appeals to some assumed but irrecoverable original contract, and his recommendation to a friend, in 1709, to use Locke's *Two Treatises* as a guide to 'the measure of your obedience, and the bounds of their power who rule'.[45] For the most part, however, what bridged the gap between Berkeley's theory of obedience and his acceptance of the Revolution was a highly pragmatic definition of legitimacy. A rightful monarch, Berkeley argued in 1709, was one who exercised effective power with 'the consent and acquiescence of the people'. All kings *de facto* were thus kings *de jure*. Indeed if even Cromwell had had the title of king conferred on himself and his posterity by a free parliament, and if his descendants had succeeded in retaining power, then it would now be 'wickedness' to disturb the public peace by challenging his family's rule.[46] As an argument in principle this was perfectly sound. Indeed it could be argued that to ground the duty of obedience on a law willed by God to save men from the miseries of anarchy necessarily implied that such obedience was due only to effective authority, capable of discharging that function. Applied to a specific situation, however, it left much unclear. Berkeley's vague references to 'the judgement of most men' and 'the consent and acquiescence of the people' did nothing to specify how one ruler came to lose effective power and another to gain it, or to define the responsibility of those caught up in any such transfer of authority. Once again Berkeley, born in 1685 and addressing an audience at least ten years younger than himself, found it possible to gloss over this issue in a way that Wetenhall and King, senior ecclesiastics at a time when rival claimants confronted each other in arms, could never hope to do.

A similar argument for acceptance of the Revolution settlement in terms of obedience to *de facto* authority comprised one part of the political thinking of Jonathan Swift. In 1721, for example, Swift dismissed a correspondent's scruples over whether to take the oath of abjuration, declaring George I to be rightful sovereign and denying the title of all other claimants, by arguing that the oath should be understood 'as the law stands'. On this basis, he boasted, he had already convinced 'a young gentleman of great parts and virtue' to take the oath, 'and I think I could defend myself by all the duty of a Christian to take oath to any prince in possession. For the word lawful means according to present law in force.'[47] The appeal to robust common sense was characteristic; but

---

ceased to be so by 1715. G.J. Warnock, 'On passive obedience', *History of European Ideas*, 7 (1986), 555-62, argues more convincingly that in *Passive Obedience* Berkeley was carried away by his philosophical preoccupations. **45** 'Passive obedience', 15, 29-30; Rand, *Berkeley and Percival*, pp. 63-4. **46** Rand, *Berkeley and Percival*, p. 63. **47** Swift to Knightley Chetwode, 29

it also ignored precisely the issue, the relationship between *de facto* and *de jure* titles, that the oath was concerned, rightly or wrongly, to flush into the open. And indeed Swift's own comments in other contexts remained more than a little equivocal. In 1737, for example, he presented the deposition of James II as having constituted the lesser of two evils.

> As to what is called a revolution principle my opinion was this; that whenever those evils which usually attend and follow a violent change of government were not in probability so pernicious as the grievances we suffer under a present power, then the public good will justify such a revolution, and this I took to have been the case in the Prince of Orange's expedition, although in the consequences it produced some very bad effects, which are likely to stick long enough by us.[48]

An earlier sermon, in 1726, was similarly guarded: 'that unhappy prince [James II] ... did not only invade our laws and liberties, but would have forced a false religion upon his subjects, for which he was deservedly rejected, since there could be no other remedy found, or at least agreed on.'[49]

Some private memoranda help to clarify the issue, suggesting that Swift's own belief was that the crisis of 1688 should have been resolved by leaving James on the throne while giving his daughter Mary effective power as regent.[50] It is against this background that we must consider the comments made in the unpublished pamphlet which Swift composed in the summer of 1714 to defend the record of the Tory ministry and refute claims that there was a conspiracy to bring in the Pretender:

> Six and twenty years have almost passed since the Revolution, and the bulk of those who are now in action either at court, in parliament, or public offices, were then boys at school or the universities; and look upon that great change to have happened during a period of time for which they are not accountable. The logic of the highest Tories is now, that this was the establishment they found, as soon as they arrived to a capacity of judging; that they had no hand in turning out the late king, and therefore have no crime to answer for, if there were any.[51]

Swift's invocation of 'the highest Tories' leaves it unclear how far this was an argument he wished to impute to others, and how far it also underpinned his

---

April 1721 (*Swift Corr.* vol. 2, p. 384). **48** Swift to Pope, 10 Jan. 1721 (*Swift Corr.* vol. 2, p. 372). **49** Swift, *Prose Works*, vol. 11, pp. 229-30. **50** F.P. Lock, *Swift's Tory Politics* (London 1983), p. 82. **51** 'Some Free Thoughts upon the Present State of Affairs' in Herbert Davis and Irvin Ehrenpreis (eds), *Political Tracts 1713-19* (Oxford 1953), p. 92.

own acceptance of Anne, and later of George I, as the 'prince in possession'. But in either case his comments spell out once again the crucial role of the passage of time in reconciling abstract political principle and practical political allegiances.

V

To analyse the writings of leading Irish commentators on the Revolution is straightforward enough. One can summarize their arguments, tease out the underlying assumptions, draw attention to evasions and inconsistencies. What is more difficult to determine is how significant a section of Irish Protestant opinion they represented.

It should be immediately apparent that the selection of authors considered so far has been a seriously unbalanced one. All but one (Cox) were clergy of the established church. In terms of later political allegiances Cox, Vesey, Synge and Swift were all to be positively identified with the Tory party. Wetenhall and Berkeley, while less politically engaged, were clearly no Whigs. Neither, on closer examination, was William King. Nor is there any easy way of correcting this Tory and clerical slant. It has long been recognized that the ideas of John Locke, with the one exception of the extensive if mainly unacknowledged borrowings of William Molyneux's *The Case of Ireland*, received remarkably little attention in Ireland in the decades after 1688.[52] But what is equally striking is the absence of any significant body of writing offering a positive defence of the Revolution even in the cautious terms adopted by mainstream Whig writing in England.[53]

This imbalance in the Irish literature can in part be explained by practical considerations. Conditions during 1688-91, whether in Ireland itself or among Irish Protestant refugees in England, were hardly conducive to abstract political speculation. By the time normal political life had been restored, there was little for Irish writers to add to what was already an extensive literature in defence of a constitutional settlement now firmly established. At the same time there is one episode at least which suggests that the absence of a more substantial Whig literature may have reflected, not just chronology and circumstance, but the political preferences of a large section of Irish Protestant opinion. In

---

[52] Patrick Kelly, 'Perceptions of Locke in Eighteenth-Century Ireland', *Proceedings of the Royal Irish Academy*, 89C (1989). [53] Eccleshall ('Anglican political thought', 59) confirms the absence of recognizable Whig writing in the post-Revolution period. He refers to 'an upsurge of Whiggism' in 'the turbulent years before the Hanoverian succession', but the examples he cites, with the single exception of William Stoughton (see below), all date from *after* 1714.

1709 William Stoughton, a prebendary of St Patrick's cathedral, was chosen to preach that year's 30 January sermon, on the execution of Charles I. Convention, and the liturgy of the festival, required that the preacher should present Charles as the innocent, indeed saintly, victim of cruelty, ambition and irreligion. Stoughton, however, offered only a perfunctory comment on the dead king's private virtues, and on the extent to which the problems of his reign had been the fault of sycophantic and self-interested counsellors, before insisting that a king was nevertheless accountable for his failings in government. It was true that Cromwell and his allies had been wrong to depose and execute Charles I. But their offence had been in seeking to overthrow the constitution and establish a dictatorial commonwealth. If instead they had executed Charles in order to replace him with a prince of greater virtue and capacity, 'they would have had the credit both of native and neighbouring examples; and at least some plausibility of reason to urge for such a practice and their justification'. From this at least partial endorsement of regicide, Stoughton turned to contemporary politics, launching into a strongly worded denunciation of the doctrines of passive obedience and the divine right of kings. In 'an hereditary and successive monarchy' such as that of England, he argued, kings ruled by 'the consent of the people, the legitimacy of descent, the right of succession, and the coronation oath'. The audience's ancestors had left their posterity 'a noble freedom', and had never held back from risking life or fortune when 'weak or wicked princes endeavoured to break through the laws that fenced them in'. There was thus no reason why 'the people should continue fettered and chained up by the obligation of their oath of fealty' when a prince broke the contract 'which is the supreme condition on which he is their king'.[54]

Stoughton's 30 January sermon stands in sharp contrast to that of Samuel Synge two years earlier. Synge had stressed the dissimilarities between the execution of Charles I and the overthrow of James II. Stoughton, an Irish clergyman serving as chaplain to the lord chancellor of a newly appointed Whig executive, blatantly subordinated the intended symbolism of the day to an exposition of contractarian theory and the right of resistance. The two sermons thus vividly illustrate the depth of the ideological divisions which the events of 1688 had brought into the open. In an Irish context, however, Stoughton's provocative exposition of undiluted Whig doctrine won few supporters. According to William King, by now archbishop of Dublin, the sermon 'has made a very great clamour in this city, and has occasioned many reflections'; '... so far as my acquaintance reaches [it] is universally condemned.'[55] Nor was it only Tories who repudiated his performance. King reported that Irish Whigs 'are as angry as can

---

[54] William Stoughton, *A Sermon Preached before the State in Christ Church, on Monday the 31st of January 1708/9* (Dublin 1709). [55] King to Marsh, 9 Feb. 1709 (TCD Ms 2531, p. 52); King to Richard Freeman, 9 Feb. 1709 (ibid., p. 50).

be, and look on it as a mischievous libel on them, to have it thought that they approve such doctrines'. The sermon, he repeated to Swift, 'had an ill-effect on the minds of most here; for though they espouse the Revolution, they heartily abhor [sixteen] forty-one'.[56] King's judgement is confirmed by a later statement from Stoughton himself, who complained that following the controversy he had been 'disappointed in a considerable pretension under this government, by those persons who both approved of and employed their credit to obtain it for me in the preceding one'.[57] This uniform condemnation suggests that the caution and unease expressed in most Irish writing on the Revolution was shared by a wider Protestant opinion. It is likely that only a small minority, most of them probably clergymen, felt obliged to engage in the sort of detailed examination of the finer points of law and conscience suggested by Wetenhall and King before making their choice between James and William. Yet even those who had accepted the Revolution fairly unhesitatingly seem to have lacked enthusiasm for too explicit an exploration of its wider implications.

It would be easy to describe this position as conservative, reflecting perhaps the stronger attachment to traditional ideas of monarchy and obedience characteristic of a provincial society. Fully to understand the complexity of the Irish Protestant response to the Revolution, however, it is also necessary to take account of a further distinctive characteristic shared by most of the writings considered here. This is the extent to which an unwillingness to indulge in abstract speculation on the limits of government was matched by a pragmatic acceptance of the realities of political power. Vesey and Cox, as we have already seen, defended the Revolution in terms which subordinated all other criteria of legitimacy to the ability to provide effective government. Cox, developing the logical implication of such a stance, also dismissed as meaningless any attempt to distinguish between *de facto* and *de jure* authority. The *de facto-de jure* distinction was likewise explicitly dismissed by Swift, and with particular force by Berkeley, who reminded a friend in 1709 that 'the present royal line' had its beginnings in William the Conqueror, 'who by conquest had the same title to the crown that a highwayman has to your purse'.[58]

To this frankness about the basis on which the Revolution was to be justified can be added a less obvious, but equally striking realism about the nature of the event itself. Most commentators, both in England and in Ireland, were anxious to interpret the removal of James II in terms that did not seem to weaken the foundations of government and social hierarchy. In England this anxiety extended to a general reluctance to characterize what had taken place

---

56 King to Edward Southwell, 16 Feb. 1709 (TCD Ms 2531, p. 61); King to Swift, 10 Feb. 1709 (*Swift Corr.* vol. 1, p. 124). 57 William Stoughton, *A Sermon Preached ... 31st of January 1708/9 ... Humbly Dedicated to the Honourable House of Commons* (n.d.), dedication. 58 Berkeley to Percival, 21 Oct. 1709 (Rand (ed.), *Berkeley and Percival*, p. 64).

in terms either of a dissolution of government or of armed resistance. A war between a monarch, however tyrannical, and his subjects was self-evidently an alarming precedent to acknowledge. To say that a dissolution of the existing government had taken place in 1688 would be almost equally dangerous, implying that what had followed, the conferring of the crown on William and Mary, was an exercise of popular sovereignty. It was here that Irish apologists for the Revolution, despite their obvious concern not to provide a licence for insubordination, were significantly less inhibited. Archbishop Vesey presented the events of 1688 in terms of the people providing themselves with a new government after being left in the equivalent of a Lockeian state of nature. So too, despite his timidity on the subject of hereditary succession, did Samuel Synge. Moreover Synge was also prepared to define what had taken place in terms of a just war. This had been waged primarily by William of Orange to protect the religious liberties of his fellow Protestants, to save all Europe from the imperialist designs of Louis XIV, and to safeguard his wife's hereditary claim to the throne. But the conflict had not been entirely between rival dynasts. Otherwise Synge would not have found it necessary to add the potentially much more explosive proposition that a people abandoned by their ruler 'for their own safety may erect a new government; and having done so may by arms defend both it and themselves ... even against their former prince himself'.[59]

Despite their obvious concern to minimize the radical implications of the events which they discuss, the leading Irish apologists for the Williamite settlement thus share both a marked concern with effective authority as opposed to legitimacy, and a notably greater willingness than their English counterparts to discuss the whole episode in terms of war and of the breakdown and reconstitution of the political order. Both characteristics can in part be seen as reflecting the very different face of Ireland's revolution: the bloody civil war of 1689-91 did not lend itself to euphemism in the way that the largely symbolic confrontation in England did. But the Irish response can also be seen in a longer perspective. In the mid-seventeenth century, between 1641 and the 1660s, Irish Protestants had already seen their very survival as a minority in a predominantly Catholic kingdom threatened by the upheavals of English politics, as monarchy went to war against parliament, was defeated and abolished, and then restored. Throughout that succession of crises their predominant response appears to have been to support the body or individual – king or parliament, Cromwell or a restored Charles II – that had effective command of English political resources and so was best placed to provide protection.[60] History, in other

---

[59] Synge, *The Case of King Charles the First*, p. 28. For further discussion of this point Eccleshall, 'Anglican political thought', pp. 53-4. See also ibid., pp. 60-1. [60] For a fuller discussion of this point, see S.J. Connolly, *Religion, Law and Power: The Making of Protestant Ireland 1660-1760* (Oxford 1992), p. 11.

words, had already taught Irish Protestants the lesson formulated in almost identical terms by both Cox and King: that it was not for them to dispute the titles of princes. By the same token the recipe for self-preservation through support for strong *de facto* authority, stated explicitly by Cox and implied by others, largely summed up the political practice of two generations or more.

VI

The spectrum of opinion and allegiance revealed by the Irish debate in the immediate aftermath of the Revolution was thus a relatively narrow one. Irish Whigs, while committed to the defence of the Protestant succession, were circumspect in their discussion of the principles on which James II had been removed. Irish Tories may have agonized about the implications of overthrowing a legitimate monarch, but few of them carried their scruples to the point of rejecting the outcome. In England 6 bishops of the established church, and some 400 of the lower clergy, resigned their sees and livings rather than take the oaths of allegiance and supremacy under William and Mary. In Ireland, by contrast, the nonjurors comprised a single bishop and a mere handful of other clergymen.[61] Among the laity, equally, most unbiased observers agreed that Protestant Jacobites were rare.[62] In the second decade of the eighteenth century, however, the picture changed dramatically. What had previously been a muted constitutional debate exploded into contentious life, as rival Whig and Tory interpretations of the Revolution were debated in an atmosphere of intense mutual suspicion and fears of a possible return to civil war.

The depth and bitterness of these new divisions over the meaning of the Revolution are vividly illustrated in the sermon by John Winder, prebendary of Swift's old parish of Kilroot in Co. Antrim, which was preached at St Mary's church, Dublin, on 30 May 1714 and subsequently published 'at the request of many loyal gentlemen'. 30 May, the anniversary of Charles II's birth and also of his entry into London to resume the throne in 1660, was along with 30 January a major event in the royalist liturgical calendar. Winder rose to the occasion with a vigorous reassertion of the absolute necessity of submitting to the authority of true religion and civil government, the 'two hinges whereon depend the temporal and eternal welfare of mankind'. By civil government he made clear that he meant monarchy. God might permit supreme power to become lodged in an aristocracy or a democracy, and such power was not to be annulled or despised. But its origins nevertheless lay in wrong doing:

---

61 McGuire, 'The Church of Ireland and the "Glorious Revolution"'. **62** Connolly, *Religion, Law and Power*, pp. 242-3.

for 'tis most certain, there was never yet any such thing as a free people by nature; that is, any people who were born under no rules, and who were naturally at liberty to choose their own governments, or even their form of government.

This explicit rejection of contract theory did not lead Winder to reject the deposition of James II. But he insisted that he was nevertheless 'a mere stranger to what they call Revolution Principles':

When a man's house has been on fire, the people have pulled down the next neighbours, and have used irregular and uncommon methods to prevent a general destruction. But it does not from thence follow that my neighbour's house must be blown up every time the mob cries fire. If so 'tis but saying the word to the rabble, who love to have it so, for the sake of plunder in the hurry, and the work may soon be done.

The men who had made 'that happy Revolution' had had no such thoughts. But since then 'these republican principles were new vamped up, and foisted in under the cover of that single unavoidable act'.[63]

Winder's sermon is an unusually explicit statement. But his combative rejection of a perceived attempt to make the events of 1688 the basis of subversive doctrines was echoed by other preachers and writers. In the same year, for example, another Anglican and Tory polemicist, William Tisdall, vicar of Belfast, likewise complained of Whigs who drank toasts to 'our sovereign lords the people' and to Oliver Cromwell, thus promoting 'such Revolution Principles as overturned the constitution and brought the best of princes to the block'.[64] Berkeley's decision three years earlier to preach on the delicate subject of passive obedience was likewise in response to what he saw as dangerous notions concerning the limits of obedience. Whigs, for their part, responded in kind, reading into quibbles over the nature of the Revolution evidence of a lack of commitment to the Protestant succession, if not of positive attachment to the cause of the exiled Stuarts.

Three main reasons may be suggested to explain this eruption of disagreement regarding the constitution. Of these the first has already been explored. Swift and Berkeley, it was suggested earlier, typified a process whereby the natural or deliberate blurring of historical memory permitted a younger generation to revive in a pure and uncompromising form doctrines of passive obedience and resistance which in the immediate aftermath of 1688 had had to be

---

63 John Winder, *The Mischief of Schism and Faction to Church and State* (Dublin 1714), pp. 8, 13-14.   64 [William Tisdall], *The Nature and Tendency of Popular Phrases in General* (Dublin n.d. c.1714), pp. 7-8.

partly abandoned or at the very least heavily qualified. In doing so they provided the basis for a sharp clash of ideologies with upholders of the alternative Whig view of the Revolution, which may also have gained in clarity as the doubts and compromises of actuality faded from memory.

The second reason for the reappearance of the Revolution as a focus of party conflict was that differing interpretations of the events of 1688 came to have implications for an increasingly uncertain future. James II had died in 1701. However there remained the son born to his queen in June 1688, whose parentage had been questioned but never properly investigated. From 1702 the claim of 'James III' to be the rightful king of England, Scotland and Ireland was backed by France, once again at war with Britain. Meanwhile, following the death of Queen Anne's only surviving child, the act of settlement (1701) had vested the succession in the electress Sophia of Hanover and her heirs. At some future point it would thus become necessary to choose between rival claimants. Against this background an argument like Winder's analogy between the constitutional crisis of 1688 and a burning building, however ingenious, seemed to leave the future dangerously open. To speak of the rejection of James II as a 'single, unavoidable act', or to shuffle off responsibility for his removal by references to abdication or the workings of divine providence, inevitably raised the question of how those concerned would behave when, as seemed likely, a choice had once again to be made between the claims of hereditary succession and the preservation of a Protestant monarchy.

For Whigs the problem was somewhat different. Since the issues that had been debated in 1688 were likely to recur in the near future, some definition of the Revolution in terms of positive principle seemed essential. But how was that definition to be framed without seeming to provide a charter for recurrent instability and defiance of authority? In England in 1710 the Whig ministry blundered into a crisis wholly of their own making, when they prosecuted the high church preacher Henry Sacheverell for having allegedly cast doubt on the principles of the Revolution, only to find themselves struggling, under the disapproving eyes of Queen Anne, to define what those principles were in terms that did not leave them open to charges of endorsing republicanism, anarchy and sedition.[65] At very nearly the same time Whig members of the Irish parliament entangled themselves in a less dramatic but equally revealing controversy. This began when the Whig majority in the House of Commons, just a few months after the Stoughton affair, voted to attach to a grant being made to Trinity College, Dublin, a set of resolutions commending the college for its adherence to the principles of the Revolution. Trinity was well known as a centre of high church, Tory, and allegedly Jacobite opinion. The college authorities had recently expelled a student for denouncing the memory of

65 Geoffrey Holmes, *The Trial of Doctor Sacheverell* (London 1973).

William III.[66] From a Whig point of view the Commons resolutions thus added a gratifying sting to the tail of an act of generosity towards a hostile institution, while at the same time expressing support for the minority of allies within it. When parliament next met, in 1711, however, the House of Lords responded with an address to the queen insisting that she could never have intended that her bounty should be used 'to promote (in general) Revolution Principles; principles which ... do, in a great measure, maintain and justify the execrable murder of King Charles I ... and on which may be founded any rebellion against your majesty or your successors'. When first pressed on this point the Commons had hastily retreated, insisting that the reference had been only to the 'late happy revolution'. But that merely gave their opponents more ammunition. The College's support for the Revolution, the Lords pointed out, had already been mentioned in the offending resolutions. A subsequent reference to 'principles', therefore, 'cannot in good reason or grammar be referred to the late Revolution'. Moreover 'it is the known nature of principles, to be as well the rule and guide of future, as of past actions.'[67] It was an argument to which there was no answer. And it neatly summed up the main reason why theoretical disagreements about the events of two decades earlier had suddenly become the basis of such violent animosities.

The third key to an understanding of the increasing virulence of party conflict is to recognize that systematic doctrinal argument was only one level of political expression. Behind or beneath the sermons, pamphlets and treatises produced in the name of the two parties was another world in which political ideas were articulated through symbols, catch phrases and face to face encounters across dinner tables or at public meetings, and where partisans on both sides expressed themselves with none of the restraint that generally governed the printed word. On one side, for example, Tory students at Trinity College vandalized the statute of King William III that stood in front of the college gates, jeered and hissed at loyal speeches on occasions like 5 November, or paraded the streets singing Jacobite ballads.[68] On the other a defender of the Tory administration, writing in 1712, offered a vivid if clearly partisan account of Whig drinking culture, with its toasts

> to the pious memory of Oliver Cromwell ... Gregg's fate to all Sacheverell's friends, or plague, pestilence and famine, battle and murder, and sudden death to all archbishops, bishops, priests and deacons etc or any other of those healths, or any other of those curses, which are played

---

66 Connolly, *Religion, Law and Power*, pp. 239-40. 67 *Journals of the House of Lords* (Dublin 1780), vol. 2, pp. 414-15. For the wider background see L.A. Dralle, 'Kingdom in Reversion: The Irish viceroyalty of the earl of Wharton', *Huntington Library Quarterly*, 15 (1951-2), 404-5, 428. 68 Connolly, *Religion, Law and Power*, pp. 239-40.

off at glorious memory feasts, at sessions, assizes, tholsel, or any other solemn assemblies, to regale republicans and atheists, or to choke honest men.[69]

The ease with which the rituals of a social gathering could bring underlying political animosities to the surface is vividly illustrated in the Revd Francis Higgins' account of the dispute that erupted at a dinner for justices of the peace following a meeting of the quarter sessions for the county of Dublin in 1711. This began with a first, relatively oblique exchange when Higgins, a celebrated Tory polemicist just restored to the commission of the peace, qualified a toast crediting King William with having preserved their lives and liberties by adding 'under God'. A fellow diner replied that ''tis in God we move, and live, and have our being', adroitly using conventional piety to undermine any appeal to a purely providential interpretation of the Revolution. Real animosities flared when Lord Santry proposed a toast 'To all honest gentlemen who make the laws the rule of their obedience', to which Higgins added 'and when they can't obey, will patiently suffer'.

> This put my Lord into a passion, which he thus vented.
> Sir, what do you mean by that, Sir?
> *Mr Higgins*. I mean, Sir, that where we cannot obey, we must not resist. There have been strange doctrines relating to obedience maintained of late; and I think every man who is honoured with her Majesty's commission ought to be tender of the royal prerogative.
> *Mr Upton*. Sir, the prerogative is part of the law of the land, and it is common law.
> *Mr Higgins*. I know it is, Sir.

From this the exchange of toasts degenerated into a verbal brawl, with Santry and others denouncing Higgins and going on immediately afterwards to present him before the grand jury of the county as 'a common disturber of her majesty's peace, and a sower of sedition and groundless jealousies amongst her Majesty's Protestant subjects'. For his part Higgins alleged that as tempers rose he had heard a Colonel Foster and Sir Richard Bulkeley proclaim 'that the crown of England was elective, that her Majesty held it from the people, and if she did not rule according to law, she was accountable to the people, and may be deposed as her father was'.[70] Once again the essential point was that inter-

---

[69] Joseph Trapp, *Her Majesty's Prerogative in Ireland ... Asserted and Maintained* (London 1712), p. 45. William Greg, a clerk in the office of first minister Robert Harley, had been executed for treason after being caught passing information to the French. [70] Printed reply of Revd Francis Higgins to the presentment made against him by the grand jury of Co. Dublin, 5 Oct. 1711, PRO(L) S.P.63/367/15-18.

pretations of the events of 1688 had inescapable implications for both present and future. But these implications, on this occasion as no doubt on many others, were highlighted by the combined effects of alochol and personal friction.

VI

What, finally, were the implications of the Revolution, and of the debates arising out of it, for the development across the eighteenth century of a distinctive Irish political culture? In the decades after 1714, the impact of earlier events can be detected in three main areas.

The first of these was the continued use of the slogans and catch phrases of pre-1714 party conflict. At the level of practical politics, in the competition for place and profit and the search for efficient and reliable men of business, the distinction between Whig and Tory had by the 1720s ceased to have much relevance.[71] But in some quarters at least the political language of Anne's reign retained a certain resonance for much longer. Charles Lucas, for example, accused his opponents on Dublin corporation of demanding 'passive obedience and non-resistance to the mighty lords and rulers of this undone city', and pointedly recalled the involvement of the father of one of his opponents in the attempts of a Tory faction in Anne's reign to dominate municipal government. 'The old latent party spirit' of Sir Constantine Phipps, the Tory lord chancellor who had sought to impose a mayor by overriding the votes of the corporation, 'was to be stirred up, and fired to make another furious effort, for the late exploded cause'.[72] During the Money Bill dispute of the mid-1750s, likewise, an opposition writer complained of men in power 'whose ancestors, as well as themselves, were distinguished for their virulence of anti-revolutional [sic] principles'; 'notorious Jacobites hold the superiority over long-tried Whigs'. While this was so 'the leaven of 1710 must spread through every branch of the community'.[73] As late as 1794 the United Irishman William Drennan, on trial for sedition, could protest that he feared 'the Jacobite more than the Jacobin, and the revival of those doctrines of passive obedience, non-resistance and epidemic Toryism which produced one revolution, and may provoke another'.[74] Nor was

---

[71] Patrick McNally, 'The Hanoverian accession and the Tory party in Ireland', *Parliamentary History*, 14/3 (1995). See also the same author's *Parties, Patriots and Undertakers: Parliamentary Politics in Early Hanoverian Ireland* (Dublin 1997). [72] Charles Lucas, *A Letter to the Free Citizens of the City of Dublin*, 2nd edn (Dublin 1749), p. 17; Charles Lucas, *A Nineteenth Address to the Free Citizens and Freeholders of the City of Dublin* (Dublin 1749), pp. 5-6. [73] *Seasonable Advice to the Friends of Ireland on the Present Crisis of Affairs* (Dublin 1755), p. 21; *A Few Words More of Advice to the Friends of Ireland on the Present Crisis* (Dublin 1755), p. 13. [74] J.F. Larkin (ed.),

it only opposition writers who resorted in this way to the labels of an earlier era. Defenders of the established order also turned to past controversies for rhetorical ammunition, at times with bizarre results. One critic of Lucas, pointing to the dangers of inciting the mob against its lawful governors, recalled 'the seditious sermons delivered from the pulpit by that hellish agent of France and Rome, the detestable Sacheverell'.[75] An MP in 1779, outraged at the concern shown by some of his colleagues concerning the wishes of their constituents, referred to 'men of passive obedience and non-resistance who wanted to be pushed forward by the crowd'.[76]

Side by side with this largely rhetorical use of the slogans of an earlier political era, secondly, went a more substantive appeal by opponents of the political establishment to the precedent or principles of 1688. Lucas, for example, supported his insistence on the virtues of the balanced constitution with an outspoken comment: 'that the Lords and Commons have jointly a right to institute anew the royal estate, whenever the trust reposed in that magistrate is betrayed, or whenever a vacancy happens from other causes, the present family on the throne can testify.'[77] In the same way the Presbyterian minister Alexander MacLaine, preaching in Antrim in 1745, told his congregation that 'the end of government is no other than the good of the governed' and that all government had its source in the consent of the people.

> Nobler principles upon which to act, and more generous motives, can never enter into the heart of man, than to deliver a nation from the chains of merciless tyranny and slavery, and to advance and effectually secure their happiness and prosperity. These were the motives upon which James the Second was resisted, and permitted to banish himself; and these are motives which will for ever justify resistance in the same circumstances.[78]

Nicholas Archdall, writing in 1751 against proposals for a union of Great Britain and Ireland, acknowledged Ireland's subordination to the English crown but observed that its inhabitants 'ever since the late revolution in eighty-eight ... have considered themselves as a free people'.[79]

Already by the 1740s and 1750s, then, the Revolution could be cited either to legitimize criticism of authority or to validate a claim to certain essential lib-

---

Trial of William Drennan (Dublin 1991), p. 134.   **75** John Taylor, *Lucas Detected: Or, a Vindication of the Sheriffs and Commons of the City of Dublin* (Dublin 1749).   **76** Sir Henry Cavendish, quoted in R.B. McDowell, *Irish Public Opinion 1750-1800* (London 1944), p. 83.   **77** [Lucas], *A Second Letter to the Citizens of Dublin* (Dublin 1749), p. 16.   **78** Alexander MacLaine, *A Sermon Preached at Antrim, December 18, 1745, Being the National Fast* (Dublin 1746), pp.11-12, 14-18   **79** N. Archdall, *An Alarum to the People of Great Britain and Ireland: In Answer to a Late Proposal for Uniting these Kingdoms* (Dublin 1751), p. 6.

erties. As yet, however, its use in either capacity was limited. One central reason was the continued dominance of the doctrine of the ancient constitution. According to this view 1688 was important, not as a political turning point in its own right, but as the latest in a line of successful defences of liberties inherited from the distant past. Henry Brooke, for example, writing in the persona of a former opposition spokesman rallying support for the Hanoverian dynasty in the crisis year of 1745, had no doubts about the legitimacy of the Revolution:

> Whatever may be the original foundation of right in any monarchy to dominion, popularity can alone be the confirmation thereof; nor is there any power divine or human to support a prince who appeals from the welfare and good will of his people.

The great merit of the Hanoverian dynasty, in fact, was that its future was so completely bound up with the Revolution: 'our interest and the interest of the ruling family is one; we have no liberty, but by supporting them in the succession; they have no title, but by securing to us our liberties'. But Brooke, like others, believed that these liberties had been transmitted from the city states of ancient Greece to republican Rome, to the Gothic peoples of northern Europe, and eventually to the British Isles, where they had been preserved across centuries by repeated constitutional struggles.[80] In the same way Robert Molesworth's celebrated exposition, in 1721, of the principles of a true Whig included a firm and unqualified defence of the Revolution. 'Our constitution', Molesworth wrote, 'is a government of laws, not of persons. Allegiance and protection are obligations that cannot subsist separately; when one fails the other falls of course.' It followed that

> A right Whig ... thinks no prince fit to govern, whose principle it must be to ruin the constitution ... the exercise of an arbitrary illegal power in the nation, so as to undermine the constitution, would incapacitate either King James, King William or any other from being his king, whenever the public has a power to hinder it.[81]

Yet the constitution Molesworth referred to was once again 'the true old Gothic constitution'[82], whose extinction in the rest of Europe he had charted in his earlier *Account of Denmark* (1694). For Molesworth, in fact, the events of 1688 were less a triumph than another narrow escape from disaster: 'all we pre-

---

[80] Henry Brooke, *The Farmer's Letters to the Protestants of Ireland* (Cork 1745), Letter 5, pp. 5-6; Letter 2, p. 3; Letter 6, pp. 1-5. [81] Robert Molesworth, *Franco-Gallia, or an Account of the Ancient Free State of France and Most Other Parts of Europe, before the Loss of their Liberties*, 2nd edn (London 1721), Translator's Preface, p. xxxiii. [82] Ibid., p. vii.

tended to by the late Revolution (bought with so great expense, yet not too dearly paid for) was to be as we were, and that every one should have his own again; the effecting of which may be called a piece of good luck, and that's the best can be said of it'. This was the true 'real Whig' position, in which the problem with the Revolution was that it did not go far enough, so that the task for the future was to find ways 'to preserve our commonwealth in its legal state of freedom, without the necessity of a civil war once or twice every age'.[83]

Attempts by critics of the political order to draw on the rhetoric of the Revolution did not go unchallenged. The third significant development of the period after 1714 was the attempts of another group of authors to redefine the events of 1688 in a manner that supported authority rather than defining its limits. Thus Theophilus Bolton, vicar general of Elphin, preaching in 1721, used the anniversary of the Irish rebellion of 1641 to review the Christian doctrine of obedience. He rejected as the mistaken inventions of an earlier age the doctrines of unlimited passive obedience and the inherent superiority of hereditary monarchy, arguing that religion had nothing to say on the relative merits of particular forms of government. Instead the powers of magistrates were defined by the laws of the society concerned. A ruler who refused to govern by those laws could legitimately be resisted, and if he persisted his subjects were released from all obligation to obey him. However, Bolton went on to give this quasi-Lockeian argument a distinctive twist, concluding that since the Revolution had been founded on this Christian principle, the government it had created was manifestly of divine right.[84] Robert Clayton, bishop of Killala, preaching in 1732, offered a more blatant redefinition of traditional Whig doctrine. His starting point was the virtues of a mixed monarchy, 'a just balance between the three constituent parts of the legislative power, the king, the lords and the commons'. But he went on to argue that under the Hanoverian monarchy the threat to this balance did not come, as in the past, either from the Crown or from the aristocracy. Indeed 'it is a great weakness to imagine that acts of tyranny and arbitrary power are always confined to the persons of monarchs'. Instead the main danger now lay with 'the commonality, who are easily misled with popular cries', and with 'the violence of popular assemblies'. It was easy to oppose and find fault with those in authority. But the events of Charles I's reign had shown how such criticism could create a 'spirit of enthusiastic madness' which would throw down 'the boundaries of religion, of liberty, of property and of government'.[85]

---

83 Robert Molesworth, *An Account of Denmark as it was in the Year 1692* (London 1694), preface. See also *Franco-Gallia*, translator's preface, p. ix.   **84** Theophilus Bolton, *A Sermon Preached in St Andrews, Dublin* (Dublin 1721), p. 39 (wrongly numbered p. 35).   **85** *A Sermon Preached at Christ Church Dublin on the Thirtieth of January 1731/2 ... by Robert, Lord Bishop of Killala* (Dublin 1732).

Clayton's sermon, deftly shifting the emphasis of the traditional doctrine of mixed monarchy and explicitly repudiating the parliamentarians of the 1640s, vividly illustrates the transformation of Whiggery from an ideology of opposition to one of oligarchic rule. By contrast another defence of the established order looked back to an entirely different tradition of political argument. Samuel Davey, writing against Lucas in 1749, went out of his way to attack the claim that the king held his title 'by the suffrages of a free people'. In fact, he insisted, 'the empire of Great Britain, of which the kingdom of Ireland is a part, is not an elective but an hereditary monarchy'.

> His Majesty's title to the crown of these realms by no means depend[s] on or is owing to the suffrages of the people. The throne is his real and apparent right, and that of his family by due course of inheritance.

Neither did the king's title owe anything to the act of succession. That a papist could not possibly be head of the Church of England was self-evident, even in the absence of a statute to say so: this was proved by the attempt to exclude James during his brother's reign. What had happened in 1714, therefore, was that, the house of Hanover being the eldest Protestant branch of the royal family, 'reason and the nature of the thing pointed them out as immediate in succession to the throne on the failure of issue in Queen Anne, independent of the suffrages of the people'.[86] This reading of history, glossing over the failure of the Exclusionists and the three unchallenged years that James II had spent on the English throne, and presenting a highly sanitized account of most of what had followed, was stronger on assertion than credibility. Its reiteration as late as 1749 suggests that opposition references to 'the leaven of 1710' were not wholly fanciful.

The limited use of 1688 as a reference point among opponents of the existing political order in the decades after 1714 can be contrasted with its prominence in the opposition rhetoric of the last quarter of the eighteenth century. It was in this period, as Patrick Kelly has shown, that the ideas of John Locke, largely absent from Irish political writing following their early introduction in Molyneux's *Case of Ireland*, began to be frequenty cited.[87] Meanwhile patriot spokesmen began to appeal with increasing boldness to 1688 as a precedent for aggressive self-assertion. Henry Grattan, in 1782, cited the Revolution as grounds for rejecting any claim which the English parliament could make to impose her laws on Ireland. England herself had 'considered the right of kings

---

86 Samuel Davey, *A View of the Conduct and Writings of Mr Charles Lucas* (Dublin 1749), p. 4.
87 Kelly, 'Perceptions of Locke'. For the argument that the Revolution was central to the self image and political thinking of Irish Protestants from much earlier in the century see James Kelly's essay below, p. 188.

as defeasible, and the birth-right of the subject as indefeasible, and she deposed a king who had, under the authority of precedent and adjudication, invaded the indefeasible right of the subject, out of which right she formed not only a revolution but a dynasty'. Two years earlier he was even more direct:

> The king has no other title to his crown than that which you have to your liberty; both are founded, the throne and your freedom, upon the right vested in the subject to resist by arms ... any authority attempting to impose acts of power as laws, whether that authority be one man or a host, the second James, or the British parliament.[88]

In the same way William Drennan, in 1785, defended the extra-parliamentary campaign of the Volunteers by invoking 'the soul of the immortal Locke, and the spirit of reform which dictated the terms of the revolution', as well as 'that glorious innovation on the customary rules of succession, which placed the crowns of three kingdoms on the head of a German elector'.[89] Henry Flood, in 1781, responded defiantly to the accusation that he was a 'speculist' by appealing, not just to 1688, but to the tradition of republicanism and regicide from which the Whigs of the immediate post-Revolution era had been so anxious to disassociate themselves : 'The hireling of a court might say, that Hampden and Sidney were speculists; the revolution itself speculative. But it was such a speculation as established the liberties of England.'[90] At a more popular level a writer in an opposition newspaper in 1776 complained that the court kept up 'the farce of joy' in celebrating King William's birthday on 4 November, although 'in their hearts they hate revolution principles'.[91]

By the end of the eighteenth century two further developments had brought extra complexity to the use of the terminology and symbolism of the Revolution. The first, common to both Great Britain and Ireland, was the adoption of the term 'Whig' as the name of a particular political association: in England, the party led by the marquis of Rockingham, in Ireland the Irish Whig parliamentary grouping, linked to Whig Clubs in Dublin, Belfast and elsewhere, created in 1789. The following year John Leslie, standing for election in County Antrim against two candidates put up by the Northern Whig club, protested openly at this brazen act of appropriation. 'A Whig, he said, was a popular appellation, and he believed himself to be one; that if he was returned to parliament he would support the Protestant religion, he would protect the rights

---

88 *The Speeches of the Right Hon. Henry Grattan*, Daniel Madden ed. (Dublin 1874), pp. 61, 49. **89** William Drennan, *Letters of Orellana, an Irish Helot* (Dublin 1785), p. 30. **90** *Irish Parliamentary Register*, 2nd edn (Dublin 1784), vol. 1, p. 112 (29 Nov. 1781). **91** Quoted in James Kelly, '"The glorious and immortal memory": commemoration and Protestant identity in Ireland 1660-1800', *Proceedings of the Royal Irish Academy*, 94C, no. 2 (1994), 46.

of the people against the encroachments of the Crown, and the prerogatives of the Crown against the encroachments of the people.'[92] If such scrupulous even handedness between crown and people was a further reminder of how far the term 'Whig' had travelled from its origins in resistance to the perceived threat of absolutism in the reigns of Charles II and his brother, the summary of what Whiggery had meant in practice for the greater part of the previous century was nevertheless fair enough. But such protests could do nothing to prevent the new nomenclature from becoming firmly established.

The second development, specific to Ireland, was the capture, from the 1790s, of the cult of King William III by the forces of Protestant sectarianism. A Williamite commemorative tradition, centred on celebrations of the anniversary of his birth (4 November) and of the military victories at the Boyne and Aughrim, had been kept alive throughout the eighteenth century. For most of this period, as Jacqueline Hill has shown, William was celebrated not just for his defeat of Catholicism but for his intervention to rescue British and Irish constitutional liberties from the encroachments of Stuart absolutism. From the 1790s, however, against a background of revived sectarian animosities, his cult became increasingly the property of Protestant supremacists.[93] This had implications, not only for the new Protestant conservatism taking shape at this time, but also for the status of the Revolution as a political reference point. As the saviour of parliamentary liberties was swallowed up by the Protestant champion, so too was the memory of 1688 by that of 1690, with consequences that remain evident in Irish political symbolism and rhetoric down to the present day.

A final episode illustrates something of the scale and nature of the transformation that took place. In 1813 Nicholas Purcell O'Gorman, a leading Catholic barrister, appeared as defence counsel at the trial in Derry of Cornelius O'Mullan, a priest serving as curate in one of the city's parishes. O'Mullan had been suspended from his office by the bishop of the diocese, Charles O'Doherty, and had allegedly instigated a riot in order to prevent O'Doherty from taking possession of the parish church. The trouble between the two men had begun when O'Mullan criticized O'Doherty for having attended a civic banquet at which a toast had been drunk to the glorious and immortal memory of William III. Coming to this part of the controversy, O'Gorman offered a pointed discussion of the different political meanings of the contentious toast:

> The brave ancestors of the people whom he now addressed had shut their gates in the despot's face, and their descendants had reason to be

[92] *A Collection of the Authenticated Public Addresses, Resolutions and Advertisements Relative to the Late Election of Knights of the Shire for the County of Antrim* (Belfast 1790), pp. 10, 29, 52. [93] J.R. Hill, 'National Festivals, the State and "Protestant Ascendancy" in Ireland 1790-1829', *Irish Historical Studies*, 24 (1984), 30-51.

proud of commemorating the glorious act. Had he then been in existence, he would have been proud to have lent his aid to the 'Glorious Revolution' – he would have rallied round the Orange standard and breathed his last in the breaches of our walls before the tyrant should have entered. His ancestors were unfortunately shut up within the walls of Limerick, fighting in the cause of tyranny.

If O'Mullan and others now objected to toasting the glorious and immortal memory, this was because its meaning had been perverted. 'William gave liberty to England, but to Ireland a party, and the sacred memory of the champion of freedom was degraded to the mere watchword of a faction.'[94]

O'Gorman's words cannot, of course, be detached from their context. As his reference to the brave ancestors of his audience indicated, he was pleading O'Mullan's case before a Protestant jury to whom the issue of the glorious memory would have been a matter of particular concern. But other aspects of the context are also important. O'Gorman was not just a Catholic lawyer. He was a leading member of the Catholic Committee, newly radicalized by the controversy over the veto and the resulting seccession of the gentry-led conservative wing of the movement. His dispatch to Derry to defend an assertive junior priest in conflict with a conservative, accommodationist bishop was itself a reflection of the quickening of Catholic political life. In this context his willingness to identify the war of 1689-91 in such unqualified terms as a conflict between tyranny and liberty provides striking testimony to the place which the Revolution, however belatedly and for however short a time, had come to hold in Irish political rhetoric. At the same time the remarks that followed looked forward all too accurately to the very different way in which the events of 1688 and after were to be remembered in the decades that lay ahead.

---

[94] *An account of the trial of the Rev. Cor. O'Mullan* (Derry 1814), p.13.

Corporatist ideology and practice in Ireland, 1660–1800

JACQUELINE HILL

I

If the term 'corporatism' means anything in the Irish context, it probably conjures up the vocationalist ideas that were current in the 1920s and 1930s, inspired largely by continental European beliefs in a more harmonious medieval and early modern past. In Ireland the supporters of vocationalism envisaged occupational groups electing self-governing corporations, which would play a central role in society and the economy, and form a barrier against the excesses of state bureaucracy and the threat of Communism. Such ideas had only a limited impact on intellectual debate and the political system, although the 1937 constitution was given a 'vocationalist veneer', notably in its provisions for Senate elections.[1] The fact was that, in contrast to the position in certain European countries, in early twentieth-century Ireland corporatism had few backers among those who exercised political power. Its rejection in Ireland reflected the extent to which Irish society took its political ideas from Great Britain. But at another level the tradition that was being rejected was in fact a part of Irish political history as well as European, in the form of the ideology and practice explored in this paper.

In medieval times an earlier variety of corporatism had flourished in Ireland as elsewhere in western Europe, and still retained considerable vitality in the early modern period. The neglect of systematic study of Irish political thought has tended to obscure its presence, but some understanding of its nature and significance is essential to any rounded picture of Ireland and its institutions during the eighteenth century. This paper sets out to consider what corporatism was, to survey its presence in Ireland from the 1660s to the act of union, and to analyse what was happening to corporatist culture and practice in that period. It concludes with an assessment of how far corporatism had declined by 1800, and what kind of ideas and values were taking its place.

---

[1] Joseph Lee, 'Aspects of corporatist thought in Ireland: the commission on vocational organisation, 1939-43' in Art Cosgrove and Donal McCartney (eds), *Studies in Irish History Presented to R. Dudley Edwards* (Dublin 1979), pp. 324-46.

II

Corporatism was a view of the polity as made up not of individuals but of 'orders' or associations, oath-bound bodies differentiated by function or calling, including guilds, municipal corporations, colleges and estates, each with distinctive rights and privileges. The ideology had its origins, and received some of its theoretical underpinnings, from Christian theology, and accordingly was imbued with Christian beliefs about hierarchy, harmony and social order. This was exemplified by the 'chain of being' that linked the highest body with the lowest, all typically under the regulation of the sovereign. Organic metaphors, such as 'the body corporate' or 'the body politic' were common, and served to soften the inherent inequality of the system:[2] a body had to have feet as well as a head, and all must know their proper stations. (Hence the importance attached to precedence, and distinctive dress for the various orders and corporations.) Smaller bodies, such as guilds, were regarded as forming groups in larger ones, such as urban corporations, which in turn were represented in estates or orders. Three estates were usually recognized (though in some countries there were four): the first estate, the clergy ('those who prayed'); the second estate, the nobility ('those who fought'); and the third estate, which consisted not of the entire population, but an urban elite or bourgeoisie comprising the 'free' citizens ('those who worked').[3] The legal rights of corporations had evolved during medieval times, and typically included the right of perpetual succession, to sue and be sued, to own land, use a common seal and make bye-laws.

The system had emerged in western Europe after the collapse of the Roman empire, and served to fill the consequent vacuum in authority: the institution of monarchy was still relatively weak, and as a result the pre-Reformation church came to exert much influence. However, corporatist culture was by no means incompatible with the Protestant Reformation (which in fact was responsible for reinvigorating corporate traditions of fraternity and community), and remained so prevalent in western Europe down to the overthrow of the *ancien régime* that German historians coined the term *Standestaat* to describe it.[4] By the early modern period the place of corporations in the state was beginning to attract systematic attention from political thinkers, with some, such as Bodin, arguing that such bodies depended on the approval of the sovereign, and others, such as Althusius, contending that they were legitimized by their members' 'common consent'.[5]

---

[2] Georges Duby, *The Three Orders: Feudal Society Imagined* (Chicago and London 1980), pp. 57-8, 313. [3] Ibid., pp. 13, 354-5. [4] A.R. Myers, *Parliaments and Estates in Europe to 1789* (London 1975), p. 11; Antony Black, *Guilds and Civil Society in European Political Thought from the Twelfth Century to the Present* (London 1984), ch. 9. [5] Jean Bodin, 1530-96; Johannes

III

The tendency of historians to play down the importance of corporatism in English political development[6] has also extended to Ireland and other countries subject to the English crown. However, now that English historians are beginning to look afresh at the later seventeenth and eighteenth centuries, some reassessment is taking place. Claims that England in this period possessed many of the hallmarks of an *ancien régime* – as exemplified by the cultural hegemony of the established church and the preeminence of aristocratic values – have been contentious, but have also stimulated a lively debate which has prompted new research.[7] The description of Ireland as an *ancien régime* has as yet attracted less criticism,[8] but there is much work to be done before a fuller picture emerges.

At a superficial glance the view that Ireland, along with England, was exceptional by continental standards seems persuasive. There was a parliament, certainly; but its vocational underpinnings appeared to be weak and blurred. The bishops of the established church sat in the House of Lords, while representatives of the towns – who by the seventeenth and eighteenth centuries were more likely to be landed gentry than merchants or tradesmen – had no separate estate of their own but sat with the gentry in the House of Commons. (Scotland, by contrast, possessed the convention of royal burghs, which continued to meet even after the 1707 act of union with England.) However, the vocational nature of the estates, and particularly the claim of the church to represent a distinct order in society, was strengthened by reference to another body, Convocation, whose two houses represented the higher and lower clergy. Convocation had met on several occasions in the seventeenth century, and the Williamite era witnessed renewed calls for it to meet simultaneously with parliament and make regulations for the church. These demands were realised between 1703 and 1711 during the reign of Queen Anne.

Further down the scale came the corporate towns or boroughs, whose royal charters conferred powers of self-government. Since Irish Protestants in this

---

Althusius, d. 1638. See Black, *Guilds and Civil Society*, ch. 11. **6** Myers, *Parliaments and Estates in Europe*, p. 9. **7** See e.g. J.C.D. Clark, *English Society 1688-1832: Ideology, Social Structure and Political Practice during the Ancien Régime* (Cambridge 1985), *passim*; Frank O'Gorman, 'The recent historiography of the Hanoverian regime', *Historical Journal*, 29 (1986), 1005-20; Robert Hole, *Pulpits, Politics and Public Order in England 1760-1832* (Cambridge 1989), ch. 16; H.T. Dickinson, *The Politics of the People in Eighteenth-Century Britain* (London and New York 1994), pp. 1-9. **8** See e.g. S.J. Connolly, *Religion, Law, and Power: The Making of Protestant Ireland 1660-1760* (Oxford 1992); C.D.A. Leighton, *Catholicism in a Protestant Kingdom: A Study of the Irish Ancien Régime* (Dublin, 1994); Jacqueline Hill, *From Patriots to Unionists: Dublin Civic Politics and Irish Protestant Patriotism* (Oxford 1997). For a restatement of the colonial model, see Kevin Whelan, 'An underground gentry? Catholic middlemen in eighteenth-century Ireland', *Eighteenth-Century Ireland*, 10 (1995), 7-68.

period were as much an urban as a landed people, this was an important element in the polity. The composition of the 'body corporate' of such towns varied from place to place depending on the terms of the charter, but might include some combination of freemen (notably in towns with craft guilds), burgesses, aldermen, mayors, provosts and sovereigns. In the case of parliamentary boroughs, there was a right of representation in parliament. Borough electorates varied in size from a handful of voters to several thousands in the capital city, but were always smaller than the whole body of town dwellers, and did not include even all the Protestant inhabitants. In the case of Trinity College, the body corporate (and hence the electors for the college's two parliamentary seats) comprised the provost, fellows and foundation scholars.[9]

As was common elsewhere, such bodies were linked by a formal commitment to uphold the interests of the established church. Thus all corporation officials were subject, along with members of parliament, to the provisions of the test act of 1704,[10] which required them to be in communion with the established church. In addition, such officials were required from 1692 to take the oath of supremacy, acknowledging the supremacy of the king over the church, and the so-called 'declaration against popery', which involved a disavowal of transubstantiation and the invocation of the saints.[11] On church holidays it was the custom for members of such bodies to attend services of the established church in their corporate capacity. As for Trinity College, whose foundation charter in 1591 charged it with promoting both the study of the liberal arts and 'the cultivation of virtue and religion', from Charles I's reign onwards fellows were obliged to have taken holy orders and (with only two exceptions) to be celibate, and even the students were required to attend prayers three times a day, and to receive holy communion according to Anglican forms.[12] In this way the system served to promote not Protestantism as such, but specifically the established episcopal Church of Ireland.

The corporatist nature of these institutions was reinforced by dress codes. For the aristocratic elite, taking its cue from its European counterparts, a standard court dress had evolved by the mid-eighteenth century; and in the corporations, the church and Trinity College the various hierarchies were marked out by distinctive gowns.[13] Public processions, such as viceregal cavalcades, anniversary parades, the riding of town franchises – to maintain urban bound-

---

9 Kenneth Milne, 'The Irish municipal corporations in the eighteenth century' (unpublished Ph.D. thesis, TCD 1962), ch. 1; W. MacNeile Dixon, *Trinity College, Dublin* (London 1902), p. 150. 10 2 Anne, c. 6 (4 Mar. 1704). 11 An act for abrogating the oath of supremacy in Ireland, and appointing other oaths (3 Will. & Mary, c. 2 (Eng.) (24 Dec. 1691)). 12 The celibacy rule was strictly enforced down to the mid-eighteenth century: Constantia Maxwell, *A History of Trinity College Dublin 1591-1892* (Dublin 1946), pp. 40-1, 151, 190. 13 Ibid., p. 132; 'Oath of a comon councillman', Dublin Corporation Archives, Book of oaths, MR/32, p. 8.

aries against the encroachment of the other estates[14] – were opportunities to reinforce these distinctions, with the different orders taking their places according to their stations. Funeral processions furnished another example. Following the death of Dublin MP Charles Lucas in 1771, the procession to St Michan's parish church was headed by representatives of the church, including diocesan clergy and members of Trinity College (the vice-provost and scholars); behind them came the coffin, attended by members of Lucas' family; after which there followed members of the nobility, the speaker of the House of Commons, and then in turn the lord mayor, aldermen, sheriffs, masters and wardens of the guilds, and members of the corporation's lower house, or city commons.[15] Observance of precedence within the different orders was equally important. At parliamentary elections in the early decades of the century, the Dublin freemen were apt to be reminded to deliver their votes according to their guilds, beginning with the oldest and most prestigious, the merchants guild, 'and proceeding according to their stations'.[16]

However, it is one thing to show the existence of the institutions and forms of corporatism. It is another to show that they represented anything more than the vestiges of a once vibrant medieval reality. After all, this was the age of the Enlightenment, a period when, it is assumed, Lockeian individualism was gaining ground over corporate privileges, when older values such as 'the divine right of kings' were giving way to parliamentary sovereignty, and when the confessional state was being subjected to the test of reason and experience. No doubt these tendencies were all present, but undue emphasis on them has tended to obscure the strength of the desire to protect, and in some cases revive, older varieties of corporate rights and privileges.

To begin with the church, the characteristic corporatist assimilation of heavenly and earthly institutions was invoked at the beginning of our period, when the dual restoration of monarchy and established church was perceived as marking the end of an unnatural and ungodly era of civil war, regicide and republic. The anthem at the ceremony for the installation of twelve bishops in St Patrick's cathedral, Dublin, in 1661 proclaimed

> Angels look down, and joye to see
> Here, as above, a Monarchie
> Angels look down, and joye to see
> Here, as above, a Hierarchie.[17]

---

[14] See Lennox Barrow, 'Riding the franchises', *Dublin Historical Record*, 33 (1979-80), 135-8; idem, 'The franchises of Dublin', 36 (1982-3), 68-80.   [15] *Freeman's Journal*, 7-9 Nov. 1771.   [16] *Faulkner's Dublin Journal*, 10-14 Oct. 1729.   [17] Quoted in R.B. McDowell and D.A. Webb, *Trinity College Dublin 1592-1952: An Academic History* (Cambridge 1982), p. 22.

The intimate connection between church and state was a hallmark of the restored monarchy: Charles II was urged to foster the episcopal reformed church because it could be relied on to teach passive obedience and was dependent on the monarchy for its survival.[18] His brother James II ignored this advice, and lost his throne in the revolution of 1688-9. Although there was no significant 'non-juror' element in the Irish church after the Revolution (unlike the situation in England, where hundreds of clergy and even some of the bishops refused to take the oaths to the new monarchs, William III and Mary), the ousting of a lawful king inevitably dealt a blow to the morale and self-confidence of the Church of Ireland. Subsequently the 1690s and the early decades of the new century witnessed a desire among church leaders, which to a considerable extent transcended party affiliations, to restore the authority and rights of the church and reassert its role as the spiritual arm of the state in maintaining doctrinal orthodoxy, discipline and the social order. Both 'high' and 'low' churchmen defended the status of the Church of Ireland as a distinct 'national church', with its own Convocation, not dependent on that of the Church of England.[19] As during the Restoration period, leading churchmen again stressed the obligation of dissenters of all kinds (Protestant as well as Catholic) to conform to the church: there could be no *right* of toleration.[20]

Differences of emphasis over how to achieve these goals, and whether or not to proceed as part of a wider 'British' crusade against current evils, were manifested in sessions of the Irish Convocation between 1703 and 1711. They added fuel to the 'rage of party' that characterized the reign of Queen Anne, with Whig politicians criticizing what they regarded as the excessive claims of Tory churchmen. Church insistence on maintaining the sacramental test, and assertions by the lower house of Convocation of its rights (ahead of those of parliament) to regulate tithes, were particularly contentious, and Convocation was forced to back down. One Whig statesman claimed that 'this country is very near as much under the power and influence of the clergy as the people of Italy are', and even among the clergy themselves some were critical of what one called 'making the clergy a distinct corporation from the laity'.[21] However,

---

18 Conal Condren, 'Casuistry to Newcastle: "The prince" in the world of the book' in Nicholas Phillipson and Quentin Skinner (eds), *Political Discourse in Early Modern Britain* (Cambridge 1993), p. 177. **19** On the church in this period, see F.R. Bolton, *The Caroline Tradition of the Church of Ireland* (London 1958); S.J. Connolly, 'Reformers and highflyers: the post-revolution church' in Alan Ford, James McGuire, and Kenneth Milne (eds), *As By Law Established: The Church of Ireland since the Reformation* (Dublin 1995), pp. 152-65; D.W. Hayton, 'The high church party in the Irish convocation 1703-1713' in Hermann J. Real and H. Stover-Leidig (eds), *Reading Swift: Papers from the Third Munster Symposium on Jonathan Swift* (Munich 1998), pp. 117-40. **20** In the early part of the century Protestant dissenters faced persecution if they attempted to set up new congregations: Connolly, *Religion, Law, and Power*, p. 164. **21** Connolly, 'Reformers and highflyers', pp. 158, 161; Hayton, 'The

the church maintained a high profile by promoting a drive for moral reform, backed up by new legislation passed in 1695 and 1704 against sabbath-breaking and against cursing and swearing: the lower house of Convocation would have liked to go even further in imposing moral discipline on society at large. There was also some support for reviving projects from the previous century to win converts by ensuring the availability of Irish-language versions of the scriptures, and by promoting educational initiatives. But Convocation's assertiveness had inflamed an anticlerical spirit among members of parliament, and strengthened erastian tendencies among some politicians.[22] Thus debates about the church's corporatist role and privileges were central to early eighteenth-century Irish politics, and continued to reverberate thereafter.

Although convocation was not in fact to meet again after 1711, the habit of referring to 'the king and the three estates of the realm' lingered on.[23] A toleration act of 1719 exempted Protestant dissenters from the obligation to attend services of the established church, but formal repeal of the test act was achieved only in 1780.[24] And it was with corporatist arguments that Richard Woodward, bishop of Cloyne, underpinned his famous defence of the church's privileges in *The Present State of the Church of Ireland* (1786), which succeeded in fending off reform of the tithe system for a generation. Woodward argued that the ecclesiatical constitution was inextricably linked to the civil: 'they were formed so precisely on the same model, that the whole was likened to a double cone, united by the authority of the Crown'.[25]

The corporatist nature of the eighteenth-century Irish aristocracy has been obscured by the absence (as in England) of fiscal exemptions and reserved office, and by the decay of the seigneurial system; though it should be remembered that many manorial courts survived, with jurisdiction in petty criminal and civil matters.[26] Noble privileges were more evident in respect of rank than of corporate status, at least for peers (such as trial by peers, certain legal immunities, and membership of the House of Lords, where counsel could be offered to the monarch). Corporate privileges – such as the right to bear arms and to possess a coat of arms – had a tendency in the course of the century to be encroached on by those who lacked the classic *ancien régime* qualification of noble birth; some, at least, of the new Protestant settlers were keen to have pedigrees made out.[27] Since the gentry enjoyed few privileges of rank, they placed a high value

---

high church party', pp. 138-9.   **22** Connolly, 'Reformers and highflyers', pp. 156-7, 173-4. **23** Edward [Tennison], *A Sermon Preached in Christ-Church, Dublin ... on the fifth day of November, 1733: Being the Anniversary-Thanksgiving for the Happy deliverance of the King, and the Three Estates of the Realm of England* (Dublin 1733).   **24** 6 Geo. I, c. 5 (2 Nov. 1719); 19 & 20 Geo. III, c. 6 (2 May 1780).   **25** Richard Woodward, *The Present State of the Church of Ireland* (Dublin 1787 edn), p. 11.   **26** Such courts were sometimes under church control: Milne, 'The Irish municipal corporations', pp. 49-51.   **27** Francis G. James, *Lords of the Ascendancy: The House of Lords and its Members, 1600-1800* (Dublin 1995), ch. 5; Katharine

on landownership as a badge of their own noble status. However, the point has been made that the boundaries of the Irish 'landed' class were less obvious than was the case in England, thanks in part to the presence of large numbers of middlemen (including Catholics) who let out land on behalf of the great owners but who owned little land themselves. Given the resulting ambiguities, the gentry compensated by displaying a fierce attachment to the code of honour, reflected in the prevalence of duelling. Lavish hospitality, too, and conspicuous excess in the consumption of food and drink, were much in evidence.[28]

The cleft in society occasioned by religion clearly weakened the cohesiveness of the aristocratic elite. Nevertheless, the effects of this should not be exaggerated. The resident Irish peerage in the late seventeenth century, for instance, has been described as having begun 'to meld into an aristocratic elite whose sense of identity transcended diverse ethnic origins and even different religious affiliations'.[29] Catholic peers who were protected by the treaty of Limerick, or whose outlawry had been reversed, continued to be summoned to the Irish House of Lords, although the oaths acted as a barrier to prevent them taking their seats. The titles of other Catholic peers were not recognized, and some individuals were disciplined for using their titles; yet respect for the hereditary nobility ensured that such peers were socially accepted. And although the penal laws in principle debarred all Catholics from the right to bear arms, statutory exceptions were made in 1705 for certain Catholic noble families in consideration of their antiquity and lineage. Catholic middlemen, if they had Protestant undertenants, could wield political influence.[30]

As for institutional rights, both houses of the Irish parliament displayed determination in the 1690s and periodically thereafter to defend and indeed to strengthen their rights. While the House of Commons pursued its sole right to prepare money bills, the upper house was chiefly concerned with establishing its appellate jurisdiction. These issues led to clashes with the executive and the London parliament, which were only temporarily halted with the passing of the declaratory act by the British parliament in 1720. This formally set out the latter's claim to make laws binding on Ireland, and denied the appellate jurisdiction of the Irish House of Lords, but this act in turn was repealed in 1782. It should be noted that there was nothing in these clashes of an anti-monarchical nature. William Molyneux's *The Case of Ireland's being Bound by Acts of*

Simms, 'Charles Lynegar, the Ó Luinín family and the study of Seanchas' in Toby Barnard, D. Ó Cróinín and K. Simms (eds), *'A Miracle of Learning': Studies in Manuscripts and Irish Learning. Essays in Honour of William O'Sullivan* (Ashgate 1998), pp. 266-83. On privileges of rank and corporate privileges, see M.L. Bush, *The English Aristocracy: A Comparative Synthesis* (Manchester 1984), ch. 2. **28** Connolly, *Religion, Law, and Power*, pp. 59-73; James Kelly, *That Damn'd Thing Called Honour: Duelling in Ireland, 1570-1860* (Cork 1995). **29** James, *Lords of the Ascendancy*, p. 36. **30** Ibid., pp. 91-2; Connolly, *Religion, Law, and Power*, p. 147.

Parliament in England, Stated (1698) made it quite plain that if anything the idea was to urge the monarch to exercise greater power in his capacity as king of Ireland, by strengthening the rights of the Irish parliament.[31]

At the municipal level the role of craft guilds in the regulation of trade continued to be recognized not merely by guild members and the municipalities but by the Irish parliament, which in 1707 adopted resolutions calling on the guilds to enforce the apprenticeship laws on all freemen.[32] The crown, too, remained well-disposed, issuing a charter of incorporation to the last of the Dublin guilds, the apothecaries, in 1747. Such recognition was of crucial importance, because corporatist ideology took it for granted that rights and functions went together: it was as a consequence of their economic functions that freemen of guilds enjoyed the political privileges of representation on municipal corporations and a parliamentary vote (and incurred corresponding obligations, such as the payment of certain taxes and filling of offices). Occasionally impatience was expressed by parliament over the restrictive effects of guild monopolies, but it is significant that a drive to give statutory recognition to customary guild rights concerning regulation of trade found general support in the Irish parliament. This campaign began in the 1760s in response to a concerted movement by Catholic merchants and traders to opt out of the quarterage system by which the guilds attempted to regulate all tradesmen following particular trades, whether they were freemen or not. Since there were craft guilds in several of the larger towns, including Cork, Waterford, Limerick and Kilkenny, as well as in some of the smaller ones, this campaign had something of a national flavour.[33]

The quarterage system had originated in the seventeenth century, at a time when confessional pressures and the growing cost of freedom suggested the need for a category of tradesmen who, while not incurring the costs or taking the oaths of freemen (which bound them among other things to protect the secrets of the trade), might nevertheless have their right to trade recognized by

---

31 Isolde Victory, 'The making of the 1720 declaratory act' in Gerard O'Brien (ed.), *Parliament, Politics and People* (Dublin 1989), pp. 9-29; James, *Lords of the Ascendancy*, pp. 68-72; James McGuire, 'The Irish Parliament of 1692' in Thomas Bartlett and D.W. Hayton (eds), *Penal Era and Golden Age* (Belfast 1979), pp. 1-31; William Molyneux, *The Case of Ireland's being Bound by Acts of Parliament in England, Stated* (1698), ed. J.G. Simms (Dublin 1977), pp. 127-8. **32** Freemen were those who on payment of fees and taking of oaths had become free of their guild by right of birth, apprenticeship, or special grace (in some towns the status could be obtained by marriage). In guild towns, freedom of the guild was usually a prerequisite to freedom of the town or city corporation. See Milne, 'The Irish municipal corporations', pp. 29-30; Hill, *From Patriots to Unionists*, ch. 1. **33** Maureen Wall, *Catholic Ireland in the Eighteenth Century: Collected Essays of Maureen Wall*, ed. Gerard O'Brien (Dublin 1989), ch. 2; Hill, *From Patriots to Unionists*, p. 28; David Dickson, '"Centres of motion": Irish cities and the origins of popular politics' in *Culture et Pratiques Politiques en France et en Irlande xvie-xviiie Siècle* (Paris 1990), p. 116.

the guilds. Quarter brothers, most of whom were Catholics, were entitled, on payment of a quarterly fee to the guild representing their trade, to follow their trade and enjoy some advantages of freedom, including (occasional) welfare benefits and conviviality, as long as they did not flout guild regulations. Evidence from Dublin suggests that the quarterage system was still working with some success in the early decades of the eighteenth century – a period when Protestants still represented a majority of Dublin's growing population – and that as late as the 1750s the guilds continued to take for granted that it was enforceable.[34] But during that decade Catholic merchants, who were excluded from full freedom by the prescribed oaths, increasingly resisted payment, in which they received some support from the common law. The guilds counter-attacked by launching their own campaign, backed by several of the corporate towns, to obtain statutory backing for quarterage. The chief defender of guild privileges, Charles Lucas of Dublin, produced a ringing endorsment of corporatist values in order to boost the campaign:

> The more refined the policy of nations, and the higher their sense and estimation of freedom are found, the greater has their solicitude ever proved to build, extend, strengthen and adorn cities; and in order to induce men to inhabit, to cultivate, to improve and to defend them, it has ever been found necessary to indue a certain society of men with certain franchises, privileges, immunities and pre-eminencies, superior to foreigners or extern men, to invest them with powers, distinct from the ordinary subjects, particularly with a property in the soil, and the local government of the city, and sometimes with an exclusive right to trade.[35]

The Irish parliament was sympathetic, and on several occasions, the last in 1778, passed bills to endorse the guilds' rights to quarterage. But under Poynings' Law Irish legislation had to be approved by the privy council in London, and by the 1770s the government was turning against guild rights. In England, political economists such as Adam Smith and Josiah Tucker were critical of guilds for their monopolistic tendencies, and for representing an obstacle to 'free trade'. Accordingly, after a long struggle, the campaign was lost. Although the episode has been discussed chiefly in terms of confessional issues – the rights of (Protestant) freemen to enforce payments from (Catholic) tradesmen – the implications of the quarterage dispute went deeper. As Lucas recog-

---

34 Hill, *From Patriots to Unionists*, ch. 1. For an example of a guild oath, see 'The book of bye-laws of the corporation of sadlers' (1767), NLI MS 81, p. 4. **35** Charles Lucas, *The Liberties and Customs of Dublin Asserted and Demonstrated upon the Principles of Law, Justice, and Good Policy*, 2nd edn (Dublin, 1768), p. 7.

nized, what was at stake was the customary corporatist link between rights and functions; if the functions were lost, this called in question the legitimacy of the guilds' other privileges, and left them open to the charge of being merely bastions of what at the end of the century would be designated 'Protestant ascendancy'. Such charges were the more justified because once their regulatory powers over trade had been undermined, the guilds became less scrupulous about admitting freemen who did not follow the trade they were supposed to represent. Admission to freedom came to rely more on birth than on apprenticeship. Older guild traditions of fraternity, conviviality, mutual obligations and benefits did not cease, but politicization became increasingly prevalent, with the Dublin guilds in particular playing an active role in both local and national elections.[36]

In the corporatist polity, the next layer up from the guilds was formed by the corporate towns, whose charters granted extensive powers of local self-government. During the Restoration period, fear of the wealth and independence of London (and the memory of London's role in the civil wars) seems to have been responsible for a marked suspicion of urban corporations. Charles II was warned that 'every corporation, is a petty free state, against monarchy'.[37] In Ireland, too, no opportunity was spared to emphasize that corporations received their powers from above, handed down by royal charter. Sir Ellis Leighton, secretary to Lord Berkeley, the lord lieutenant of Ireland, who had contrived to be appointed recorder of Dublin, made the point forcefully in a speech to Dublin corporation in 1672:

> Corporations are the creatures of the monarchy, and therefore they have a particular obligation beyond other subjects at large to depend upon the monarchy and uphold it. Your charter is to the lord mayor, sheriffs and commons: this is the creature of the monarchy ... The table of aldermen ... ought to outvy all the rest of the corporation in that common duty of depending upon the king. They ought to have no politic maxims of their own, ... but leaving all affairs of state ... to the piety and prudence of the prince ...[38]

Dublin corporation's own constitution, as reflected in the oaths to be taken by freemen of the city, did indeed enjoin the oath-taker to be 'good and true' to the monarch and his heirs. However, the oath also enjoined freemen to

---

[36] Wall, *Catholic Ireland*, ch. 2; Leighton, *Catholicism in a Protestant Kingdom*, ch. 4; Hill, *From Patriots to Unionists*, chs. 7-8. [37] Quoted in Condren, 'Casuistry to Newcastle', 177; J.A.W. Gunn, *Beyond Liberty and Property* (Kingston and Montreal 1983), p. 47. [38] J.T. and R.M. Gilbert (eds), *Calendar of Ancient Records of Dublin* [hereafter *C.A.R.D.*] (Dublin, 1889-1944), vol. 5, pp. 559-60.

maintain 'the fraunches [franchises] and customs of this city'.[39] These two sources of authority came into conflict over the introduction by government of a measure for ensuring that Irish corporations did not fall under the control of Protestant dissenters, who were believed to harbour republican tendencies. In the absence of a corporation act for Ireland, the earl of Essex as lord lieutenant issued what became known as the New Rules (1672) for regulating Irish corporations. The main feature of these rules was to stipulate that elections of the chief officials must receive the approval of the Irish privy council. In addition, oligarchical, or 'close', tendencies in the corporations were enhanced, strengthening the power of (self-selecting) mayors and aldermen at the expense of assemblies of freemen (courts of d'oyer hundred), just as earlier in the century the Crown had given a more oligarchical complexion to Trinity College. This also made it easier for local landed families to exercise control over such towns.[40]

The effects of the New Rules on Irish corporations varied considerably. In some towns, including Cork, Limerick, Kinsale and Ardee, courts of d'oyer hundred retained some residual powers into the early eighteenth century.[41] The Rules' controversial nature is well illustrated by the case of Dublin, where their introduction led to unrest in the city for some years, with certain guild representatives on the corporation's lower house (the 'city commons') boycotting the quarterly assemblies of the corporation. Petitions were circulated, attacking the New Rules; and these turned out to be vehicles for the expression of corporatist values that alarmed the government. The Rules were condemned as 'destructive to many charters and privileges ... granted to this city and the several guilds and corporations therein', and contrary to 'the good of the city'. A statement from guild members belonging to the established church declared that they had never opposed the authority of the king or the lord lieutenant. But in view of their 'unalterable detestation of the New Rules', they felt that to attend the assemblies would amount to overthrowing their charters and injuring their guilds 'by whom only we are bound in conscience to be regulated in matters of this nature'. Not surprisingly, in the margin beside this passage a government official noted 'by this they declare themselves to be free states'.[42] Such sentiments were all the more disturbing because they appeared to be shared by members of the established church, Catholics and dissenters.

It took some years before Essex was able to bring the city commons to accept the New Rules, and they continued to be unpopular. Essex expressed his regret at the fact that the lower house contained such large numbers (ninety-six guild representatives, and up to forty-eight others who had served the office of sheriff). He argued that the city would be much more peaceful if the city

---

[39] *C.A.R.D.*, vol. 1, p. 261. [40] Milne, 'The Irish municipal corporations', pp. 12-13. [41] Ibid., pp. 41, 44. [42] Hill, *From Patriots to Unionists*, pp. 53-4.

commons was a smaller body, with members drawn exclusively from the wealthier section of the trading community. Such a change was to be initiated in the Jacobite charter for Dublin (1687), and although following the Williamite reconquest the position reverted to the *status quo ante*, the oligarchical tendencies remained. And the guilds too were affected; in Dublin it became common for the guild officials, notably the master and wardens, to be chosen not by the body of guild freemen, but by the guild's council, which included serving officials and those who had just gone out of office.[43]

During the following century the spectacular growth of Dublin served to highlight the weaknesses of an oligarchical city government, and by the 1740s a challenge to oligarchy in the urban corporations and guilds was under way, mounted by elements from within the corporatist world of privilege, using the language of corporatism itself. The key here was the issue of election and consent. Charles Lucas (1713-71), the champion of the rights of the lower house of Dublin corporation, and of the rank-and-file freemen of the guilds, made use of a number of political languages, including classical republicanism and Lockeian contract theory, but corporatism was fundamental to his perception of political life in Ireland. Following Giraldus Cambrensis and several English commentators, he envisaged pre-Norman Ireland as a country that lacked 'civility' or (as Lucas put it) was sunk in 'Gothic Barbarism', without liberty or security for property. The transformation came about when Henry II of England gave permission to his 'British subjects' to go to the help of the dethroned Dermot MacMorrough, king of Leinster, whereupon many of 'the more *free and civilised People of England*, our *Progenitors*, came *voluntarily* to the assistance of this *Irish* Prince'. Some of these adventurers were granted land by MacMurrough, and this paved the way for the introduction to Ireland of 'arts and sciences', the inseparable attendants of liberty. At the same time, several cities and towns corporate were established,

> with as ample *powers, privileges, free-customs, liberties*, and *immunities*, as any of those in *England* ... and (to complete the whole), MAGNA CHARTA, a great *charter* of *rights* and *liberties*, was granted to the *whole nation*, agreeable to that of *England*, after whose manner, for the further security of the *rights* and *liberties* of the *whole*, PARLIAMENTS were instituted, wherein the *people* gave their suffrages, by representatives appointed among themselves, by *free* and *uncorrupted elections*.[44]

---

43 Ibid., pp. 55-70.   44 Charles Lucas, *Divelina Libera: An Apology for the Civil Rights and Liberties of the Commons and Citizens of Dublin* (Dublin, 1744), pp. 9-11. The most detailed study of Lucas' campaign is Sean Murphy, 'The Lucas affair: a study of municipal and electoral politics in Dublin, 1742-9' (unpublished M.A. thesis, University College, Dublin 1981).

In this way corporatism formed an integral part of Ireland's national constitution. Lucas acknowledged that it was only under James I that these laws could be said to have applied to the whole of Ireland, but he insisted that when James established 'civil liberty' in Ireland he was instituting 'a *legal*, not an *imperial* government'. Thus Lucas' corporatism had more in common with that of Althusius than of Bodin. There was certainly room for monarchy – indeed, Lucas was prepared to heap praise upon monarchs who ruled by consent – but this was monarchy of a regulated or 'mixed', rather than an absolutist, kind.[45]

For Lucas, the chief expression of the rights of the people was to be found in the setting up of urban governments and the framing of municipal constitutions. There are signs of Lockeian influence in his depiction of the 'men of Bristol' arriving in Dublin and deciding 'as is common to people left in a sort of a state of nature' to begin the process of forming a civil constitution by 'choosing a chief magistrate to preside over them'. However, following that first crucial act, Lucas argued that the people had held on to ultimate power by maintaining an assembly of freemen (in Dublin's case, this was the court of darein hundred), in which the (free) citizens could exercise a veto on decisions of the quarterly meetings of the corporation, and take some share in election of officials. What he objected to was that over time, and with the connivance of various monarchs (culminating in the New Rules), the aldermen had increased their powers in the corporation, setting themselves up as 'a sort of nobility'. The New Rules were incompatible with the city's ancient constitution, and had been introduced 'without the consent of the *people*'.[46]

Lucas was an eclectic thinker, who drew on various political languages to make his case. What marked him out as a champion of corporatism was his insistence that the rights he sought to revive were those of working tradesmen who had been admitted free of their guilds. Their rights had been confirmed in royal charters and parliamentary statutes, and it was these rights that set them apart from the mass of the population:

> the franchises granted as an encouragement to industrious trading men in this and other cities, and towns corporate in this kingdom, are, in every instance, strictly to be defended and supported: As by them alone the *freemen* are distinguished and put upon a par with the greatest *freeholders* in the country.[47]

And Lucas was ready to defend these rights even against fellow Protestants who did not qualify for freedom according to guild regulations. Moreover, although

---

45 Lucas, *Divelina Libera*, pp. 11, 54. 46 Ibid., pp. 14-15, 18, 20; idem, *A Remonstrance against Certain Infringements on the Rights and Liberties of the Commons and Citizens of Dublin* (Dublin 1743), p. 21. 47 Lucas, *A Remonstrance*, p. 35.

he was apt to be anticlerical in his outlook, he defended the established church of which he was a member on the grounds that it was established by law.[48]

The overturning of the aldermanic oligarchy in Dublin took almost twenty years to achieve, and when the Irish parliament finally passed an act to reform Dublin corporation[49] the rights that were extended to the city commons (a share in the election of lord mayor and of new aldermen) and the guilds (the right to elect their own representatives on the city commons) fell some way short of the reforms that Lucas and his supporters had been calling for. However, they did go some way towards reinstating the principles of election and consent. The election of Lucas himself for one of the city seats in parliament put the seal on the success of the anti-oligarchical campaign, and several of the guilds restored to the whole body of freemen the rights of electing the master and wardens. The example of Dublin gave heart to anti-oligarchic campaigns by freemen in other towns and cities, including Limerick, Bandon and Cork, where the control of Lord Shannon over the corporation was successfully challenged in the 1760s.[50] These developments had wider political effects, contributing to the rise from mid-century onwards of extra-parliamentary support for the patriots and later for the Volunteers. And although by the time of the American revolution some of the more advanced radicals had begun to outgrow corporatism, the eventual winning in 1782 of legislative independence, by which the British parliament gave up its claim to pass laws that were binding on Ireland, represented a triumphant vindication of corporatist values.

IV

> It may be observed ... that all these sovereigns [the Protestant episcopalian monarchs of Germany and northern Europe] at the time that they emancipated themselves from papal oppression, were limited in the exercise of their own power, by privileges of the states, or different orders of their subjects; and thus religious and civil liberty, seldom to be found apart, went hand in hand.[51]

In drawing attention to the role of corporatist privilege in well-constituted societies, Bishop Woodward was highlighting what for many contemporaries had been its primary political justification: as a check on royal absolutism. Wood-

---

[48] Ibid.; Hill, *From Patriots to Unionists*, p. 89. [49] 33 Geo. III, c. 16 (17 May 1760). [50] Milne, 'The Irish municipal corporations', pp. 16-17, 156, 162; Éamon O'Flaherty, 'Urban politics and municipal reform in Limerick, 1723-62', *Eighteenth-Century Ireland*, 6 (1991), 113; Ian d'Alton, *Protestant Society and Politics in Cork, 1812-1844* (Cork 1980), p. 93. [51] Woodward, *The Present State of the Church of Ireland*, p. 10.

ward, of course, as noted above, was using such arguments to justify maintaining the privileges of the established church; hence his insistence on the congruence of the Church of Ireland with civil and religious liberty. Likewise, the independence of the aristocratic order was commended, even by those who themselves lacked noble status, as integral to a proper constitutional balance[52] and hence the preservation of liberty. As for the corporate towns, they too were defended by their supporters as 'bulwarks of liberty'.[53]

Conversely, the language of corporatism was always available to attack what was perceived or presented as undue or irregular privilege. The use of the term 'priestcraft', signifying the excessive and dangerous privileges of the clerical estate, was widespread in Ireland as well as England, and was frequently directed at the clergy of the established church: such attacks might come from within the church itself as well as from Catholics, dissenters, deists and atheists.[54] Similarly, when the oligarchical Dublin aldermanic board was stigmatized as an 'aristocracy',[55] the charge was meant to convey, not just that its members had pretensions above their station, subverting the natural order of society, but that they threatened to unbalance the city's constitution.

The use of such language in itself signifies that Ireland fitted into the *ancien régime* model of eighteenth-century European society. It is worth noting, however, that the incidence of such attacks bore no straightforward relationship to the vitality of corporatism at any particular time. Henry Grattan's attacks on 'the encroachments of the [Anglican] priest' in the 1780s,[56] for instance, were made at a time when the real privileges of the established church were weaker than they had been at the beginning of the century.

Indeed, by the last quarter of the century several of the traditional forms of corporatism were losing ground. Admittedly, the Irish parliament had gained in status since the constitutional settlement of 1782-3, which acknowledged that only the king, (Irish) lords and (Irish) commons could make laws for Ireland.

---

52 Charles Lucas, *The Rights and Privileges of Parliaments Asserted upon Constitutional Principles* (Dublin 1770), pp. 4-6. The idea of a 'balanced' constitution owed much to civic republicanism: J.G.A. Pocock, *The Machiavellian Moment: Florentine Political Thought and the Atlantic Republican Tradition* (Princeton 1975). 53 Lucas, *The Liberties and Customs of Dublin Asserted*, p. 7. 54 For the idea that 'priestcraft' could flourish in Protestant countries see [Robert Molesworth], *An Account of Denmark, as it was in the year 1692* (London 1694). See also, e.g., [Charles Lucas], *A Sixteenth Address to the Free Citizens and Free-Holders of the City of Dublin* (Dublin 1748), pp. 4-8, 21; [Arthur O'Leary], *Mr O'Leary's Defence, Containing a Vindication of his Conduct and Writings* (Dublin 1787), p. 52. On the wider significance of 'priestcraft', see Mark Goldie, 'The civil religion of James Harrington' in Anthony Pagden (ed.), *The Languages of Political Theory in Early-Modern Europe* (Cambridge 1987), p. 213; J.A.I. Champion, *The Pillars of Priestcraft Shaken: The Church of England and its Enemies 1660-1730* (Cambridge 1992), ch. 1. 55 Lucas, *A Remonstrance*, p. 36. 56 Speech on tithes, 14 Feb.1788, in *The speeches of the Right Hon. Henry Grattan ... with a Commentary by Daniel Owen Madden*, 2nd edn (Dublin 1853), p. 125.

However, the status of the Irish parliament as a corporatist institution was being undermined by the rising demand that it represent a wider public opinion. In any case, legislative independence was swept away with the act of union. And meanwhile the state was undercutting the legal basis for the purely confessional aspects of corporatism. The repeal of the test act (1780), which in respect of Protestant dissenters formally abolished the sacramental test for public office, and the introduction of an oath (1774) by which Catholics could testify allegiance to the monarch and enjoy freedom of worship and conduct schools (1782), was part of this process. No longer could the established church, now contending with the evangelical challenge, claim exclusive rights in the spiritual field, and Convocation was unlikely to be revived. The guilds' failure to win statutory backing for their trading role facilitated the formation of non-denominational chambers of commerce and called in question the basis of the urban distinction between the free and the unfree; and the encroachment on the local government role of urban corporations by the creation of statutory bodies for particular municipal purposes weakened the claim of the chartered towns to enjoy exclusive rights of self-government.[57] Ancient customs that reinforced corporatist values, such as the riding of town franchises, were dying out.

These developments might have been expected to open up the possibility of restructuring Irish society on liberal, or even radical, lines, in which differences of religion could be consigned to the past. In the 1790s this was, indeed, the programme of the United Irishmen, for whom corporatist and confessional privilege were obsolete in an age of reason.[58] That their message failed to have much appeal for the rich and powerful was not surprising. More serious was the failure to win more than minority support from urban Protestants, including the Protestant freemen. While this is sometimes depicted as the result of government manipulation, there is a simpler explanation to hand. Although some aspects of the corporatist world had been weakened, the associated political privileges were still substantially intact. This was notably the case in respect of the Protestant freemen. Since mid-century such Protestants had campaigned to win greater participation within the political system, with a good deal of success. Working through guilds and corporations, they had invoked 'ancient rights' in order to play a more active role in local government, to break free of deference when voting in local or parliamentary elections, and, along with Protestant farmers and the minor gentry, to take up arms (through the Volunteers) to make political points. Moreover, since freemen were increasingly being

---

[57] L.M. Cullen, *Princes & Pirates: The Dublin Chamber of Commerce 1783-1983* (Dublin 1983) chs 3-5. Statutory encroachment on Dublin corporation's functions assumed significant proportions from the mid-1770s: Jacqueline Hill, 'The shaping of Dublin government, 1690-1840' in Peter Clark and Raymond Gillespie (eds), *Capital Cities: Dublin and London* (forthcoming). [58] Nancy J. Curtin, *The United Irishmen* (Oxford 1994), ch. 1. [59] Hill, *From*

created simply on the grounds of birth, regardless of occupation, the effect was to broaden considerably the base of the 'aristocratic' elite. Lacking landed wealth – sometimes wealth of any kind – and conscious of being greatly outnumbered by urban Catholics, these new members of the elite were bound to cling all the more strongly to confessional values as a badge of their status.[59]

Moreover, thanks to the relaxation of the penal laws against Protestant dissenters, the elite had become less narrowly Anglican but more 'Protestant' in the wider sense of the term. Far from shrinking, the rift between Catholics and Protestants had become wider. This was what led Edmund Burke, in his capacity as a friend of the Irish Catholics, to deplore the assimilation of Protestants in general into a 'master caste', monopolizing 'every franchise, every honour, every trust, every place down to the very lowest and least confidential'.[60] What Burke was describing was the outcome of a process whereby the ranks of the lower nobility had expanded to embrace significant sections of the middle and lower classes; and religion, from being just one of the badges of privilege, had assumed central importance.

In these circumstances, neither the rhetoric of the United Irishmen, nor the government-inspired extension of political rights to Catholics in 1793 (making Catholics eligible for membership of guilds and corporations, allowing them to take degrees in Trinity College, to bear arms, and to exercise the parliamentary franchise on the same terms as Protestants)[61] were likely in themselves to have much success in breaking down the Protestant exclusivity of the elite. Some rural Catholics, certainly, might obtain the parliamentary franchise, if their landlords (secure in the knowledge that parliament remained a Protestant monopoly, and assuming that deference would bind tenants to the landlords' interest) were prepared to grant freehold tenures. But in respect of the guilds and corporations, where freemen stood to be swamped if the Catholic middle classes were admitted in any numbers, the results were meagre.[62] This ensured that over time, more and more urban Catholics would cease to strive to enter the world of corporatist privilege and instead seek to overturn it. By the 1780s and 1790s the invocation of 'natural rights' and 'common justice' by some of their spokesmen heralded a significant shift in political discourse, and in the 1790s the very principle of confessionalism in politics came under sustained attack in certain quarters.[63] This struck at the heart of the *ancien régime* as it had evolved in eighteenth-century Ireland, paving the way for the rise of liberalism, which in the nineteenth century would go far towards eclipsing the values associated with corporatism.

Patriots to Unionists, pp. 192-211; Dickson, '"Centres of motion"', pp. 101-11. **60** Edmund Burke, 'A letter to Sir Hercules Langrishe' (1792) in *The Works of Edmund Burke* (London 1884-99), vol. 3, pp. 304-5; see also Leighton, *Catholicism in a Protestant Kingdom*, ch. 4. **61** 33 Geo. III, c. 21 (9 Apr. 1793). **62** Hill, *From Patriots to Unionists*, ch. 8. **63** Leighton, *Catholicism in a Protestant Kingdom*, ch. 7.

This short survey has argued that corporatist institutions, practices, ideology and language were ubiquitous in eighteenth-century Ireland. Unlike civic republicanism, corporatism was not chiefly a language of opposition; nor, unlike the divine right of kings, was it chiefly a language for upholding absolutism. As a political ideology, its strength lay in the fact that it could be invoked both by the supporters and by critics of the status quo; and it could be reinforced by other contemporary political languages, such as Lockeian contract theory and civic republicanism.[64] Corporatist institutions might have been in decline by the last decades of the century, but when in 1792 the United Irishmen urged their supporters to rally behind 'universal emancipation and representative legislature' corporatism's appeal was still deemed strong enough to be worth renouncing: 'we address you without any authority save that of reason ... Here we sit, without mace or beadle, neither a mystery, nor a craft, nor a corporation.'[65] And if traditional forms of corporatism were in decline, new varieties -albeit lacking royal charters and the customary vocational dimension – were springing up.

One such case was freemasonry. Freemasonry had little to do with working masons – reflecting, rather, the growing popularity of clubs and voluntary associations – but with its oaths, its conviviality, its cult of brotherhood, its structures of election and consent, it clearly owed much to craft guild culture.[66] A close relation of freemasonry was the Orange Order, founded in 1795. The institution was oath-bound, fraternal, protective of its secrets, its officials dependent on election and consent. But, unlike at least some freemasons, the Orangemen insisted on maintaining the exclusively Protestant character of the elite as it had evolved in Ireland in the course of the century; and the assistance they offered the king against his enemies was conditional: 'as loing as he ... Maintanes the prodestand Religion'.[67] Although the conditional element was later dropped from the oath,[68] there must have been many occasions from the 1790s onwards when government ministers, despairing of managing such loyalists, might have echoed their predecessors' verdict on the Dublin guilds in the 1670s: 'by this they declare themselves to be free states'.

---

64 For use of such languages, see Hill, *From Patriots to Unionists*, pp. 83-105. **65** Quoted in Rosamond Jacob, *The Rise of the United Irishmen, 1791-94* (London 1937), p. 151. **66** Petri Mirala, '"A large mob, calling themselves freemasons": masonic parades in Ulster, 1770s to 1830s' (paper delivered at symposium on 'Crowds', Queen's University, Belfast, 21-2 Sept. 1998). **67** 'Bye laws and Regulations of the Orange Society meeting in Ballymagerney' (1798), cited by R.H. Wallace, 'History of the Orange Order' in *The Formation of the Orange Order 1795-1798: The Edited Papers of Colonel William Blacker and Colonel Robert H. Wallace* (Belfast 1994), p. 68. The 'conditional' nature of the oath suggests the influence of Lockeian contract theory, which was being invoked for conservative as well as radical purposes in the 1790s. See Patrick Kelly, 'Perceptions of Locke in eighteenth-century Ireland', *Proceedings of the Royal Irish Academy*, Sect. C, 89 (1989), 30-3. **68** *Report from the Select Committee [on] ... Orange Lodges, Associations or Societies in Ireland*, Parliamentary Papers, 1835 (377), vol. 15, p. 36.

Protestant dependence and consumption in Swift's Irish writings

ROBERT MAHONY

I

An old Irish nationalist witticism holds that unionists are loyal not so much to the Crown as to the half-crown, the largest silver coin commonly circulating before decimalization in 1971. Unfairly as the joke elides the political principles of Irish Protestants, it yet highlights the link between allegiance and economics among their traditional concerns. That connection was of utmost significance to Jonathan Swift, who though hardly the first commentator on Irish affairs to look at money and trade – Richard Lawrence and Sir William Petty, to name only two, preceded him by a generation – became the best-known writer in eighteenth-century Ireland to give patriotic advocacy and protest an economic footing. In Swift's consideration of economics, indeed, what matters most is his rhetoric: Petty was a more thorough economist, but a dull writer; Swift, an amateur in economics, was a surpassing rhetorician. That Swift's contribution to Irish political thought was primarily rhetorical, however, should not detract from its genuine importance. For rhetorical formulations clear the path that popular political expression follows; a shift in popular articulation is predicated upon altering the rhetorical pathways. Measured in terms of practical effect, Swift did not succeed in making that alteration during his lifetime, which he found very disappointing, though he was gratified by the popular reputation as a patriotic hero his efforts had gained him. Only over time did it became evident that he had indeed inspired a shift in Irish popular political expression.[1]

Swift's rhetorical achievement, however partial, can be discerned even from a very brief comparison with that of Richard Lawrence. Lawrence's *The Interest of Ireland in its Trade and Wealth, Stated* (1682) anticipates Swift by some forty years in identifying as serious economic defects the prevalence of idleness in the countryside, absenteeism among landlords, the bestowal of public offices mainly on those not born in Ireland, and notably the 'excessive consumption of foreign growth and manufacturies'.[2] Nevertheless, the impact of Lawrence's work

---

[1] For a fuller discussion of this phenomenon, see Robert Mahony, *Jonathan Swift: The Irish Identity* (New Haven 1995).   [2] Richard Lawrence, *The Interest of Ireland in its Trade and Wealth, Stated* (Dublin 1682), p. [ii].

was fleeting; not only was his style far from memorable, but his rhetorical anti-Catholicism clouds his diagnosis. Addressing mainly an Irish Protestant audience, he attributed these and other Irish ills to the influence of the Catholic clergy, manifesting a reflexive anti-Catholicism at once personal and altogether conventional in his day:[3] when difficulties arose in Ireland, one would not have to seek far for their cause. The Catholic clergy were of course more evident and comfortable in the early 1680s than they had been in the 1650s, but their numbers were inadequate to affect the Irish economy very substantially. The Catholic landed class of the 1660s -70s, moreover, whose economic proclivities the clergy would most have reflected and influenced, had been prostrated economically during the Cromwellian era, their holdings usually reduced and often displaced from Munster or Leinster to the poorer land of Connacht. By the early 1680s they had made little progress in recovering their economic position despite prolonged litigation, nor would they. They might live away from their now less productive estates (though few were based in England or further abroad), or indulge themselves with imports; their tenants might have seemed idler than those on better land who, frequently settlers themselves, served the more recently-established Protestant gentry. But for more than a generation before Lawrence's *Interest of Ireland*, Catholics had not dominated the Irish economy, and they were certainly not among the non-Irish granted public office. What would appear to have exercised Lawrence's rhetorical reflexes was the palpable presence of Catholic clergy and gentry, obscuring for him their loss of economic power and influence.

Forty years later, when Swift in his *Proposal for the Universal Use of Irish Manufacture* (1720) addressed the now mostly Protestant Irish gentry and merchant classes, he was no more effective than Lawrence in countering their taste for imports, nor in inspiring them to attend to the other ills of Ireland that Lawrence had indicated. But Swift was luckier in his circumstances and capitalized upon that with a more accurate, as well as stylistically more appealing, rhetoric. In the first place, he was subtly questioning the economic value of Ireland's political dependence upon Britain, by arguing for economic self-reliance at a time when there was widespread Irish Protestant resentment at British restrictions upon Irish trade and political autonomy. Although his audience ignored his prescriptions, Swift's pamphlet quickly gained him a popularity Lawrence never had. Swift's rhetoric also, however, offered a means of discussing and analysing the British-Irish relationship by concentrating upon its economic features, without resorting to the longstanding convention of anti-Catholicism. That rhetorical convention, though stale, was often populist; Swift's perception that the ways Britain and Ireland interacted in the 1720s were

---

[3] For Lawrence's background, see T.C. Barnard, 'Crises of identity among Irish Protestants, 1641-1685,' *Past and Present* 127 (1990), 39-83, esp. 59-68.

in everyday respects economic led him to employ a ramblingly down-to earth, hence equally populist, style for his alternative rhetoric, which avoided rehearsing Irish religious differences. Neither Swift nor Lawrence was, then, effective in a purely practical sense; but Swift's breaking with rhetorical convention enabled his becoming in time, if not so obviously in his own day, a 'leader of public opinion in Ireland', to adopt the title of W.E.H. Lecky's 1861 study.

Pleased as Swift was by his popularity, his intention in writing on Irish affairs from 1720 was to change the way his audience, in the main Irish Protestants like himself, thought about themselves in relation both to Britain, their ethnic and his preferred homeland, and, more indirectly, to the Catholic majority in Ireland. Hence his practical objective was intertwined with his rhetorical method. Swift's consideration of Irish affairs is nowhere comprehensive and systematic, since he commonly addressed particular circumstances, so that the overall diagnosis to be gathered from his numerous pamphlets and briefer comments must in part be inferred. But the conclusion is nonetheless clear. Irish Protestants, though dominant in Ireland, were a minority in the country and therefore depended for their ultimate security upon Britain. The British government took that dependence as affording it multiple opportunities to restrict Irish trade and otherwise foster the British consumption of the Irish economy. Resent though they did such British oppression, Irish Protestants nonetheless had no recourse but to seek their prosperity by oppressing their tenantry in turn. This was to Swift's mind ultimately self-destructive: their own economy consumed by Britain, they exacerbated that consumption at the expense of the poor, breeding poverty, idleness, duplicity and thievery.

In outlining the relationships between Britain and Ireland, and within Ireland, as primarily economic Swift sidesteps the religious issue, the factor that conventionally, in his time and earlier, had framed understanding of these relationships. Most of the gentry and indeed the rich were Protestants of British stock, while most of the poor were native Irish Catholics, a situation resulting largely from the success of England's planting of Protestant settlers in Ireland during the sixteenth and seventeenth centuries, together with its (and their) victories over Ireland's Catholic leadership in that period. But religion in this sense obscured rather than clarified the economic issues that Swift saw at stake, because it encouraged the Irish Protestant dependence upon Britain that enabled Britain's exploitation of Ireland. Swift's articulating the pressures upon and within Ireland as economic does correspond to his calling as a Christian minister: that alone would justify his attacking oppression. Yet, while he bridled at oppression and personally practised numerous charities, he was not opposed to riches and manifested little sympathy for the poor, despising their propensity for lying and theft. More than his Christian vocation, what informs his rhetoric is a fairly rudimentary political economy: Britain's self-interest accounts for its economic and political oppression of Ireland, provoking in turn the exploitation of the poor within Ireland. The remedy is for those better off in Ireland to awaken to its self-interest, and thus the necessity for economic self-reliance. This would break the vice of oppression, foster industriousness among the poor and, though implicitly, relax the psychological grip of Irish Protestant dependence upon Britain.

Indeed, Swift realized full well the hold of anti-Catholicism upon Irish Protestant self-understanding, for this informed that crippling sense of dependence. His economic rhetoric is not airily dismissive of the issue, but instead brings into play the disastrous nature of the connection he perceived between dependence and consumption in the Irish Protestant mentality that throughout his Irish writings he mainly addresses. The rhetoric of Swift's Irish writings is largely informed by this connection between dependence and consumption. That he regarded dependence as degrading is apparent throughout his writing career: Martin and Jack are ridiculous in their slavish imitation of Peter before they break with him in *A Tale of a Tub*; Gulliver's obsequiousness toward the Lilliputians is patently risible; and in 'A Beautiful Young Nymph going to Bed', the cosmetic and prosthetic evidences of the prostitute Corinna's attempts to remain enticing render her pathetic instead. Irish Protestants are degraded as well by their dependence upon Britain; it corrupts them psychologically and economically. All the same, satirical as Swift occasionally becomes in his Irish writings, they are usually not satires *tout court*; Irish Protestants might well exhibit the human perversity that his satires often target, but in his earlier Irish writings he is more committed to arguing for an effectual remedy. Embracing it would entail a profound psychological shift in his audience, which therefore he attempts to encourage indirectly in these earlier Irish works, the *Irish Manufacture* pamphlet and the *Drapier's Letters*. In particular, while religion was an inescapable factor in the nexus of external and internal oppression besetting Ireland, Swift considers both sorts of oppression overtly in economic terms, as varieties of consumption. After the mid 1720s, he alters his method, generally becoming more direct about the link between consumption and dependence (though treating them, and especially consumption, satirically indeed in *A Modest Proposal*), and, while continuing to eschew anti-Catholic rhetoric, manifesting his disappointment that his Irish Protestant audience would not heed his recommendation of self-reliance.

II

Consumption and dependence are multiply linked in Swift's understanding of the Irish condition: they mark the country's relationship with England (as he usually termed Britain) as well as its internal political, religious and economic relationships. Their history in the former relationship dates to its earliest years.

After Pope Adrian IV in 1155-6 assigned the governance of Ireland to the English crown, and King Henry II allowed his restless lords to invade the country at the request of a claimant to an Irish throne late in the next decade, he insisted upon their renewing their fealty to him once they had succeeded, effectively taking title to the country that the pope had privileged him to govern. To insure their dependence upon him, that is, he consumed what his lords had conquered. Thereafter, the country's status as a dependency of the English crown was explicit in its inclusion among the kingly dignities, initially 'Lord of Ireland,' a title granted to Henry's son, John, who kept it upon succeeding to the crown, and 'King of Ireland' from 1540, under Henry VIII. But the Anglo-Norman colonization of Ireland was never comprehensive, and the English government embarked upon a more ambitious colonial project in the later sixteenth century and throughout the seventeenth. To buttress the security of England from continental Catholic aggression, the 'Old English' descendants of the earlier settlers, who remained Catholic despite the Reformation, were gradually displaced from political power and social position by English and Scottish Protestant settlers. This Protestant colonization encountered considerable sporadic opposition for a century after the 1590s, but was at length a very successful project in consumption, for by 1700 the great bulk of Irish territory was in the hands of loyal Protestants. By planting Protestants in Ireland, then, by removing Old English Catholic officials and expropriating land from Catholic occupiers for newer settlers who professed the reformed religion, by, in other words, consuming Catholic Ireland, England forestalled her own consumption by Catholic Europe.

But England's consumption of Ireland was not limited by the demands of security from external aggression. As Swift saw the matter, after England colonized the country with Protestants, it yet restricted the economic benefits they could gain as colonists. To protect English mercantile interests from Irish competition, free trade was denied to Ireland; to satisfy English political interests, major posts in the Irish administration and established church were staffed by Englishmen, restricting opportunities for the younger sons of the Protestant gentry. Their dependence upon England kept Protestants from resisting this perpetuated English consumption of Ireland, much though they resented it. Protestant landowners instead pursued their own prosperity by rackrenting their tenant farmers, which produced widespread rural poverty, a result we would now term economically counter-productive. Swift oversimplifies this account of Ireland's condition in a letter of 1726 to Lord Peterborough, to emphasize his perception that the intertwining of consumption and dependence was destroying the possibility that Ireland as a whole might prosper. England had ultimate responsibility for this catastrophe, and it would have been forestalled, he implies, if the government in London had considered his own people, the descendants of those who completed the conquest of Ireland in the seventeenth century, 'to be on as good a foot as any subjects of Britain, according to the practice of all other nations, and particularly of the Greeks and Romans'.[4]

What he seems to mean, at least with respect to Greek colonization, we may elucidate by recalling a passage from Thucydides' history of the Peloponnesian War. Corcyra was at war with Epidamnus, and Corinth had joined the war on the side of the Epidamnians, even though Corcyra had originally been colonized from Corinth. Both Corcyra and Corinth had sent representatives to Athens, which had a defensive treaty with Corinth: the Corcyrans to dissuade the Athenians from joining the fight, the Corinthians to persuade them to do just that. The Corinthian representatives contended that their treaty bound the Athenians to come in on their side, and argued further that Corcyra, having been colonized from Corinth, did not have the standing to make a case for Athenian neutrality. The Corcyrans replied to the latter contention: 'If they object in justice, in that you receive their colony, henceforth let them learn, that all colonies, so long as they receive no wrong from their mother City, so long they honour her; but when they suffer injury from her, they then become alienate: for they are not sent out to be the slaves of them that stay, but to be their equals.'[5] Though from a late twentieth-century perspective, ancient Greek colonization encompassed more oppressiveness than this classic description suggests, especially if native peoples were involved, this was long the standard statement of the case. It provided the classical foundation for any such argument as Swift's that Ireland deserved to be treated as England's equal, since those dominant in Ireland were not sent there as colonists 'to be the slaves of them that stay' in England, 'but to be their equals'. As Henry Maxwell noted in 1703, this holds all the more in a case like that of Ireland, whether the country be considered a conquest or an 'annexed government':

> The design of maintaining conquests or annexed government by colonies, is to avoid the great expense and hazard that attends their being maintained by a standing force. From which design it plainly follows, that after colonies are once settled, and have a constitution given to them agreeable to that of their mother country; they must afterwards be indulged the liberty of making their own laws, provided they be not repugnant to the laws of their mother country.

This was the precedent established by Roman as well as Greek practice, and Maxwell added, 'The Romans gave them [colonies] another privilege, and that

---

4 Swift to Peterborough, 28 April 1726 (*Swift Corr.* vol. 3, p. 132). 5 Thucydides, *Eight Bookes of the Peloponnesian Warre*, translated by Thomas Hobbes (London 1629), p.20. Swift's executor, the Revd John Lyons, recorded his abstracting Hobbes's Thucydides at Moor Park in early 1698, cf. *The Battle of the Books*, ed. Hermann J. Real (Berlin 1978), p.129. My thanks to Hermann Real for acquainting me with this reference.

was to be governed by their own magistrates, and for these reasons the Romans were always most faithfully served by their colonies.'[6]

In his letter to Peterborough, Swift was not basing his case for Irish equality upon its character as a kingdom *per se*, an area of longstanding debate which most Englishmen considered as having been settled by the declaratory act of 1720, which determined that Ireland was a 'depending kingdom' bound by statutes of the Westminster parliament. Rather he asserts that a sense of equity ought, by universal but especially classical practice, to govern the relationship of colonists with their mother-country. Throughout the letter, Swift complains that England has refused to observe such equity, that Thucydidean idea of fairness. Obviously this idea can be related to that of Ireland's distinctness as a kingdom: the country became a kingdom, after all, during the reign of Henry VIII, long after it had come under English political dominion. But the argument for distinctness – with its implications of autonomy – he tends to press in works meant primarily for Irish readers, sympathetic to the notion that the declaratory act was bad law (a procedure he adopts in the *Drapier's Letters*); Swift seems to have considered that the point to make to his noble British friend (really intending the letter to be read by Walpole, the prime minister) was that the people the government was oppressing were the descendants of those British Protestants 'sent out' to colonize Ireland in the seventeenth century, who in fact bore the brunt of conquering Jacobite Ireland within, in 1726, living memory. They should have the rights long since conceded to the British people whence they had sprung, rather than be denied such rights like the native Irish their forbears had defeated.

But if England was ultimately responsible for distorting the Irish economy, Swift also saw the connection between dependence and consumption in the self-awareness of Irish Protestants as inducing them to compensate themselves irresponsibly for English restrictions. Not only did they behave as though they had no choice but to accept, albeit resentfully, England's economic interference, but they seemed to Swift not to have discerned sufficiently that their sense of dependence underlay their own internal consumption of Ireland. When addressing his Irish Protestant audience, then, his rhetorical methods included capitalizing upon their resentment at English economic interference even to the point of exaggerating its extent; showing them that accepting such interference had led them in turn to distort their own economic behaviour with consumptionist practices detrimental to their long-term economic interest; and insisting that self-sufficiency offered an alternative to their both accepting English interference and adopting compensatory economic distortions. Swift's prescription of self-reliance involves more than Irish Protestants' cultivating 'moral self-dis-

---

[6] Henry Maxwell, *An Essay towards an Union of Ireland with England* (London 1703), p. 5. I am indebted to Sean Connolly for bringing this reference to my attention.

cipline and frugality';[7] rather, it is the only means of halting their self-destructive complicity – of which they were inadequately aware – in England's ongoing consumption of Ireland.

Hence, while Swift argued in his letter of 1726 to Peterborough, and often elsewhere, that England should allow free trade to Ireland and more often appoint Irish Protestants to official positions, he also pressed those Protestants, whom he termed 'the people of Ireland,' to become self-sufficient. At the least, as Swift argued in the anonymous *Proposal for the Universal Use of Irish Manufacture* of 1720, his first published work addressing Irish affairs since becoming dean of St. Patrick's Cathedral in 1713, Irish landlords should cease rackrenting their tenantry so as to afford imported English and foreign goods. This practice diverts to other countries, particularly England, the proceeds from Irish rents. Instead, the gentry and merchants should support Irish domestic industries, especially the production of wool. The self-reliance he advocated had patriotism in its favour, as well as justice of the sort a Christian minister should press for, since it would diminish the fact of dependence and its oppressive effects. But adopting it meant forwarding the self-interest of individuals in the long rather than the short term, what we might describe as delayed gratification, never a welcome proposition. Inasmuch, further, as this would entail a different, more just relationship between landlord and tenant, it also ran counter to the ideological inclination of colonialism in Ireland. Given that the colonists were Protestant, and those they dominated mainly Catholic, this inclination may be seen as equating Protestant dominance or supremacy in Ireland with the subordination or oppression (or, indeed, consumption) of Irish Catholics.

The roots of that ideologically-privileged equation ran deep. Catholics had rebelled in 1641 and massacred thousands of Protestant settlers; the number of victims probably totalled between three and four thousand, but was massively inflated at the time, rising into the hundreds of thousands: by 1647, it was officially alleged, 154,000 had died by rebel hands, and the poet John Milton in 1649 gave an estimate of 'more than 200,000'.[8] The massacres renewed legendary characterizations of the native Irish as barbarians, and since their inspiration was attributed to Catholic clergy, old barbarism could be linked to the old religion. Popularized in such accounts as Sir John Temple's *Irish Rebellion* (1646), the massacres of 1641 assumed an enormous significance in Protestant self-understanding as a people at risk. Vengeance might be the Lord's, but the

---

7 Patrick Kelly, '"Conclusions by no means calculated for the circumstances and condition of Ireland": Swift, Berkeley and the solution to Ireland's economic problems' in Aileen Douglas, Patrick Kelly and Ian Campbell Ross (eds), *Locating Swift: Essays from Dublin on the 250th Anniversary of the Death of Jonathan Swift, 1667-1745* (Dublin 1998), p. 59.   8 Jane Ohlmeyer, *Ireland from Independence to Occupation: 1641-1660* (Cambridge 1995), p. xx; Milton, *Observations upon the Articles of Peace...* (London 1649), p. 49.

Scriptures could also encourage them to inflict it themselves.[9] Catholic bloodthirstiness justified the retributive zeal of Oliver Cromwell in suppressing the rebellion, and lay behind an Irish parliamentary statute of 1662 fixing 23 October, the date the rebellion began in 1641, for annual commemoration in every Church of Ireland parish. The service rubric for that commemoration recalled the extent of the massacres and gave thanks that God had seen fit to avert a complete annihilation of the Protestants of Ireland by sparing a remnant.[10] It was no great leap from this rhetorical fixture in Protestant self-awareness to the idea that Providence had appointed that remnant to rule over the Catholic natives. This notion may be gathered from the tenor of the published commemorative sermons for 23 October that have survived, especially after James II's Irish regime of 1689-91, which caused Protestants to fear a reprise of the 1641 massacres, was defeated by King William III.[11] In the ensuing years, the sermons mix gratitude for providential deliverance with an increasingly positive consciousness of Protestantism as a minority faith, even the faith of an elect. And they hail the Irish parliament's enactment of a penal code to defend that faith by curbing Catholic landownership and ecclesiastical organization. From the perspective these sermons generate, by holding Catholicism at bay the penal laws represent the Protestant mission – obviously endorsed by Providence – to consume Catholic Ireland.

This is not to say that the tenor of the 23 October sermons in their aggregate reflects accurately Protestant perceptions of Catholics in Ireland, or indeed, the actual operation of the penal laws. For, though mandated by statute for delivery in every Church of Ireland parish annually, only a few such sermons appeared in print, delivered to congregations of Irish Protestant notables in Dublin and London. Comprising insufficient evidence from which to generalize about Protestant attitudes in the country at large toward Catholics or the penal laws, they form instead a homilitic genre, with a commemorative purpose tied to events on a specific date long past. But as that date had become symbolic, these surviving sermons do evidence a privileged rhetoric, an official liturgy of sorts, for remembering the historical event and learning the lesson it teaches. In this rhetorical context the penal laws figure metaphorically as an embodiment of Protestant Ireland's having learned that lesson, a bulwark against the repetition of that event. That rhetoric was consumptionist: its terms pre-

---

9 See *That Great Expedition for Ireland by way of Underwriting Proposed* (London 1642), p. 14, quoted in Raymond Gillespie, *Devoted People: Belief and Religion in Early Modern Ireland* (Manchester 1997), p. 75. 10 E.g. ' For it was thy goodness alone that we were not delivered over for a prey unto their teeth,' [Second Collect], 'A form of Divine Service to be used October 23,' *The Book of Common Prayer ... According to the Use of the Church of Ireland* (Dublin 1680), n. p. 11 See T.C. Barnard, 'The uses of 23 October 1641 and Irish Protestant celebrations,' *English Historical Review* 106 (1991), 889-920.

sented the consumption of Catholic Ireland, metaphorically facilitated by the penal laws, as the means of preventing the Catholics from consuming Protestant Ireland as they had attempted in 1641. By privileging consumpton as defence, this rhetoric also valorized the demographic status of Protestants as an Irish minority. Whatever the actual attitudes of Protestants toward Catholics, or the varied inconsistencies of the practical application of the penal laws, the rhetorical formulation that so promoted consumption by an elite had so strong an appeal to the self-interest of that elite that a departure from such rhetoric – even if this posed no challenge to Protestant supremacy – was likely to prove ineffectual in practice. The rhetoric of the sermons, that is, acquired by virtue of its nearly-liturgical repetition and its appeal at once to religious solidarity, the historical favour of Providence, and the human pleasure in consumption an ideological sturdiness that continued for much of the eighteenth century; the metaphorical value of the penal laws, among various other reasons, kept them on the statute books well after they were compromised by inconsistent application. But so promoting Protestant consumption also, as Swift saw it, confirmed Protestant dependence upon England.

While it was the link between consumption and dependence that energized Swift to challenge and displace them by advocating economic self-reliance, he was not the first to find fault with the rhetoric of consumption as religious defence. Even as the penal laws were initially being formulated in their eighteenth-century shape in the aftermath of the Jacobite collapse – and so before they came into metaphorical play within the rhetoric of consumption – Bishop Wetenhall of Cork and Ross, in a 23 October sermon of 1692, questioned the religious and indeed practical value of the Protestant preference for consumption over a serious effort to convert the Catholic natives:

> had we Protestants been as industrious, first, ourselves to have lived according to the truth and power of the reformed religion, and then to have instructed the Irish therein, as we were to secure ourselves the Irish lands; had we been as careful to make them knowing good Christians, as ourselves rich and great; we had, in all probability, never seen the rebellion of forty one *nor* the tyranny of the late eighty-eight, and following years.[12]

No large-scale project for converting the Catholic natives, such as Wetenhall seems to insinuate would optimally have defended and advanced Protestantism, ever took place. To be sure, as S.J. Connolly has summarized in *Religion, Law and Power*, there were stirrings in this direction as the penal laws made headway, offsetting somewhat their coerciveness as an instrument of conversion.[13]

12 Wetenhall, *A Sermon Preached Octob. 23, 1692* ... (Dublin 1692), p. 17.   13 See S.J.

Both houses of Convocation in the Church of Ireland, bishops as well as parish clergy, approved resolutions in 1703-4 and again in 1709 supporting evangelization among the Catholics at large, through preaching and other forms of instruction in the Irish language. In addition, John Richardson, a County Cavan clergyman, attracted significant support in 1711 for a project of printing religious materials in Irish and establishing charter schools to advance literacy and religious instruction in English. But concerns lest the Irish language be thereby encouraged, and fear that the Church of Ireland lacked the resources necessary for effecting such proposals, foredoomed their coming into practice, though similar schemes surfaced from time to time afterwards. As Connolly notes, 'it is clear that many Protestants were indifferent, to say the least, to the conversionist schemes of men like Richardson'.[14] Even the charter school movement, fostering the education of Catholic children in basic skills and Protestant doctrine, had only a limited and faltering effect. Thus, though whatever might forward spiritual motives for conversion was officially wlecomed and certainly made some progress, the penal laws became over the years a prominent metaphor for the advancement of Protestantism, not least for their practical effect of converting Catholic landowners to the established church.[15] And that is to say that in the rhetoric of colonialist ideology, consumptionism remained dominant for generations after Wetenhall cautioned against it.

Indeed, as Connolly has noted, both Archbishop Edward Synge of Tuam and Archbishop William King of Dublin compained in 1719 that a great many Protestant landowners would, in Synge's words, 'rather keep the Papists as they are, in an almost slavish subjection', for thus were more tractable.[16] The penal laws might have little actually to do with the Catholic poor, but the consumptionist ideology they represented had become so entrenched that Archbishop Synge's son, Bishop Edward Synge of Clonfert, in a 23 October sermon of 1731, was deeply concerned by the unwillingness of most Catholics to follow their self-interest, embrace that ideology and convert. From this he perceived an ideological defect: in fact the penal code gave Catholics in his time greater reason to hate Protestants than their forefathers had in 1641, even while their loyalty to the Jacobite pretender, and a natural barbarity as bloodthirsty as their ancestors', made them a formidable threat to Protestantism. Yet the remedy he proposed – though Synge was himself not at all the most rabidly anti-Catholic among Church of Ireland bishops – was all the greater stringency in the penal laws, since 'the great law of self-preservation directs and empowers us to use

---

Connolly, *Religion, Law and Power: The Making of Protestant Ireland* (Oxford 1992), pp. 294-307.   14 Connolly, *Religion, Law and Power*, p. 306.   15 Connolly notes (*Religion, Law and Power*, p. 309) that conversions during the penal era could account for the transfer of about ten per cent of Irish land from Catholic to Protestant hands.   16 Quoted in *Religion, Law and Power*, p. 309.

proper means to secure ourselves against' that threat.[17] The true reformed religion, that is, was best defended by penal laws enabling the consumption of Catholic Ireland, even though (or, by Synge's logic, *because*) such legislation perpetuated and deepened the Catholic hatred of Protestants that latently threatened the security of the reformed religion. Synge's exercise in circular logic evinces neatly the rhetoric of Protestant self-perception, as a people simultaneously empowered and endangered, which made the ideology of consumption so formidable despite its contradictory ramifications. Historical victimhood, as a condition of Protestant identity, meant victimizing the historic aggressor. And the primary arena for the exercise of that ideological imperative was economic.

Swift himself believed in Protestant supremacy, but considered the penal laws adequate to protect it. He was palpably reserved about some of the implications of the ideology of consumption, however, as actually or potentially subverting that supremacy. He was certainly suspicious of the anti-Catholic rhetorical gloss customary in articulating such ideology, for not only was it superfluous but it also distracted attention from the real economic and political underpinnings of Protestant supremacy. The sermon of 1731 by the younger Synge, for instance – who, Swift told Laetitia Pilkington in the 1730s, 'I knew was not an honest man'[18] – ascribed the barbarous poverty of most Catholics to an inveterately perverse hatred of Protestants, which blinded them to the economic advantages of converting. With a clearer sense of economic motivations, Swift complained repeatedly that peasants were brutalized by their landlords' rackrenting, which had so curtailed economic activity in the countryside as to promote idleness, begging and thievery. And their landlords rackrented because English prohibitions upon Irish exports left them no quicker avenue to prosperity, however self-destructive this was in the long run. Swift actually had little sympathy for Catholics as such or for their faith and he railed against the poor as liars and thieves. But he nevertheless regarded their condition as resulting from poverty rather than from their religion. The security of Protestant Ireland hardly demanded the utter impoverishment of the Catholic natives, and was indeed ultimately endangered by it.

If Protestant supremacy be taken narrowly, moreover – as Swift thought proper – to embrace members of the established church rather than dissenters, privileging anti-Catholic rhetoric to defend it posed another danger. Unsympathetic to Catholicism, Swift was fiercely bigoted against Presbyterians, the largest body of dissenters, who outnumbered episcopal Protestants in the north of Ireland. Regarding them as religious fanatics and political republicans whose forebears had torn England asunder in the seventeenth century, he favoured the continuance of political sanctions against them and little lamented the emigra-

---

[17] Edward Synge, *A Sermon Preached ... the 23rd of October, 1731* (Dublin 1731), p. 13. [18] Laetitia Pilkington, *Memoirs*, ed. A.C. Elias (Athens, Ga. 1997), vol. 1, p. 282.

tion of many of them to the American colonies. He feared their numbers in Ireland as a greater threat to the established church than Catholicism posed, since the penal laws precluded a Catholic political resurgence. In 1732, disdaining to indulge in anti-Catholic rhetoric, he voiced the suspicion that the 'dreaders of Popery' who did so had as their real object weakening or dismantling the establishment he stoutly defended.[19] Exaggerating the popish menace could persuade members of the Church of Ireland to make common cause with the Presbyterian interest, blurring distinctions between the two main Protestant churches that he was determined should be maintained. His poem of 1733 'On the Words "Brother Protestants and Fellow Christians"' satirized this phrase, favoured by Presbyterians referring to the Anglican establishment, likening it to what might be spoken by detritus caught up with the farmyard apples in a rural flash flood:

> A Ball of new-dropt Horse's Dung,
> Mingling with Apples in the Throng,
> Said to the Pippin, plump, and prim,
> *See, Brother, how we Apples swim.* (11-14)[20]

Swift's loathing of Presbyterianism is a constant in his career from the early *Tale of a Tub* (1704). In his Irish writings from the period before the 1730s, however, it is most apparent in some of his sermons, and muted in the pamphleteering of the 1720s. There was in fact little occasion to articulate this antipathy more openly until the Presbyterians in 1731 mounted a campaign for the repeal of the test act which barred them from public office. And in the earlier years of his deanship, when he was widely suspected in government circles of Jacobite sympathies, it would have been imprudent to suggest that Protestant supremacy was more in danger from Presbyterians than from Catholics. Economic issues prompted his writings on Irish affairs in the 1720s, and for his challenge to prevalent habits of consumption to evince a sanguine attitude toward the ancient Catholic threat would have revived suspicions of his Jacobitism, rendering his argument ineffective. That argument would instead have to focus upon the economic implications of the ideology of consumption without recourse to its religious dimensions.

III

What enabled Swift to intervene in Irish politics with this approach, after six years as Dean of St Patrick's spent 'in the greatest privacy'[21] and professed igno-

---

[19] Swift, 'Queries Relating to the Sacramental Test' (1732) in Swift, *Prose Works*, vol. 12, p. 259. [20] *Poems of Jonathan Swift*, ed. Harold Williams, 3rd edn (Oxford 1958), vol. 3, p. 811.
[21] Swift to Alexander Pope, 10 January 1721 (Swift, *Prose Works*, vol. 9, pp. 25-26).

rance of the political world, was an outburst of Irish Protestant resentment at their dependence upon England. A controversy over Irish parliamentary prerogatives had prompted the British ministry to enact the declaratory act in 1720, defining Ireland's subordination to the London parliament. In the *Proposal for the Universal Use of Irish Manufacture* Swift did not address forthrightly the furore continuing in Ireland around the notion of Ireland's dependency; rather, he invoked such patriotic resentment indirectly while echoing a chorus of contemporary exhortations to the Irish to support their own industries by purchasing Irish goods only. In fact he hints broadly enough that resorting to self-reliance, which would enable them to take their economy into their own hands, was tantamount to rejecting their dependence upon England. With calculated offhandedness, for instance, he makes the circumspectly inflammatory comment that he had heard 'the late Archbishop of *Tuam* mention a pleasant observation of some body's' recommending burning everything English except their people and their coal.[22] The advice is not his; its source is dead or forgotten, and he doesn't himself actually espouse it, but the point is made, the more by his adding that he would not be sorry to see the people stay at home, and hoping soon to do without the coal. The clarity of such apparent indirection harnesses the resentment of Irish Protestants to his implicating them, by their dependence upon England, in the ruin of their own economy.

But the response to his pamphlet was hardly what he had recommended. The Irish administration condemned the work as seditious and apprehended the printer, who refused to betray the anonymous author (widely known to be Swift), and whom a jury refused to convict. This was a victory for the freedom of the press, yet popular acclaim for Swift's defiance of English authority over Ireland's economy, and protest at the surrogate prosecution of his printer, did not translate into any alteration in the preference of the Irish gentry and merchants for imported goods. Happy to criticize England, they were averse to disciplining their own consumption. By advocating patriotic self-sufficiency as the counter to indiscipline, Swift had attempted to strike the chords both of consumption and resentment at dependence in Protestant self-awareness as he perceived it; but only one sounded, however loudly. This may have cautioned him against focussing again on the excesses of Irish Protestant consumption when writing the *Drapier's Letters* some years later. The occasion itself called for a different approach, however, a forthright emphasis upon the English consumption of Ireland that Irish Protestant dependence emboldened. Hence, without mentioning dependence as Irish Protestants' historical bulwark against Catholicism, Swift implicates it instead as the avenue the ministry in London takes to insult them and threaten their economic security. Implicitly again, as in the

---

[22] Swift, *Prose Works*, vol. 9, p. 17.

Irish Manufacture pamphlet but without the concomitant of sacrifice or deferred gratification for the common good, self-reliance is the means of defying that insult.

To supply an apparent need for small coins in Ireland, the Walpole government, through the king, had awarded a patent to an English fabricator, William Wood, for a very substantial minting order. Fearing that the free exchange of Wood's copper coins would displace gold and silver in current circulation, major Irish authorities, including parliament, decried the project as destructive to Ireland's economy. These protests had all been couched in assertions of loyalty to the king, concurring with which Swift entered the controversy. Disguising himself for a series of open letters as a trader in woollens, to underscore the ostensible simplicity of his advice, he held that Ireland could at once demonstrate loyalty to the king himself and refuse to accept the coins the king had licensed Wood to mint. For coppers were a convenience rather than legal tender: it was not obligatory in law to accept them in payment for any debt or goods. The Irish need not injure their own commerce by taking coins that would drive out gold and silver; moreover, Wood's solicitations for the patent were untoward, and in issuing it the king was badly advised by the ministry. Nonacceptance is presented as an altogether loyal refusal to innovate — though in fact it is a form of self-reliance and thus strikes at the psychology of dependence.

The second and third letters lay greatest stress upon the insult — to the Irish generally in the second and to the Irish parliament in the third — offered by Wood (and, by no great extension, by the ministry that arranged his patent). Wood expresses his contempt for the Irish in the very phrasing even of efforts to conciliate them; they ought to resent such an insult, which bespeaks his low birth — and, implicitly, the obtuseness of the government in empowering a man of such humble origins to threaten the economic ruin of Ireland. Of course, the Drapier is also implying that the Irish Protestant psychology of dependence invites such behaviour even from the tools of the English ministry. The fourth letter, much celebrated in Swift's day and by generations of nationalists later, continues in this vein, if far more eloquently. And here the inference that Ireland ought not to be dependent is carried more clearly than before. The Drapier describes Ireland and England as obliged to share the same king, but denies any basis except English power for the dependence of Ireland upon England or its subjection to the parliament in London. Thereby he affirms Ireland's loyalty to the king, while running counter to the declaratory act of 1720. Swift's insistence upon that loyalty implies its reciprocation by right, which means that the king must not abandon a loyal people. As the Protestant sense of dependence upon England derived from fear of the consequences if England abandoned them, his implication confutes the possibility of any such abandonment. That understanding of reciprocal loyalty, of course, takes monarchy literally, ignoring the supremacy of parliament, recently manifested in the Declaratory Act, in constructing national policy for Ireland.

The prominence of loyalty as a concept in the fourth letter problematizes the tendency in the Irish nationalist tradition to take literally its being addressed 'To the Whole People of Ireland'. To maintain that here Swift simply becomes a patriot comprehensively Irish, transcending religious antagonisms by speaking to the whole body of Catholics as well as Protestants, contradicts the tenor common to his Irish writings, in which 'the people' are most distinctly the Protestants of Ireland. Yet his insistence particularly in this letter that the people of Ireland have been outstandingly loyal to the present king and his family, which most Protestants would think contestable if Catholics were included, could indeed be understood as recognizing that Catholic Ireland, for all its covert Jacobitism, was overtly quiescent in the face of the Hanoverian succession. Such loyalty, of course, however outward, is hardly what the nationalist tradition would celebrate. Swift could, alternatively, be inserting an ironic note with his insistence upon the loyalty of the 'Whole People,' but this would compromise his hailing in this and the other letters the real loyalty of Irish Protestants to the English connection through the crown. A sounder alternative is to find Swift shifting the import of the 'Whole People' between the Protestants of Ireland and the entire population, rather as the speaker in *A Tale of a Tub* shifts between the 'Tale-teller'and other voices, subtly to satirize here the English tendency to continue perceiving the people of Ireland as disloyal, whereas the kingdom is in fact now in the hands of a loyal Protestant population indeed.[23]

In the face of the popular agitation to which Swift had contributed, the London ministry eventually conceded defeat and withdrew Wood's patent. Swift was lionized by the people, hailed as the 'Hibernian patriot,' and it was with this wind in his sails that he completed *Gulliver's Travels* early in 1726. Ireland is prominent in Part III, the last of four parts to be written (probably after the Wood's coinage affair), as Balnibarbi, a land oppressed by the floating island of Laputa, or England. Less specific to Ireland, Gulliver's degradingly ingratiating dependence can be taken as satirizing a distortion typifying colonial self-awareness, while in the Lilliput episode, at least, the burden of his consumption has a distorting effect on the local economy as well. But though Gulliver exhibits insufficient self-reliance, he does not demonstrably resort to irresponsible consumption, the link Swift had implied in the *Irish Manufacture* pamphlet of 1720. That link emerges clearly again, however, in Swift's letter to

---

[23] For a more sophisticated and compelling elaboration of the traditional nationalist understanding of Swift's addressing the 'Whole People of Ireland', however, see Carole Fabricant, 'Speaking for the Irish nation: The Drapier, the bishop, and the problems of colonial representation,' *ELH*, 66 (1999), 337-92.

Lord Peterborough in April 1726, when he was visiting London, which gives an account of his meeting with the prime minister.

What brings the conection of dependence and consumption to light with such explicitness in this letter is, in part, the fact that it was written for an English reader, but more because whatever hopes Swift might have had from his interview with Walpole were obviously and very precipitously dashed. The meeting had barely begun before Walpole 'enlarge[d] very much upon the subject of Ireland, in a manner so alien from what I conceived to be rights and privileges of a subject of England, that I did not think proper to debate the matter with him so much as I otherwise might, because I found it would be in vain'.[24] Thus the letter to Peterborough, which it was intended that Walpole should read, lays out the grievances of Ireland as Swift had not done in the meeting. That these are Protestant grievances is clear from the prefatory assertion of the people's 'extraordinary loyalty' and the initial complaint that they are despised, as if all Irishmen, though they are descendants of the British conquerors of Ireland. Beyond this the recital emphasizes the denial to Irish Protestants of free trade and access to office in church and state, while England gains hugely from commerce and rents paid to absentees. More than simply misgoverned, Ireland is being consumed by England, which forces 'the whole body of the gentry' to follow suit within Ireland:

> All they have left is ... to rack their tenants ... to such a degree, that there is not one farmer in a hundred throughout the kingdom who can afford shoes or stockings to his children, or to eat flesh, or drink anything better than sour milk or water, twice in a year, so that the whole country, except the Scotch plantation in the north, is a scene of misery and desolation.[25]

Writing for the eyes of the king's chief minister, Swift asserts the direct relation of English to Irish Protestant consumption within the context of dependence. His clarity is the product of despair, however: rather than consider any form of palliation, England, he now knows for certain, is intent to continue consuming Ireland.

IV

The tone of despair itself continues in Swift writings over the next three years, between his interview with Walpole and *A Modest Proposal* (1729). With a directness he had formerly avoided in addressing his local, Protestant audience,

---

24 Swift to Peterborough, 28 April 1726 (*Swift Corr.* vol. 3, p. 132). 25 Ibid., p. 133.

he elaborates the thesis he had laid out for Peterborough. The admonitory tone of the earlier writings is absent, nor, though dependence remains a central issue in *A Short View of the State of Ireland* (1727-28) and *Maxims Controlled in Ireland* (1729), where he certainly points to English responsibility for the condition of the country, does he evoke resentment overtly at England's interference. A degree of hopelessness pervades both works, probably because of the onset of agricultural depression and famine, and perhaps traceable as well to the ill-success of his meeting with Walpole. But it is hopelessness controlled by an expository tone, as he adjusts his criticism of dependence and consumption to demonstrate that Irish conditions are uniquely perverse. The *Short View* lists the generally-accepted reasons for any country's prosperity, some the gifts of nature, others the result of a rational political and economic system. In Ireland, that system is so distorted that even the gifts of nature are of no avail: 'The conveniency of ports and havens, which nature hath bestowed so liberally upon this kingdom, is of no more use to us, than a beautiful prospect to a man in a dungeon.'[26] The diagnosis is familiar, but here Swift advocates no remedy; his irony runs simply, too, to stress the country's literal perverseness : 'There is no one argument used to prove the riches of Ireland, which is not a logical demonstration of its poverty.'[27] Despair in such a situation becomes itself logical. He does not complain that the self-sufficiency he formerly promoted has gone unheeded by his audience; it is as though the perverseness imposed upon and distorting the country makes good advice itself irrational.

Despair is even more muted in *Maxims Controlled*. Swift notes at length the common wisdom guiding economic thought: it is a sign of wealth in a country if the necessities of life are expensive; low interest rates signify an abundance of money; increasing urban construction indicates that the country flourishes; people are the riches of a nation. But the facts of Ireland's economy confute each of these. Prices of life's necessities have been driven up as an effect of rack-renting; interest is low because the country lacks sufficient currency, and trade in general is depressed; construction in Dublin has been impelled mainly by speculation; and the population of Ireland, far from contributing to the nation's wealth, is so frequently beset by idleness that half the people live by begging and thievery. Here, indeed, remedies like selling the unnecessary population into slavery, or transporting them, can be dreamt of. But these are only dreams; the speaker is left to confess that when he learns of the death of some country wretch, he finds himself pleased. The bitterness of *Maxims Controlled* is nonetheless restrained; it would seem from the 'Verses on the Death of Dr. Swift,' begun around this period, that he might already be taking some compensatory solace from his reputation as 'the Hibernian patriot', even if his audience was demonstrating no likelihood of taking his advice to rely upon themselves.

26 Swift, *Prose Works*, vol. 12, p. 8.   27 Swift, *Prose Works*, vol. 12, p. 11.

Bitterness and fantasy, though, colour *A Modest Proposal*, written and published in 1729. Swift's most famous short satire, its very success can tempt literary commentators to regard it as transcending Ireland altogether. It becomes a satire upon inhumanity, or more specifically upon the 'projecting' mentality that is so fixated upon the remedy proposed for a given defect that morality is (almost comically) overridden. But the *Proposal* does in fact as well as ostensibly deal with Ireland, and reflects at once his sense of despair at its condition and his bitterness at the irresponsibility producing that desperate state. For here, quite directly, Swift takes up the theme of consumption, whose perverse results he had explicated in the *Short View* and *Maxims Controlled*. The portrayal of poverty with which he opens the *Proposal* is more intensely drawn than in the earlier works, and focusses, as Swift hasn't before, on children. The excess of appetite, in the begetting of children and more immediately in respect to their wanting (in both senses) sustenance, points to the theme of consumption, but it is that of the poor themselves to which the Proposer draws our attention. Only by an inversion as yet unprompted in the reader could that reader understand who is to blame for the state of the poor as described; we have no reference to rackrenting, for instance. Only when the Proposer gives his recommendation that the rich could consume the poor directly, by literally feeding upon the offspring of the poor, is that inversion of blame triggered, and then – odd though it may seem – subtly. For the Proposer's focus now is on the good of the commonwealth: he seems intent on realizing the maxim that people are the wealth of the nation. The trope of cannibalism, however, represents the apogee of consumption: 'I grant this food will be somewhat dear, and therefore very *proper for landlords*; who, as they have already devoured most of the parents, seem to have the best title to the children.'[28]

What is proposed, therefore, literalizes Protestant consumption of the Catholic poor; no simple cause-and-effect explication, as in the letter to Peterborough or the *Short View*, showing how rackrenting impoverishes rural Ireland, has the effect of this consumptionist fantasy. But the trope of cannibalism has a deeper resonance, reaching to the justification of Protestant consumption in the ideology of Protestant supremacy. That ideology has as its basis the fear that, left unprotected as in 1641, Protestant Ireland would be consumed by the Catholics, for they are barbarous, bloodthirsty and filled with hatred for Protestants. The cannibal, of course, is the very type of the barbarian, and legendary descriptions of the native Irish, as well as the polemics and sermons of the sixteenth and seventeenth century, often present them as cannibals. Allowed free rein, Catholics would literally or figuratively consume the Protestants. It is the mordancy, the 'toothiness', of this rhetoric of fear, fundamental to the

---

[28] Swift, *Prose Works*, vol. 12, p. 112.

defensive ideology of Protestant consumption, to which Swift's trope of cannibalism most specifically responds. That trope is one of Swift's best-known examples of satiric imagery, and working even beyond ridiculing the ideology of Protestant consumption, it functions also to *invert*, as Swift's satire does so often. We can understand that the whole of the *Proposal* rests upon thematic inversion – Swift is not the Proposer, the remedy proposed is not his, and, toward the end of the piece, the Proposer echoes various remedies Swift *had* proposed in earlier works, all of them aiming at self-sufficiency, simply to discard them as nowhere at all so efficacious as his recommendation of cannibalism. The inversion suits, in fact, the perverseness Swift has ascribed to Ireland in the *Short View* and *Maxims Controlled*. Finally, however, since the whole work pivots on the technique of inversion, inverting the objects of ideologically-imputed cannibalism – that is, proposing that Protestants become the cannibals – evokes its very opposite. For Catholics now become the objects of cannibalism *because* they are barbarously less than human: they can be eaten because prospectively, in the supremacist ideology that underlies the consumptionism mocked here, they are man-eaters themselves. So invertedly, the threat of Catholic consumption is itself invoked; and even justified, as Protestants are placed on the same plane as those they fear.

The *Modest Proposal*, Swift's bitterest comment on the Irish economy, is also one of the greatest and best-known satiric works in any language, a literary monument at the intersection of Swift's advocacy of reforms and his despair at gaining their adoption. It is rather fortuitous than the product of thematic development and aesthetic precision, that such an artistic achievement should come at the end of a decade more devoted to Irish affairs than any other period in Swift's writing career; but it is also true that nothing he wrote about Ireland before or after it meets the same literary standard. And by modern moral standards, the last of such works noticed here, the sermon 'Causes of the Wretched Condition of Ireland,' probably dating from the early 1730s, seems to degenerate into peevishness. Swift begins by indicating England's general culpability for Ireland's economic distortions, to be sure, and that more specifically of absentee landlords, yet hopeless that such factors can be altered, after touching quickly upon the preference for imports and luxuries among the gentry, he devotes himself at length to the character of the poor. Though hating oppression, Swift never considered that its victims were by that token more virtuous than their oppressors, an attitude discernible even in the *Modest Proposal*. On the contrary, the disposition of the poor to laziness, begging and thievery, and the dishonesty of servants, are themes that recur through his lesser-known Irish writings. But here, since he can expect no remedy for this issuing from landlords' treating tenants more justly, his proposals that education in charity schools be restricted to the children of the deserving poor, and that rural beggars be forced to stay in their own parishes lest they migrate to the city, seem by comparison niggardly, almost trivial. They hardly invoke the themes of consumption and dependence in the grander forms of *Irish Manufacture* or the *Drapier's Letters*. Yet these themes are very much sounded. English and Irish Protestant economic distortions are seen as the ultimate source of the defects of the poor, while even among them the fact is seen to operate that dependence causes distorted consumption. There is an implicit analogy, indeed, to the relation between England and Ireland, and between Irish Protestants and Catholic tenants, in the recognition that the dependence of the poor upon society at large accounts for their consuming from it, as beggars and thieves, disproportionately to their contributing to it. Here, however, the effect of economic distortions among the poor — which is to say, their own self-indulgence — can be somewhat corrected by selective education and by equalizing the burden of charity upon society. And here, too, Swift's recommendations — since it is a sermon, they are undisguisedly his own — seek to adjust Irish Protestant self-awareness. Only this time they look to the manner in which the practice of charity might be altered to increase its efficacy. For undifferentiated kindness merely blunts the edge of conscience, without relieving the weight of oppression.

But even these suggestions went unheeded. There is an element of the counterintuitive in Swift's efforts on behalf of Ireland for over a decade. Though he left his most memorable formulation of the human inclination to perverse thinking and action to 'On Poetry: A Rapsody', written in 1732:

> But *Man* we find the only Creature,
> Who, led by *Folly*, fights with *Nature*;
> Who, when *she* loudly cries, *Forbear*,
> With Obstinacy fixes there. (19-22)[29]

his satires had targeted human perversity well before he began to give public, albeit anonymous advice to Protestant Ireland in 1720. But the force of that obstinacy he recognized as a satirist and moralist he appears to have hesitated for some time to acknowledge as a writer on Irish economic affairs. We might say that he should have foreseen that his efforts were doomed; or we could echo the Whig literary tradition and consider that Swift's writings on Ireland were prompted mainly by hatred of the Whig government that had displaced his Tory friends and foreshortened his influence on English high politics. Perhaps, however, it is the case instead that, having gained public standing with the *Irish Manufacture* pamphlet, and increased it with the *Drapier's Lettters*, he was tempted to equate his celebrity with formative influence on the Irish Protestant self-concept, and even Whig policy. Why else would he have sought an interview with Walpole in 1726? If such was the case, he came at length to his unhappy

[29] Swift, *Poems*, vol. 2, p. 641.

senses. By 1731 he could concede in a letter to the countess of Suffolk, 'I shall not attempt to convince England of any thing that relates to this kingdom. The Drapier ... could not do it in relation to the halfpence ... looking upon this kingdom's condition as absolutely desperate, I would not prescribe a dose to the dead.'[30] And perhaps in that latter comment he realised his inability to alter the self-awareness of Irish Protestants, an emblem of the very perversity he had satirized for years.

---

30 Swift to the countess of Suffolk, 26 October 1731 (*Swift Corr.* vol. 3, pp. 500-1).

The politics of political economy in mid-eighteenth-century Ireland

PATRICK KELLY

I

The period between the defeat of the Wood's Halfpence project in 1725 and the beginnings of the Lucas affair in the late 1740s may appear a somewhat muted one in Irish political discourse, if one focuses on politics in the sense which we normally employ the term today. Yet this apparent suspension of political discourse is belied by the fact that the three decades following 1720 were the most prolific in Ireland during the eighteenth century for the production of writings dealing with what we now categorize as economics, though contemporaries considered it a branch of politics.[1] Amongst the contributors to this literature were Jonathan Swift, George Berkeley, Arthur Dobbs, Thomas Prior, David Bindon and Samuel Madden, men whose role in the Ireland of their time is generally considered of the first importance. Yet apart from Swift, the attention that has been paid to these writings both within Ireland and outside is extraordinarily slight.[2] Even Berkeley's *Querist*, for all his fame as a philosopher and the frequent tributes to him in general histories of economics, has received surprisingly little attention.[3] Given the interest generated by the spread of economic thinking elsewhere in Europe during the second quarter of the eighteenth century as a manifestation of the Enlightenment, the neglect of

---

1 E.g. George Berkeley, *The Querist, Containing Several Queries, Proposed to the Consideration of the Public*, 1750 edn, printed in *Bishop Berkeley's Querist in Historical Perspective*, ed. Joseph Johnston (Dundalk 1970), Query 562: 'Whether there can be greater mistake in politics than to measure the wealth of the nation by its gold and silver'; *A Comparative View of the Public Burdens of Great Britain and Ireland* (1779): 'there is more true political knowledge in [Berkeley's] *Queries* than in all Swift's works put together ...' 2 The only attempt to assess this literature as a whole has been Salim Rashid's 'The Irish school of economic development: 1720-1750', *The Manchester School of Economic and Social Studies*, 54 (1988), 345-69, though Rashid's concern was chiefly to compare it with Adam Smith. 3 See in particular the various articles by Joseph Johnston of 1938-40 reprinted in the introduction to his *Bishop Berkeley's Querist in Historical Perspective*; Patrick Kelly, 'Ireland and the critique of mercantilism in Berkeley's Querist', *Hermathena*, 139 (1985), 101-16; Stephen L.R. Clark, intro. to *Money, Obedience, and Affection: Essays on Berkeley's Moral and Political Thought* (London/New York 1989), and Salim Rashid, 'Berkeley's *Querist* and its influence', *Journal of the History of Economic Thought*, 12 (1990), 38-60.

these writings is all the more surprising. Ignoring Ireland in this regard cannot be attributed to the conviction that the British Isles remained untouched by the Enlightenment, since in recent decades there has been enormous interest in the Scottish Enlightenment, especially its political, economic and social writings. Hume in particular has proved a major focus for interest in the application of contemporary economic wisdom to the problems of dependent and undeveloped economies.[4] Recently John Robertson published a study of the adaptation of general eighteenth-century economic principles to such local contexts, considering Scotland and Naples/Sicily as paradigm instances of the intermeshing of the general and local manifestations of the Enlightenment.[5] Yet many of the phenomena which Robertson identifies as starting from the later 1740s in Sicily were already to be found in Ireland some two decades earlier and it is with these that I shall deal in what follows.[6]

II

The volume of economic writing published in Ireland in the decades from 1720 to 1750 (that is from Swift's *Proposal for the Universal Use of Irish Manufacture* to the second, much revised, edition of Berkeley's *Querist*) runs to more than two hundred items in Henry Wagner's 1907 bibliography of Irish economics, ranging from single broadsheets to tracts of over 100 pages.[7] Rather than consider the whole output of these three decades, however, I intend to focus on the dozen or so years from 1728, starting with the publication of Sir John Browne's *Seasonable Remarks on Trade* and continuing to the appearance of Samuel

---

[4] E.g. Istvan Hont, 'The "rich country-poor country" debate in Scottish political economy' in I. Hont and M. Ignatieff (eds), *Wealth and Virtue: The Shaping of Political Economy in the Scottish Enlightenment*, (Cambridge 1983); Andrew Skinner, 'The shaping of political economy in the Scottish Enlightenment', *Scottish Journal of Political Economy*, 37 (1990), 145-72. [5] John Robertson, 'The Enlightenment above national context: political economy in eighteenth-century Scotland and Naples', *Historical Journal*, 40 (1997), 667-97. [6] Parallels between Ireland and Italy, particularly Sicily, were, however, apparent to Berkeley and David Bindon in the 1730s: Berkeley to Prior, 7 May 1730, on the relevance of his Italian travels for understanding Irish problems: *The Works of George Berkeley*, ed. A.A. Luce and T.E. Jessop (Edinburgh, 1948-57), vol. 8, pp. 207-8; Bindon's note to translation of [J.F.Melon], *Essai Politique sur le Commerce* [1734] as *A Political Essay on Commerce* (Dublin 1738), p. 187, n.(b). [7] [Henry R.Wagner], *Irish Economics, 1700-1783: A Bibliography with Notes* (1907, reprint New York 1969). Though Wagner lists subsequent editions as separate items, this element of double counting is roughly compensated by items which he overlooked. Cf. L.W. Hanson, *Contemporary Printed Sources for British and Irish Economic History, 1701-1750* (Cambridge 1963); M. Canney and David Knott, *Catalogue of the Goldsmiths' Library of Economic Literature*, vol. 1: *Printed Books to 1800* (Cambridge 1970), and the manuscript catalogue of the Halliday Tracts in the library of the Royal Irish Academy, Dublin.

Madden's *Reflections and Resolutions for the Gentlemen of Ireland*, and David Bindon's 1738 translation of Jean Francois Melon's *Essai Politique sur le Commerce* (1734), with notes adapting it to Irish conditions.[8] These years, for which Wagner records around 100 items, are particularly illuminating in that economic issues did not become overlaid with political conflict to the extent that they had in the bank controversy of 1720-21 and again in the Wood's Halfpence affair. Consequently it is easier to appreciate the efforts to adapt the general principles of later British mercantilism to the particular circumstances of Ireland. Notable works published in Dublin during this period included Swift's *Short View of the State of Ireland* (1727-8), and *Modest Proposal* (1729), David Bindon's *Essay on the Gold and Silver Coin Current in Ireland* (1729), Thomas Prior's *List of the Absentees of Ireland ... With Observations on the Present State and Condition of That Kingdom* (1729), and his *Observations on the Coin in General* (1729), Arthur Dobbs' *Essay on the Trade and Improvement of Ireland* (two parts, 1729 and 1731), and George Berkeley's *Querist* (three parts, 1735-7). Less impressive performances came with the various writings of the metal manufacturer James Maculla, whose *Proposals for a Publick Coinage of Copper Half-Pence and Farthings* effectively launched the new round of publications starting in 1728; the extensive works of Sir John Browne covered trade and currency, as well as plans for inland navigation, while the chemist William Maple wrote on currency. Although some of this prolific publication, especially in the case of Browne, involved substantial recycling of ideas and on occasions of complete sections of text, the total output of these years testifies to a lively concern with Ireland's economic predicament, reinforced by almost universal claims to be motivated by love of country and a sense of duty to fellow countrymen. 'It is ... every man's duty to promote the happiness of the nation wherein he lives, and by such means as are honest and lawful to increase its power and wealth.'[9]

Identification of Maple as a chemist raises the question of the social background of these writers and the readership for which their works were intended. The majority of the writers seem to have come from lesser gentry or merchant backgrounds, with a strong sprinkling of clergymen. Best known of the latter was Jonathan Swift, dean of St Patrick's, while there was also Samuel Madden, sometime fellow of Trinity College, who came from a wealthy gentry background and helped found the Dublin Society for the Promotion of Agriculture and Industry in 1731, to say nothing of Berkeley, another former College fellow, promoted to the see of Cloyne in 1734. The dominant figure in the early eighteenth-century Irish church, William King, had been deeply concerned with the country's economic well-being since the 1690s; while the gen-

---

8 This important item by Bindon was overlooked by Wagner. **9** Arthur Dobbs, *Essay on the Trade and Improvement of Ireland*, part 1 (1729), p. 2; cf. Sir John Browne, *An Essay on Trade in General, and on that of Ireland in Particular* (1728), pp. 64-5.

eral culture of 'improvement' in early eighteenth-century Ireland was supported by other bishops such as Bolton of Cashel, Clayton of Cork, Hutchinson of Down and Conor, and Archbishop Synge of Tuam.[10] This degree of clerical involvement with economic questions was unusual by English or Scottish standards, though not by those of continental Europe. Amongst lay writers, some were members of parliament, notably Sir John Browne, David Bindon and Arthur Dobbs. Bindon came from a largely merchant background in Limerick, while Browne and Dobbs were primarily landowners. None of these three MPs had a university education, as their clerical confrères would have had, and as did Thomas Prior, a minor landowner in England as well as Ireland, who was also a founder of the Dublin Society. Browne also had in addition commercial interests, as did some of the other minor figures such as Daniel Webb, the foremost advocate of paper money apart from Berkeley.[11] The most socially prominent figure was Lord Perceval, future second earl of Egmont, whose brief *Some Observations on the Present State of Ireland, Particularly with Relation to the Woollen Manufacture* appeared in 1731.[12] Only one writer may possibly have been a Catholic, the William Plunkett who has been tentatively identified as author of *Agriculture the Surest Means to National Wealth* (1738).[13]

The question of intended readership is less easy to determine. Many authors, as already pointed out, sought to conceal their reasons for publication by publishing anonymously, or merely over their initials. Some indications can, however, be gathered from dedications. Several works sought to appeal directly to parliament, sometimes through dedications to the Speaker of the Commons. Others addressed the British administration in Ireland by dedicating to the lord lieutenant, while yet others again saw the lord mayor of Dublin as representing a public opinion that might be stirred in their favour.[14] More concrete indications of the potential readership for the genre are provided by three subscription lists that survive for economic titles from the late 1720s and 1730s. These were for Defoe's *Complete English Tradesman* (1726), the almanac publisher John Watson's *Two Tables of Exchange* (1727), and David Bindon's translation of Melon's *Essai Politique sur le Commerce* (1738).[15] The first two each

---

10 Cf. T.C. Barnard, 'Improving clergymen, 1660-1760' in Alan Ford, James McGuire and Kenneth Milne (eds), *As by Law Established: The Church of Ireland since the Reformation* (Dublin 1996), pp. 243-72. 11 Daniel Webb, *An Enquiry into the Reasons of the Decay of Credit, Trade, and Manufactures of Ireland* (Dublin 1735). 12 Egmont Diary, 7 Apr. 1731, HMC, *Egmont MSS* (1920-3), vol. 1, p. 172. The diary also shows David Bindon in regular contact with Egmont throughout the 1730s: ibid., vol. 1, pp. 168-388 *passim*; vol. 3, pp. 166-8. 13 D. MacDonald, *Agricultural Writers* (London 1908), p. 209; this pamphlet (p. 7) was among the earliest to refer to Berkeley's *Querist*. 14 Other writers exploited their title pages to spell out the kernel of their message, e.g. James Maculla (*A New Scheme Proposed to the People of Ireland ...*, 1728-9), and Samuel Madden (*Reflections and Resolutions for the Gentlemen of Ireland ...*, 1738). 15 Items published by subscription in Dublin at this time were mostly works of

include somewhat over 200 names (with a fair degree of overlap), mostly merchants with a sprinkling of gentry. Disappointingly none of the lists specifically identify individuals as members of parliament, though all include some MPs. The Bindon list is far more extensive, with over 500 names. It also covers a much wider range of social categories; namely nine bishops, eight peers, numerous esquires, five judges, the attorney and solicitor general, a sprinkling of TCD fellows, fourteen clergymen, four medical men, and – perhaps surprisingly – six women. What is particularly interesting is to find the names of other economic writers in Bindon's list, namely Arthur Dobbs, Samuel Madden, and Jonathan Swift; though neither Prior nor Berkeley are included.

III

Like most works of early political economy, the writings produced in Ireland in the dozen years starting from 1728 were responses to specific economic crisis. Thus a brief account of the country's economic circumstances in these years is desirable as a prelude to considering the literature. Underlying conditions in Ireland in the first half of the eighteenth century were generally unfavourable and those of the second quarter in particular extremely harsh, with such periods of amelioration as occurred too brief to make good the ground lost in the previous period of distress.[16] Eighteenth-century Ireland was a largely undeveloped agricultural economy supporting a generally under-capitalized landlord class, significant numbers of the more prosperous of whom resided permanently, or much of the time, outside the country. Such industry as existed was largely confined to the towns or to the north of the country, and those forms of production for which the country seemed best favoured by nature, the export of cattle to Britain and the manufacture of woollen cloth for export, had been debarred by English legislation in the later seventeenth century. The linen industry which English mercantilist policy had sought to substitute for the manufacture of woollens was largely in the north of the country, where the bulk of the population,

---

poetry, history, and translations, with occasional medical or legal texts. See further, F.J.G.Robinson and P.G.Wallis (eds), *Book Subscription Lists: A Revised Guide* (Newcastle-upon-Tyne 1975) and P.G.Wallis (ed.), *Book Subscription Lists: An Extended Supplement* (Newcastle-upon-Tyne 1997). **16** For the early eighteenth-century Irish economy, see the various writings of L.M.Cullen, esp. *An Economic History of Ireland*, 2nd edn (London 1987), p. 39-49; 'Landlords, bankers, and merchants: the early Irish banking world' in *Economists and Irish Economy*, ed. A.E. Murphy (Dublin 1984), and W.E. Vaughan (ed.), *A New History of Ireland*, vol. 4: *Eighteenth-Century Ireland, 1691-1800* (Oxford 1986), ch. vi; S.J.Connolly, *Religion, Law and Power: The Making of Protestant Ireland, 1660-1760* (Oxford 1992), 41-59; James Kelly, 'Harvests and hardship: famine and scarcity in Ireland in the later 1720s', *Studia Hibernica*, 26 (1992), 65-105.

though Protestant, were Scots-descended Presbyterians. Provision for the Catholic masses was often inadequate and, especially in times of difficulty, vagrancy and begging were an enormous problem. The 1720s and 1730s were particularly unfortunate in that the international market for Irish agricultural produce was generally slack, and the country experienced severe bouts of famine. The second worst period of famine in the eighteenth century occurred in the second half of the 1720s, which though less acute than that of 1740-1 cast a long shadow over the 1730s. Bad harvests from 1725 to 1728 led to starvation, vagrancy, riot, increased emigration to North America, especially from Ulster, and a general decay of trade that the improved harvests of 1730-2 were not sufficient to pull the country out of. Arrears of rents could not be paid off; difficulties occurred in the linen trade, and the fall in population from the late 1720s was not made good.[17] The major private bank failure of Burton and Falkiner in 1732 disrupted the credit and currency system, and poor harvests were again experienced from 1733 to 1736. Small wonder then that public attention both within and without parliament turned to consideration of, first, how the immediate crisis of famine might be coped with, and then to the longer-term issue of how to break through stagnation and increase the employment opportunities of the masses, though as Berkeley confided to Prior on congratulating him on the appearance of his *List of Absentees*, 'the spirit of projecting is low in Ireland'.[18]

Together with natural calamity and dislocation of international trade, early eighteenth-century Ireland suffered the further disadvantage of a highly unsatisfactory currency system. Not only were there no Irish coins as such, a matter that ill-served a commercial economy,[19] but the circulating medium consisted of English gold and silver coins, together with foreign gold and silver pieces current at rates established by government proclamation, which consistently undervalued the main currency metal, silver. This bimetallic imbalance ensured that when bullion outflows occurred because of adverse trade balances, the country experienced a severe restriction of its circulating medium. In addition Ireland was chronically short of small change; the lowest denomination English silver piece in general circulation was the sixpence, and provision for smaller sums had to be effected with base coin. The supply of copper money was seriously inadequate, being the product of various concessions to patentees going back to the 1690s,[20] and the bulk of the surviving copper consisted of below intrinsic value pieces known as 'raps' (many of which were counterfeits).

---

17 For the knock-on effects of the crisis of the late 1720s, see L.M. Cullen, 'The food crisis of the early 1740s: the economic conjuncture', forthcoming in a collection of papers on the 1740-41 famine, to be edited by David Dickson, to whom I grateful for drawing this to my attention, as to Professor Cullen for permission to refer to the paper. **18** Berkeley to Prior, 7 May 1730 (*Works*, vol. 8, p. 208). **19** As David Bindon, *Essay on the Gold and Silver Coin* (1729), p. 7, pointed out, going on to claim that Ireland was unique in Europe in this respect. **20** For details see *A Defence of the Conduct of the People of Ireland in their Unanimous Refusal of*

The deficiencies of the currency had already been the occasion of two earlier major politico/economic crises in the 1720s, namely the Bank project of 1720-1 and the Wood's Halfpence affair. The bank project was intended to create a national bank with private shareholders on the model of the Bank of England that would stimulate credit and promote liquidity in the crisis following the collapse of the South Sea Bubble in England in 1720. Combined fears of stock-jobbing and political corruption killed off the Bank project, while strongly worded resolutions from both houses of the Irish parliament effectively blocked the prospect of reviving the issue for more than a decade.[21] Not till the mid-1730s would proposals for a national bank be revived in the anonymous *A Proposal for the Relief of Ireland ... by Establishing a National Bank* (1734), followed by the first part of Berkeley's *Querist* (1735), and even then the impact of the Lords' 1721 resolution, which condemned any peer who raised the bank project in the future as a betrayer of his country, probably influenced Berkeley's opting for anonymity.[22] Other than private bankers' notes, whose currency had been ensured by acts of Anne and George I, there was little interest in developing forms of paper-credit in Ireland – in striking contrast to the remarkable creativity in the American colonies.[23] The Wood's Halfpence project had, till overtaken by broader political controversy, been an attempt to provide for additional small change through the production of halfpence and farthings by an English patentee. Its credibility had been undermined by a national campaign raising fears of the scheme as a plot to drain Ireland of its remaining gold and silver, and as an attack on the country's political liberties. Though an indignant British ministry finally withdrew Wood's patent, the need for small change persisted as did the problems over gold and silver ratios and the composition of the circulating currency.[24]

The current ratio of Irish to English money had been established in 1701.[25] While, as already stated, there were no Irish coins as such, there was an Irish money of account that valued the English shilling piece at 13d Irish, giving an exchange par of 108.33 for silver.[26] The problems of the 1720s and 30s chiefly

---

Mr Wood's Copper-Money (1724), pp. 21-3. **21** Michael Ryder, 'The Bank of Ireland, 1721: land, credit and dependency', *Historical Journal*, 25 (1982), 583-603; Irish antipathy to banks was adverted to by Maculla, *A New Scheme Proposed*, p. 7. **22** Query 226 of *The Querist* (1735 edn only) criticizes the *Proposal*, thus making clear it is not by Berkeley, as Wagner, *Irish Economics*, item 146 suggests. *Journals of the House of Commons (Ireland)*, vol. 3, p. 289 (9 Dec. 1721); *Journals of the House of Lords (Ireland)*, vol. 2, p. 270 (Dec. 1721). **23** Richard A. Lester, *Monetary Experiments: Early American and Recent Scandinavian* (Princeton, N.J. 1939) chs. 3-4. American paper issues and the particular developments in Rhode Island are discussed in detail by George Caffentzis, *Exciting the Industry of Mankind: George Berkeley's Philosophy of Money* (forthcoming Kluwer, Dordrecht). **24** Irvin Ehrenpreis, *Swift: The Man, his Works and the Age* (London 1967-83), vol. 3, pp. 187-317 *passim*. Swift's responsibility for the withdrawal should not be exaggerated. **25** Joseph Johnson, 'The Irish currency in the eighteenth century', reprinted as *Berkeley's Querist in Historical Perspective*, ch. 6. **26** L.M. Cullen, *Anglo-*

derived from two factors. First, the failure to rate foreign coins in strict proportion to their metallic content gave rise to disparities which affected gold more extensively than silver. Second, when the gold-silver ratio had been changed in Britain in 1717 with the reduction of the guinea from 21s. 6d. to 21s. 0d., no corresponding readjustment was made in Ireland. As a result silver was now seriously undervalued and various foreign gold coins, particularly large denomination Portuguese pieces, were over-valued in proportion to the guinea. What was ignored by contemporaries, however, was that even with the more realistic gold-silver ratio established in 1717, silver was still undervalued in Britain and would continue in short supply throughout the century.[27]

IV

The main areas on which Irish writers of the late 1720s and 1730s concentrated their attention were the currency, and what they called 'trade', a term sometimes employed as a synonym for commerce, and sometimes as a sort of shorthand for a concept that as yet had not been clearly articulated, namely the economy. The third most important field of economic discourse in this period was agriculture.[28] Under these three headings Irish writers also engaged with questions of employment, poor relief, the problem of luxury, and the economic role of the gentry. The conceptual framework in which the discourse was conducted was that of later mercantilism with an emphasis on promoting the circulation of gold and silver money as the key to stimulating economic activity, the objective of providing for the employment of the population, and a privileged role accorded to foreign trade in the promotion of national wealth. Only with Berkeley would the fixation with gold and silver and the primacy of foreign trade be rejected and a plan put forward for the solution to stagnation and unemployment through the use of paper-money issued by a publicly owned national bank, in effect harnessing the wants of the Irish poor as the motor to transform the economy. Since, however, economic processes were in no way conceived of as a self-regulating system capable of optimizing output when self-interest was allowed free play, the discussions took place in the context of a political approach to economic problems in which the successful functioning of the economy depended on proper direction by the 'statesman' or the legislature.[29]

Irish Trade in the Eighteenth Century (London 1968), pp. 155-8. **27** Albert Feavearyear, *The Pound Sterling: A History of English Money*, 2nd edn (London 1963), pp. 157-8; Cullen, *Anglo-Irish Trade*, p. 158. **28** Agriculture will be considered here only in relation to other topics such as the role of the gentry or provision of employment. **29** See further, pp. 120, 123-5 below.

Crucial to the general perception of Irish economic interests was the relationship with England. Despite the victory achieved in the Wood's Halfpence affair, virtually no one in the 1720s and 30s, other than Swift, overtly argued that Ireland's economic salvation depended on the country being allowed to direct its own economic destiny. What is notable about the writers of the late 1720s, in contrast to earlier Irish writers, was the near consensus which emerged from 1728 as to the feasibility of Ireland's over-coming its problems within the framework of existing restrictions imposed by Britain. In place of denouncing English restrictions what was called for was acknowledgement of the importance of Ireland to the British economy, and the benefits that could (and consequently should) be allowed to accrue to Ireland within the imperial economy. For Dobbs this was a realization of the reality of British political dominance; to expect to compete with the imperial power in what was conceived to be its crucial domestic industry, the woollen trade, was accepted as futile. But Prior boldly argued that it would be to Britain's advantage to allow Irish competition even in this hallowed field.[30] Such an acceptance, however, must be matched by a realization on England's part that Ireland was of benefit to her, whether directly by the large sums dispatched to maintain Irish absentees, or by the market which she provided for a vast range of English products – as categorized by the British writer Joshua Gee in 1727.[31] To Sir John Browne Ireland and the colonies offered Britain access to cheap manufactures within the empire which could be exploited to drive their French and Dutch rivals out of the markets which they had earlier wrested from England. In an early contribution to the rich country – poor country controversy that would subsequently command the attention of Hume and others in Scotland, Browne saw trade as bringing money into a country. The enhanced standard of living would push up wages, and expose the country concerned to successful competition from poorer rivals, until the adverse trade balance in turn depressed wage levels and allowed it once more to compete with rivals themselves undergoing the same cyclical process.[32]

Successful regulation was assumed to depend on maintaining a favourable general balance of trade. A number of writers, such as Browne, Prior and Dobbs, presented detailed export and import figures from the customs records with a view to substantiating their arguments.[33] Such data were also contrasted with earlier figures, notably those in Petty's *Political Anatomy*, to assess the coun-

---

[30] Cf. Thomas Prior, *List of the Absentees of Ireland ... With Observations on the Present State and Condition of That Kingdom* (London 1729), pp. 59-65; Dobbs, *Essay*, pp. 3-4, 74-8. [31] Joshua Gee, *The Trade and Navigation of Great Britain Considered* (London 1729), ch. 13. [32] Browne, *Seasonable Remarks*, pp. 11-14; *Essay on Trade*, pp. 49-51. Cf. Istvan Hont, 'The "rich country-poor country" debate'. [33] Browne, *Seasonable Remarks*, p. 26; *Essay on Trade*, pp. 59-61; Prior, *Absentees*, pp. 37-48; Dobbs, *Essay* (1729), pp. 5-59 *passim*.

try's progress in the longer term.[34] As with earlier English writers, the balance was seen as the key to determining the country's commercial policy through the elimination of trade with countries that returned a consistent adverse balance. France was regarded as the worst example of the latter in taking raw agricultural products in return for a combination of luxury goods, such as wine and lace, and manufactures which might be produced in Ireland.[35] The relatively novel concept of assessing trade between countries in terms not of a balance of precious metals but of a 'balance of labour' (a concept introduced by Nicholas Barbon in the 1690s) was advanced by Sir John Browne, who argued that the only imports that should be encouraged were raw materials for working up for re-export. Browne is particularly interesting in that his discussion of the issue actually employs the term 'in adding value', and he clearly articulates the impact on Irish employment as the main factor to be considered in relation to assessing the balance.[36] In earlier discussions of Ireland's general balance, the amount sent to absentees had been a much disputed figure, which Prior now sought to clarify in *A List of the Absentees of Ireland, And the Yearly Value of their Estates and Incomes Spent Abroad* (1729), by establishing the precise sums paid to identified individuals (including the £900 sent to his friend Berkeley from the deanery of Derry), which amounted to an annual total of £621,500.[37] Such an enormous sum could be represented as a major benefit to the British economy, and a compelling reason for Britain's henceforth encouraging rather than discouraging Irish trade.[38]

For Arthur Dobbs, the key to Ireland's commercial relations with Britain lay clearly with co-operation rather than confrontation. Operating within an Aristotelian framework of trade as a process of mutual co-operation between nations[39] – seemingly in accordance with some providentially foreordained plan – Dobbs wished to go further than the general consensus and argued the case for political union between Great Britain and Ireland.[40] Like Browne, and later

---

34 Browne, *Essay on Trade*, pp. 64-7, 53-6. **35** *Considerations on Two Papers lately Published*, pp. 121-2; Prior, *Absentees*, p. 98; Dobbs, *Essay* (1731), pp. 16-19, 146; Berkeley, *Querist*, queries 150-61. **36** Browne, *Essay on Trade*, pp. 65-7, 53-6. For the balance of labour concept, see P. Kelly, 'Between politics and economics: concepts of wealth in English mercantilism', *Studi settecenteschi*, 5 (1984), 21-2, 28-30. **37** *Considerations*, pp. 110-2; Prior, *Absentees*, pp. 14, 81. **38** Prior, *Absentees*, pp. 63-6; Dobbs, *Essay* (1729), pp. 52-74 (esp. 66-71); *Essay* (1731), pp. 16-18. **39** 'Trade and commerce unites in interest and affection the most distant nations. As the soul animating the natural body makes members of it useful to each other ... so trade in the body politic makes the several parts of it contribute to the well-being of the whole, and also to the more comfortable and agreeable living of every member of the community ....': *Essay* (1729), pp.1-2. See further, ibid., pp. 69-70. **40** The political dimension of Dobbs's scheme is more clearly articulated in his unpublished 'An Essay on the Expediency of a Union between Great Britain and Ireland' , National Library of Ireland, MS Thom 1. See further, James Kelly, 'The origins of the act of union: an examination of unionist opinion in Britain and Ireland, 1650-1800', *Irish Historical Studies*, 25 (1986-7), 252.

Berkeley, Dobbs saw London as the centre of Ireland's monetary circulation.[41] Though Prior too took the view that economic co-operation within an imperial context could ensure the future of the Irish poor, he stopped short of a call for political union. For him, as for many others, the problem of stagnation in Irish trade was largely due to an insufficient monetary circulation. His approach was one derived from William Petty in terms of what Marian Bowley has identified as the 'necessary stock of money' concept, which Prior formulated as, 'money being the measure of all commerce, a certain quantity thereof is necessary for the carrying on the trade of each country, in proportion to the business thereof'.[42] An insufficient circulation for the volume of trade in the nation would restrict the volume of economic activity, particularly given the limitations imposed by customary times of payment for rent, wages and the settlement of commercial debts.[43] Neither Dobbs nor Prior seem to have had any confidence in the potential of credit to lift the Irish economy out of its stagnation, though they were both (especially the latter) aware of the way in which an inadequately functioning currency constricted economic activity, whether by shortage of change, insistence on the acceptance of foreign coins only by weight, or the difficulty of adapting prices expressed in the Irish money of account to the actual coins in circulation.[44] Daniel Webb, however, was prepared to accept a limited issue of small denomination paper-credit for the needs of poor tradesmen, but subject to rigorous control to prevent the issue exceeding the £30,000 he considered adequate for the successful working of the scheme.[45]

V

The question of the regulation of the currency played a substantial part in the literature of the 1720s and 1730s. The most interesting writers in theoretical terms were Bindon, Prior, and of course Berkeley (though consideration of the treatment of money in *The Querist* will be deferred till later). 'Money-matters', as Sir John Browne termed them, involved both complex technical questions involving calculations based on the weight and fineness (together giving the precious metal content) of the coins, and more fundamental issues relating to

---

[41] '... as the blood in the natural body circulates through the heart in greater quantities ... than through the extremities, so all the wealth of a nation [circulates] through the capital and centre of empire and trade': Dobbs, *Essay* (1729), p. 70; Browne, *Essay on Trade*, pp. 51-2; Berkeley, *Querist*, queries 75-7, 433.   [42] Prior, *Absentees*, pp. 18, 63-72; Marian Bowley, *Studies in the History of Economic Theory before 1870* (London 1973), pp. 48-54.   [43] Cf. more detailed discussion in Browne, *A Scheme of the Money-Matters of Ireland* (1729), pp. 11-12.   [44] See further in the following section.   [45] [Daniel Webb], *An Enquiry into the Reasons of the Decay of Credit, Trade and Manufactures in Ireland* (1735), pp. 31-6.

the functioning of the economic system. Money was also, however, an overtly political concern and of immense symbolic significance, representing in very concrete form the sovereignty of a nation – or rather in Ireland's case its subjection to Britain.[46] The controversy over Wood's Halfpence had brought the political significance of currency very much into the open, and as the letters of Archbishop Boulter (administrator of Ireland in the absences of successive lords lieutenant from 1726 till his death in 1742) make clear, left the Irish administration perforce attuned to the political implications of regulating the currency, particularly the desirability of involving parliament in any major currency decisions.[47] Possession of a mint, regarded as a *sine qua non* of a self-respecting state, had been denied by successive British administrations back to the late seventeenth century, when Newton had advised in forthright terms against setting up an Irish mint.[48] In 1698 calls for an Irish mint may have had unwelcome overtones of the recent emergency coinages of the Jacobite regime, the 'brass money and wooden shoes' of Irish Protestant ideology, so it is interesting that the Jacobite tract written by Nicholas Plunkett in 1698 also advocated the establishment of an Irish mint.[49] The economic benefits of a mint were analyzed with great perspicacity both in David Bindon's *Essay on the Gold and Silver Currency* and Prior's *Observations*.[50] For Bindon a country which lacked its own mint was on a par with one which scarcely enjoyed the benefits of money at all. A local mint enabled a favourable proportion to be kept between the large and small denominations of coin, and would avoid the problem that the available coins were not suited to prices expressed in the Irish money of account.[51] Similar arguments were put by Prior with the addition of problems arising from accepting foreign coins only by weight, which hampered market transactions as only English silver was acceptable at face value.[52]

Other writers like Browne provided an elaborate account of the origin of money and coinage, which may seem rather naive in contrast to the succinct

---

46 Cf. Swift, *The Intelligencer*, no. 19 (1728): 'Ireland is the first imperial kingdom, since Nimrod, which ever wanted power to coin their own money' (Swift, *Prose Works*, vol. 12, p. 57). **47** See *Letters Written by his Excellency, Hugh Boulter, D.D., Lord Primate of all Ireland* (Dublin 1770), esp. Boulter to Walpole, 25 May 1736. Cf. Bindon, *Essay on the Gold and Silver Coin* (1729), p. 1, for the necessity of involving parliament. **48** Newton to English lords justices, 18 Aug. 1698: 'Ireland is one of the English plantations and though it has changed the title of lordship to that of kingdom, yet it still continues ... inferior to this kingdom and subservient to its interests. We are unwilling that any opinion of ours should be made use of for promoting any design ... to make [the Irish] of equal dignity and dominion with ourselves [England] and perhaps at length desirous to separate from this Crown ...': *Calendar of Treasury Books*, vol. 14 (1698-9), p. 107. Similarly, the establishment of mints had not been permitted in the American colonies. **49** Nicholas Plunkett, 'The improvement of Ireland' (1698), ed. P. Kelly, *Collectanea Hibernica*, 35 (1992), 57. **50** Bindon, *Essay*, pp. 18-21; Prior, *Observations* (reprinted in J.R.McCulloch, *Scarce Tracts on Money* (1856), p. 336). **51** *Essay*, pp. 18-21 **52** *Observations*, p. 337.

treatment provided by Bindon (for whose work Browne expressed admiration in speaking of 'the ingenious Mr Bindon').[53] However, their intention may have been to highlight the ill-functioning of the Irish system by illustrating the important functions of money which were not adequately provided for in Ireland. The chief source for Irish writers on money was Locke's contribution to the debates which had preceded the English recoinage of 1696.[54] Some writers like Swift, who had Locke's pamphlets in his library, followed their mentor in a slavish manner, while others sought to adapt Locke to the rather different circumstances of Ireland in the 1720s and 30s.[55] Locke's principal appeal for Irish writers may have lain in his emphasis on the role of money in international trade as opposed to the concern which his contemporary opponents had displayed for money in the domestic context. Most Irish writers had a clear understanding of the way in which increasing the nominal valuation of silver coins would reduce the payments to be made by tenants and debtors in terms of silver, whereas lowering the valuation would proportionately benefit the interests of landlords and creditors. Views on the effect of revaluation on Irish prices varied, with Bindon correctly perceiving that there would be no immediate impact but that effects would be gradually passed on via the exchange process.[56]

Most writers on currency devoted some attention to the process of foreign exchange, so vital for the Irish economy the bulk of whose exchange transactions were handled through London. Like modern economic historians the anonymous author of the attack on Browne, entitled *Considerations on Two Papers, lately published*, regarded the exchange with London as a crucial indicator of the well-being of the Irish economy, terming it '... one of the pulses skilful politicians are to feel; in order to discover the true state of a national trade'.[57] Expositions of the exchange process also drew heavily on Locke for their account of technicalities such as the par.[58] Examples drawn from the exchange were made use of to illustrate the disproportionate value of different coins brought into the country – English silver, guineas, foreign gold, the higher value Portuguese moidores, and the even more overvalued new high denomination

---

53 Browne, *Scheme of the Money-Matters*, pp. 1-4, 37.   **54** John Locke, *Some Considerations of the Lowering of Interest, and Raising the Value of Money*, 2nd edn (London 1696); *Further Considerations concerning Raising the Value of Money* (London 1695); see further the introduction to *Locke on Money*, ed. P. Kelly (Oxford 1991).   **55** Locke had never had to confront the reality of the difference between 'real' and 'imaginary' money as found on the continent, a distinction obscured by the normal operations of the currency system in England though painfully obvious in Ireland. Cf. Luigi Einaudi, 'The theory of imaginary money from Charlemagne to the French Revolution', in F. Lane and J.C. Riemersma (eds), *Enterprise and Secular Change: Readings in Economic History* (London 1953).   **56** *Essay*, p. 11; Prior, *Observations*, pp. 329-31.   **57** *Considerations on Two Papers lately Published*, p. 123.   **58** E.g. Browne, *Scheme*, pp. 13-15; Bindon, *Essay*, pp. 7-9; Prior, *Observations*, pp. 312-14. Cf. Locke, *Further Considerations* (1695) in Kelly (ed.), *Locke on Money*, vol. 2, pp. 420-1.

Portuguese pieces, which Boulter in a despairing letter to Walpole in 1736 confided might soon come to make up half the current monetary circulation.[59]

Bimetallism also proved a problem; Prior flatly contradicted Locke's assertion that, since gold and silver were constantly changing their relative values, only one metal could serve as the measure of value.[60] Prior, Bindon, and even Browne appreciated the utility of different forms of money for different levels of transaction; gold for substantial dealings, silver for everyday transactions (presumably, that is, of the gentry and middle classes), and copper 'to answer [the] little occasions' of tradesmen and the poor.[61] Opinions differed as to the status of copper. Browne claimed that there was a tri-metallic system in operation in Ireland, though most writers regarded even *ad valorem* copper pieces as a mere supplement to the precious metal currency.[62] Nonetheless, whether technically money or otherwise, the question of the coinage of copper aroused strong political passions and Boulter's initiative in persuading the British ministry to allow the production of a small amount of copper change in 1736 once more awoke the alarm of Swift.[63] Swift's conviction of the malign intentions of the Dublin administration and their British masters in this respect verges on paranoia. Boulter's efforts to convince the London administration of the urgency of this and other economic and financial problems in Ireland reveal him to have been every bit as concerned for the country's well-being as Swift himself.[64]

Opposition in the Irish parliament of 1729 managed to prevent the issue of a much needed copper supplement and to force the abandonment of thoughts of revaluing foreign silver as well as gold. The administration led by Boulter favoured revaluing both foreign silver and gold, but had to drop their proposals in the light of public outcry and parliamentary opposition. In his own mind Boulter was convinced of what the most far sighted Irish writers on coinage wished for, namely the introduction of the English monetary standard in Ireland. Most of Boulter's ire over the coinage debates was reserved for David Bindon, whom he dismissed in 1729 as 'a broken merchant of Limerick'.[65] Swift's final intervention in 1736-7 angered him even further, particularly the provocative black flag flown from the steeple of St Patrick's when in 1737 the

---

59 Prior, *Observations*, pp. 306-11; Boulter to Walpole, 25 May 1737 (*Boulter Correspondence*). **60** Locke, *Further Considerations* (1695) in Kelly (ed.), *Locke on Money*, vol. 2, pp. 422-3; Prior, *Observations*, pp. 298-300. **61** Browne, *Scheme*, p. 5. Cf. Berkeley, *Querist*, queries 468-9, 571. **62** Copper was not technically money in the eyes of the law, since it was not included in the mint indentures nor could it be proffered for free coinage under the English 1663 Free Coinage Act. See Boulter to Dorset, 12 Apr. 1731; Boulter to Walter Cary, 26 Mar. 1737 (*Boulter Correspondence*). Cf. Browne, *Scheme*, p. 7. **63** Swift, *Thoughts on the Gold Coin* (1736) in *Prose Works*, vol. 13, p. 119. **64** Esp. Boulter to Carteret, 13 May, and 23 Oct. 1729; Boulter to Newcastle, 29 Sept. 1737 (*Boulter Correspondence*). **65** Boulter to Carteret, 13 May 1729; 25, 30 Apr. 1737 (ibid.). Bindon's solution involved raising the rating of the English shilling piece to 13½ d. Irish.

Irish administration at last convinced Walpole and Newcastle to allow them to reduce the value of gold in Ireland. However, this bringing Irish ratios into line with the British revaluation of 1717 together with the issue of the copper halfpence and farthings finally ended two decades of enormously disruptive monetary conditions in Ireland.[66] In passing it may be noted that Boulter was not simply prejudiced against Irish economic writers in general. In 1734 he recommended Arthur Dobbs to Walpole as one who had proved his worth in the Commons and had written a valuable work on Irish trade, though Prior's anonymous *List of Absentees* was blamed for stirring up 'the utmost grumbling against England, as getting all our money from us by trade or otherwise'.[67] Most of all, however, Boulter blamed the bankers for their influence over the Irish House of Commons, the general public, and even at times, especially through his colleague Speaker Connolly, the Irish privy council itself.[68] Ironically, though bankers were indeed generally regarded as the beneficiaries of the ill-regulated currency system, their views, which seemingly accorded with Locke's advice against altering the monetary standard, commanded considerable public influence.[69]

VI

If trade and currency were the main issues to occupy the attention of Irish writers in the late 1720s and 1730s, three further points in their writings also merit consideration, namely the significance of luxury, the role of the gentry, and the condition of the Irish poor – particularly the conviction of their innate inclination to sloth and indolence. The successive harvest failures of the late 1720s greatly exacerbated the problems of beggary and vagrancy, especially in the capital, as people fled from the land to seek what charitable relief might be available, limited though it proved.[70] This problem also raised the question of the role of landlords, including the issue of absentees. Absentees in turn brought up the question of luxury, further raising the matter of whether one could distinguish between harmful and beneficial luxury in the Irish context.

The crucial role of the landlords in the Irish economy, as potential motors of local development if resident on their estates, and parasitic consumers if absentees, whether in Dublin or abroad, was widely recognized.[71] Even in the

---

[66] Boulter to Dorset, 11 Feb. 1738; Boulter to Walter Cary, 26 Mar. 1737 (*Boulter Correspondence*). [67] Boulter to Walpole, 4 Jan. [? recte June] 1730; to Carteret, 23 Oct. 1729 (ibid.). [68] Boulter to Carteret, 25, 30 Apr. 1730 (ibid.). [69] Locke, *Further Considerations*, pp. 9-10; Kelly (ed.), *Locke on Money*, vol. 2, pp. 415-16. [70] James Kelly, 'Harvests and hardship', 82-7. [71] Prior, *Absentees*, p. 52; Madden (*Resolutions*, p. 30) speaks of the gentry as 'the principal engine of this useful work'.

later seventeenth century the Jacobite author of 'The Improvement of Ireland' had called for the gentry to reside on their estates in order to act as centres of local industry and stimulate the consumption of local produce.[72] By cultivating the appurtenances of civilization in building mansion houses, planting orchards and gardens, and growing trees, the gentry would transform the Irish countryside and through improving clauses in leases introduce much needed agricultural improvement. To Berkeley and Madden in the 1730s, as much as to Plunkett in the later seventeenth century, such local economic leadership and potential for fostering entrepreneurship was a manifestation of patriotic duty. But the Irish gentry as a landlord class had a further vital function as the reservoir from which the country's legislature was for the most part recruited. Informing oneself of the nature of trade and commerce and understanding such matters for oneself was urged on the gentry as an additional patriotic duty, particularly as merchants and bankers were identified as self-interested and unaware of the broader national interest. Some writers, however, followed Locke in stressing that since trade provided the market for the product of the land that kept up rents, and land the products on which the manufacture of commodities for export depended, mercantile self-interest did not belie the essential truth that land and trade would prosper together or suffer together.[73] To educate the gentry in their proper interest, Prior called for the establishment of professorships of agriculture, trade and 'practical matters' at Trinity College (on the model perhaps of the practical chairs of modern languages founded by George II in 1727), and Berkeley ironically queried whether ignorance should be the portion of the eldest son.[74] Education of the gentry was enormously important in the light of the prevalent model of the functioning of the economy in which successful direction depended upon the intervention of the statesman or legislature.[75] Given the widespread mistrust of the British appointed Irish administration, in practical terms only the Dublin parliament could have performed such a role.

The debate over luxury focused chiefly on the extravagant consumption of imported luxuries such as wine and fine clothes by men and women of the landlord class within Ireland, and their residence outside the country, because of which little of their incomes would be spent beneficially at home. Set alongside the problem of the poverty of the masses, gentry extravagance appeared a wilful neglect of the basic interests – nay the very survival – of their poorer fellow

---

[72] *Collectanea Hibernica*, 35 (1992), 63, 70.   [73] Browne, *Seasonable Remarks*, pp. 27-8; Berkeley, *Querist*, queries 181-3, 195-201. Cf. Locke, *Some Considerations* in Kelly (ed.), *Locke on Money*, vol. 1, p. 272.   [74] Prior, *Absentees*, p. 93; Berkeley, *Querist*, query 330.   [75] Browne, *Essay on Trade*, pp. 54-5; Prior, *Absentees*, p. 26; Berkeley, *Querist*, query 590: '... whether the soul or will of the community, which is the prime mover that governs and directs the whole, be not the legislature?'

countrymen: 'swilling their guts with French wine, that is the blood of the country', as Madden put it.[76] The Irish gentry were characterized as far more extravagant than their English counterparts – for whom the Irish gentry, whether resident amongst them or at home in Ireland, were alleged to be figures of ridicule.[77] However, Irish writers remained convinced that well-directed gentry consumption might prove extremely beneficial for the Irish economy, if the extravagant consumption were of Irish production.[78] Such demand would create a domestic market for new industries in building and decoration, as well as for labour intensive products such as carpets and tapestries that might in time become commodities for export.[79] The applicability of the distinction between beneficial and harmful luxuries was, however, rejected by Bindon in his translation of Melon's *Essai*, which argued that not only was the distinction impossible to draw but the very concept of luxury was irrelevant to commerce.[80]

The corollary to concern over gentry extravagance was the long-standing conviction of the innate idleness of the Irish poor, memorably epitomized by Berkeley as 'their cynical content in dirt and beggary'.[81] At one level this conviction of Irish idleness (stretching back well into the seventeenth century) was merely a manifestation of colonial prejudice against the subject people, but more sympathetic and perceptive commentators had sought to rationalize Irish behaviour. Petty claimed that the way in which the Irish poor had been treated by the English did not dispose them to exert themselves as everything they earned might be taken from them, while Archbishop King argued that lack of tools amongst the Irish poor made economic activity more expensive in terms of labour than in England.[82] Berkeley revealed a sympathetic perception of how misery and despair inhibit the capacity for action and stressed the importance of cultivating the habit of work from an early age.[83] Employment of this disadvantaged poor remained the major objective for all members of the Irish school; to Berkeley it was the national goal to which everything else should be subordinated but, as we shall see, he was far from convinced that only foreign trade could facilitate the necessary expansion in employment. To most writers, however, the numbers of homeless poor too often appeared like a deluge capable

---

[76] Madden, *Resolutions*, p. 20. [77] Prior, *Absentees*, pp. 23-4; Berkeley, *Querist*, queries 153-63. [78] Prior, *Absentees*, pp. 23, 32-3, 35-6; Madden, *Resolutions*, pp. 10-11. Dobbs (*Essay* (1731), pp. 41-2), however, remained hostile to extravagant consumption even of domestic products. Rather than to lavish gentry consumption, Dobbs looked to the merchant as entrepreneur for the stimulation of growth (ibid., 17). [79] Browne, *Essay on Trade*, pp. 53-4; Berkeley, *Querist*, queries 115-21, 347-424. [80] Melon, *Essay*, p. 180. [81] Berkeley, *Querist*, query 330. It is interesting to find Berkeley's epithet *cynical* taken up by Bindon in the notes to his translation of Melon's *Political Essay on Commerce*, p. 187, n. b. [82] William Petty, *Political Anatomy of Ireland* (1691), pp. 98-9; William King (1650-1729), 'Some Observations on the taxes paid by Ireland to support the government' (no date, after 1725), TCD MS 1488, p. 22. [83] Berkeley, *Querist*, queries 61, 371, 378.

of sweeping away the whole economy rather than as a resource to be exploited to promote national wealth. Even with regard to agriculture employment was treated as the primary objective, with the vast majority of writers following Boulter and the Irish parliament of 1728 in seeking to promote tillage rather than the export-oriented ranching of cattle, and to a lesser extent sheep, that international conditions made so attractive to Irish landowners in the 1730s.[84] Though many landlords resorted to removing tenants with rents hopelessly in arrears, as the low tillage prices of the early 1730s failed to produce incomes sufficient to make good the leeway of the later 1720s, none of the writers on agriculture nor of the more general commentators on the Irish economy of the time were openly prepared to advocate such a practice.[85] Such a consensus is in many ways surprising, but reflects these writers' concern with an economic policy that sought to maximize employment rather than individual incomes.[86]

VII

The most notorious production of the Irish school in these years is Swift's *Modest Proposal for Preventing the Children of Poor People in Ireland, from being a Burden to their Parents or Country: and for making them beneficial to the Publick* (1729). This disarming title and neutral, objective language conceal a proposal to fatten up and sell surplus children for the tables of the wealthy in a horrifying parody of the genre of economic projecting (in the eighteenth-century sense of the term, rather than the twentieth). This savagery reflects (among other things) Swift's despairing realization that all the well-meaning pamphlets peddling nostrums for economic development had been able to achieve little or nothing towards the solution of Ireland's problems.[87] In his earlier pamphlet *A Short View of the State of Ireland* (1727-8) Swift had compared the Irish economy, which commentators such as John Browne had claimed to be in some respects flourishing, to conditions in other countries where the same natural conditions of fertility and good harbours, a large potential labour force, etc. had made for prosperity, and demanded why the recipe had not worked here.[88] Yet

---

84 Boulter to Newcastle, 7 Mar. 1728 (*Boulter Correspondence*); Act for Encouraging Tillage passed by the Irish Parliament, 1 Geo. 2, c.1, Jan. 1728; cf. Dobbs, *Essay* (1729), pp. 25-6; Dobbs, *Essay* (1731), pp. 21, 52-4. **85** James Kelly, 'Harvests and hardship', 101-3. **86** Concern over employment also related to worry over emigration because of adverse economic conditions, which was particularly prevalent in 1727-9, with 4,200 leaving the country in these years, mostly from the north; ibid., pp. 83-4, 92-3. **87** 'Let no man talk to me of other expedients ... having been wearied for many years with offering vain idle, visionary thoughts and at length utterly despairing of success ... ': Swift, *Modest Proposal* (1729) in *Prose Works*, vol. 12, p. 117. **88** Swift, *State of Ireland* in *Prose Works*, vol. 12, pp. 5-12; Browne, *Essay on Trade*, p. 56.

for one thinker at least, wrestling with the problems of the Irish economy in these years did produce radically new ideas (if perhaps not a practical solution to the country's problems), and facilitated a significant theoretical breakthrough – namely in Bishop's Berkeley's famed *The Querist, Containing several Queries proposed to the Consideration of the Publick*, and it is to certain aspects of this culmination of the Irish writings of the late 1720s and 1730s that I wish to turn, before seeking to draw some final conclusions on the politics of political economy in mid-eighteenth-century Ireland.

Berkeley's importance to the political discourse of the 1720s and 30s lay in three main areas; his perception of the real differences between the undeveloped Irish economy and the more advanced states of Britain, France and Holland; his understanding of the potential for paper-money to transform the needs of the poor into economic demand that would provide the motor for the transformation of the Irish economy, and his proposals for a National Bank. Furthermore, in perceiving economic self-interest as a latent rather than a universally prevalent characteristic of human nature, Berkeley also confronted the crucial underlying psychological question which earlier writers had largely sidestepped; namely, how to motivate the Irish poor to become industrious.

Given the absence of any conception of the achievement of economic equilibrium through hidden harmony or the design of nature, Berkeley, like his Irish contemporaries, accorded a crucial role to the state or legislature in bringing about the necessary conditions to promote the public objective of full employment.[89] Central to this directive role was the provision of an adequate circulating medium without which industry and natural resources could not be set in motion. Unlike his Irish contemporaries, however, Berkeley's American experience enabled him to perceive that such a means of facilitating commerce need not depend on gold and silver. Through translating wants into effective demand by the issue of paper-money the state could promote real wealth without any need for resort to foreign trade. Like Prior before him, Berkeley claimed that for a poor agricultural nation such as Ireland to export the resources so desperately needed to sustain and employ its own starving masses in order to gratify the luxurious appetites of an ignorant and unheeding gentry was the path not to wealth but to destruction. 'Whether there is not a great difference between Ireland and Holland? And whether foreign commerce, without which the one could not subsist be so necessary for the other?'[90] What was necessary was to provide a solution to Ireland's problems appropriate to

---

[89] Berkeley, *Querist*, queries 329, 352. [90] Cf. Prior, *Absentees*, p. 32: 'There is no country in Europe that produces and exports so great a quantity of beef, butter, tallow, hides and wool as Ireland does; and yet our common people are very poorly clothed, go bare-legged half the year, and rarely taste of that fleshmeat, with which we so much abound ...'; Berkeley, *Querist*, queries 173, 145, 146, 108.

Ireland's circumstances, above all matching the needs of the mass of her people by providing the basic requirements of employment and subsistence. In considering the nature of wealth, Berkeley rejected the traditional mercantilist identification of wealth as gold and silver in favour of what satisfied real human needs, namely 'plenty of all the necessaries and comforts of life'.[91] This conclusion, brought home to Berkeley by his experience in Ireland and America, also seemingly accorded with his philosophical position on the non-existence of general ideas. Since, unlike gold and silver, 'real wealth' was the direct creation of human industry, it could be provided from internal resources quite independently of foreign trade: 'Might we not put a hand to the plough, or to the spade, although we had no foreign commerce?'[92]

The crucial question in creating the wealth necessary to sustain the population became therefore how to stimulate the industry of all the inhabitants of the state so as to advance the common welfare, a project equivalent to providing universal employment. As regards individual motivation, Berkeley saw that industry could only be 'stirred' by awakening the will to labour, which in turn depended on creating an appetite for the product of labour, i.e. stimulating the desire to consume. 'Whether the creating of wants be not the likeliest way to produce industry ... And whether, if our peasants were accustomed to eat beef and wear shoes, they would not be more industrious ?'[93] It is thus the business of the state to direct appetite by controlling fashion, which is far too important a matter to be left 'to the management of women and fops, tailors and vintners'.[94] However, though wealth was thus derived from human industry, unless the product of industry could be exchanged it remained incapable of giving rise to further activity in the economy. What was needed was therefore a means of transferring and exchanging the power over the industry of others represented by the product, i.e. its value must become capable of being circulated in the market through being symbolically represented by money. 'Whether it be not the opinion or will of the people exciting them to industry, that truly enricheth a nation? And whether this doth not principally depend on the means for counting, transferring, and preserving this power?' What was crucial in stimulating industry, however, was the role of monetary circulation rather than simply money as such. And like other Irish writers on money, Berkeley was concerned to maintain the level of circulation by preventing money from slipping into hoard or stagnating.[95]

Berkeley was by no means the first writer to propose the adoption of a paper currency as a means of overcoming the shortage of specie in a given country. Notable proposals along these lines had been made for England as early as the

---

[91] Berkeley, *Querist*, query 462; similar views on gold and silver had earlier been expressed in James Jocelyn's *Essay on Money and Bullion* (1718), p. 11. [92] Berkeley, *Querist*, queries 251, 109. [93] Ibid., queries 329, 352, 20. [94] Ibid., queries 590, 13. [95] Ibid., queries 31, 424, 242, 472.

Cromwellian period by William Potter and Thomas Violet, while at the beginning of the eighteenth century the later originator of the Mississippi scheme, John Law, had proposed a paper currency based on land values as the solution to the problems of the violently impoverished economy of Scotland following the collapse of the Darien scheme of the mid-1690s.[96] What was novel about the proposals in *The Querist* was the linking of the paper money solution to the problem of economic growth with the creation in Ireland of what was virtually a closed economy.[97] Such a proposal was dependent on the perception that in Ireland's case the export of raw agricultural produce in return for luxury imports deprived the bulk of the population of basic foodstuffs and prevented them from ever becoming productive members of society: 'Whether the quantities of beef, butter, wool, and leather, exported from this island, can be reckoned the superfluities of a country, where there are so many natives naked and famished?' Retaining these commodities at home would enable the unemployed masses to combine their labour with Ireland's natural resources so as to satisfy their needs, which would be transformed into effective demand through the adoption of paper-money. This would in turn bring them into the market economy, where their wants would provide further stimulus to set an expanding cycle of production and consumption on its way.[98]

The proposed paper-money, which Berkeley regarded as inherently superior to metallic coin, would be exclusively created by the state, credit being too significant a function to leave in the hands of private individuals.[99] One of the most important functions envisaged for the legislature was, therefore, the establishment and regulation of the national bank that was required to manage the crucial paper-money. Unlike the national bank with private shareholders proposed by John Law in *Money and Trade Considered* (1705), which commentators have (not altogether convincingly) seen as Berkeley's model, Berkeley was insistent that what Ireland needed was a truly national bank, that is one fully owned by the public and answering to the legislature. Since the public would be the sole shareholder and owner, the possibility of bank collapse (a fear that reflected Berkeley's concern over the crises in the private banking sector in Ireland in the early 1730s) should be virtually impossible.[100] Though responsibility for setting up the bank and laying down the principles on which it was to operate would rest with parliament, day to day management would be carried out by experienced persons appointed by the legislature and open to its constant inspection.[101]

---

96 Douglas Vickers, *Studies in the Theory of Money* (London 1960), pp. 21, 132-7; Potter's writings (which were also studied in the American colonies) were cited in Madden's *Resolutions*, p. 171, as the origin of the national bank concept. See also Anton Murphy's important re-interpretation of Law in *John Law: Economic Theorist and Policy Maker* (Oxford 1997). 97 Berkeley, *Querist*, queries 127, 129. 98 Ibid., queries 173, 119, 107. 99 Ibid., query 226, 445, 290. 100 Ibid., queries 222 (1735 edn); 223, 245. 101 Ibid., queries 120-6 (part III, 1737

The chief practical problem in running the bank would be maintaining a constant value for the bank's notes through avoiding over-issue and instead maintaining a proper balance between the volume of notes and the volume of trade. In accordance with a quantity theory of value approach (almost certainly derived from Locke), Berkeley held at one level that the total value of notes issued would be proportional to the total volume of goods traded in the economy. Against the logic of this he further argued, however, that the bank's notes needed to be backed by value of land, which would be achieved through individuals mortgaging of land in return for bank bills. This process would particularly exercise the skill of the managers, as care would have to be taken to ensure that excessive amounts of land were not mortgaged (as Berkeley asserted had happened in Scotland).[102] Given his concept of the truly national bank owned by the public and answerable to the legislature (which would thus have the whole stock of the nation behind it), it is not altogether clear why Berkeley still clung to the need to back its notes with land. Some indications why he still felt such a need may be found in the experience of the failed project of 1720-21, when public concern at the soundness of a purely commercial bank had led the proposers to modify their initial scheme by introducing an element of land backing for the notes.[103]

The apparent link between Berkeley's paper-money and his advocacy of the establishment of a closed economy in Ireland has, however, greatly puzzled commentators. Can Berkeley really have believed that Ireland would be better off behind 'a wall of brass a thousand cubits high', or was he merely stating a paradox to reinforce the claim that Ireland is the nation that has managed to impoverish itself by foreign trade.[104] Certainly given the call for the creation of labour intensive industries such as carpet-making to promote exports, it is hard to accept that Berkeley was rigorously opposed to all forms of foreign trade. On balance it would seem, therefore, that the paradox was intended to emphasize how severely unregulated foreign trade can impoverish the undeveloped economy, and must therefore be restricted to imports essential for domestic production in place of corrupting luxuries. In the long run, however, restriction of foreign trade will enable Ireland to develop so as to compete on equal terms with nations like Britain, France and Holland.[105]

VIII

This consideration of some of the more significant concerns of Irish writers on political economy in the late 1720s and 1730s has sought to illustrate how they

edn). [102] Ibid., queries 237-46 (1735 edn). [103] Ryder, 'The Bank of Ireland', 572-3. [104] Berkeley, *Querist*, queries 134, 325. [105] Ibid., queries 64-9, 170-6, 554, 172.

exploited the available English literature dealing with the subject and adapted it to the specific circumstances of Ireland. In the hands of Berkeley – for all the obscurity of *The Querist* format – Irish political economy evolved into a full-blown theory of the differences between the developed and the undeveloped economies, with the perception that prescriptions evolved in relation to the developed economy were not merely not necessarily applicable to the poorer economy but in practice actually harmful to it. Berkeley's paper-money and isolated economy offered an alternative to the wisdom of mainstream mercantilism, which by means of careful regulation sought to prevent the exposure of the undeveloped economy to the full force of competition so as to allow it to grow and eventually compete on equal terms with the mature economies of Britain, Holland and France. Groping towards the articulation of what was clearly formulated by Berkeley had been a lengthy process, traceable back in piecemeal form to what these writers regarded as the *fons et origo* of a distinctive Irish tradition of economic writing, namely, the work of Sir William Petty, on whose *Political Anatomy* so many of the writers we have considered drew.[106] As to the other sources in the broad stream of early English political economy (where Petty occupied a major place), the author who has received much consideration in this paper has been John Locke. Locke's privileged status in eighteenth-century Irish political discourse in the narrower sense, as in its intellectual culture in general, undoubtedly justifies this.[107] Locke turns out to stand much in the same relationship to political economy in mid-eighteenth-century Ireland as David Berman has shown him to do in relation to an eighteenth-century Irish philosophical tradition stretching from King to Burke.[108] Of the other sources for Irish political economy of the period the most widely cited was Charles Davenant, particularly *Discourses on the Public Revenues, and on the Trade of England* (1698), which is mentioned by Dobbs, Prior, and Madden (amongst others), and was also one of the four books of economic interest that Berkeley is known to have owned.[109] The Irish writer of the late 1720s and 1730s who was most informative as to what he read in the literature of political economy was Samuel Madden, whose *Reflections and Resolutions* (1738) cites more than two dozen different authorities. Other writers though less ready in acknowledging their sources also emphasized the importance of study as well as practi-

---

106 Cf. in particular Petty's distinction between 'local' or 'domestic' wealth (food, clothing, houses, agricultural improvements and industrial buildings and equipment) and the 'universal' wealth represented by gold and silver: *Political Anatomy* (1691), p. 15, and *Political Arithmetic* (1690), pp. 82-3. 107 P. Kelly, 'Perceptions of Locke in eighteenth-century Ireland', *Proceedings of the Royal Irish Academy*, sect. C, 89 (1989). 108 David Berman, 'Enlightenment and counter-enlightenment in Irish philosophy', *Archiv für Geschichte der Philosophie*, band 64 (1982), 148-65, 257-69. 109 *Catalogue of the Valuable Library of the Late ... Dr Berkeley Lord Bishop of Cloyne ...*, Leigh and Sotheby, 6 June 1796. Cf. Prior, *Absentees*, pp. 62-3; Dobbs, *Essay* (1731), p. 14; Madden, *Resolutions*, p. 85.

cal experience of other countries in contributing to the solution of Ireland's economic and social problems.[110]

The other issue to which I wish to advert by way of conclusion is what these economic writings of the 1720s and 1730s have to tell us about how their authors perceived their position in relation to other groups in Ireland. While the trade issue was considered in terms of co-operation and the advantages accruing from Ireland's colonial status in obviating the need for such things as paying for Ireland's own defence, the currency question, as we have seen, did raise in striking fashion the country's subordination, akin to that of the other colonies, and emphasized a problem analogous to that of Sicily as a '*regno governato in provincia*'.[111] The discussion of Irish poverty and the problem of providing employment for the Catholic masses, however, raised in striking form the gap between these middle class, mostly Anglican, merchants and intellectuals and the Catholic masses who surrounded them. Strong though the sympathies of these writers may have been for the misery of the Irish poor, their economic prescriptions also reveal a deep sense of difference from them. Even the generous-spirited Madden could write of how 'a people with the honour of having English blood in their veins, feel the burden of Irish poverty galling their backs', while Berkeley's sympathies with the misery of the poor were matched by denunciation of them as 'the most indolent and supine people in Christendom', together with a comparison of the position of the Anglo-Irish to that of Roman colonists in Britain.[112] On the other hand these middle class, Anglican writers also felt themselves cut off from the mass of the extravagant and self-indulgent Anglo-Irish landlords (some of whom Berkeley would describe in *A Word to the Wise* of 1749 in almost Swiftian language as 'vultures with iron bowels'), and the gentry were forcefully reminded that they could never hope to prosper themselves as long as the bulk of the population lived in misery.[113]

This ambiguity over their racial identity and political allegiances did not, however, extend to their economic objectives, objectives which for all their concern to promote economic development were in important respects signally different from those of Adam Smith and his successors. In this regard, as others, Berkeley was the figure amongst these writers to articulate the logical culmination of their views. For Berkeley economic activities were far from being ends in themselves; what he sought was to benefit the impoverished mass of his fellow countrymen by promoting a modest degree of prosperity, equated with eating beef and wearing shoes. Such prosperity was not envisaged, however, as threat-

---

110 Browne, *Seasonable Remarks*, pp. 27-8; Prior, *Absentees*, p. 93; and esp. Berkeley, *Querist*, Advertisement by the Author; queries 346, 495, 530.   111 Cf. Robertson, 'The Enlightenment above national context', 685.   112 Madden, *Resolutions*, p. 3; Berkeley, *Querist*, queries 19, 91, 357, 512.   113 Berkeley, *Works*, vol. 6, p. 241; *Querist*, queries 167, 255.

ening the existing social hierarchy or promoting political upheaval, let alone leading to Malthusian pressures on sustenance.[114] Moreover, since the human capacity to consume is limited, Berkeley saw an inherent contradiction between the seemingly infinite appetite for money, and the purpose which money is intended to serve in society, as well as for the individual. To become victim to the passion for limitless accumulation is the path to madness in 'gathering counters ... multiplying figures [and] enlarging denominations, without knowing what they would be at, and without having a proper regard to the use, or end or nature of things'. For whole societies the domination of such values, as during the South Sea Bubble, undermines political stability through promoting luxury and corruption, and will ultimately result in absolute government and the loss of liberty.[115] Dobbs too espoused this Christian Aristotelian stance in his rejection of luxury and extravagance as a stimulus to economic activity, while Prior and Madden backed similar views with the practical measures which they organized for the promotion of agriculture and industry. Viewed from the threshold of the twenty-first century, early eighteenth-century Irish political economy's rejection of limitless accumulation, and its firm subordination of economic activity to political and social objectives, may seem a rather more attractive alternative than it did at the beginning of the industrial age.

---

114 Berkeley, *Querist*, queries 286, 352.   115 Ibid., queries 306-9. For the political impact, see further Berkeley's earlier reaction to the collapse of the South Sea Bubble in *An Essay towards Preventing the Ruin of Great Britain* (London 1721).

Precedent and principle: the patriots and their critics

S.J. CONNOLLY

I

On 16 April 1782 the Irish House of Commons assembled to hear Henry Grattan propose an address to the king asserting Ireland's claim to legislative independence. Two earlier such resolutions had been unsuccessful. Now, however, a new ministry headed by the marquis of Rockingham was widely expected to meet Irish demands. Grattan's speech thus opened on a note of anticipated triumph:

> I found Ireland on her knees, I watched over her with a paternal solicitude; I have traced her progress from injuries to arms, and from arms to liberty. Spirit of Swift, spirit of Molyneux, your genius has prevailed. Ireland is now a nation. In that new character I hail her, and bowing to her august presence I say, *esto perpetua*.[1]

Fourteen years later Theobald Wolfe Tone, in Paris as an emissary of the United Irish movement to the republican government, contemplated the recently erected pantheon of heroes of the revolution . An Irish equivalent, he reflected, might be more selective than the French had managed to be, but nevertheless would already have some worthy occupants – 'Roger O'Moore, Molyneux, Swift and Lucas, all good Irishmen'.[2]

At first sight these two quotations provide a satisfying confirmation of the continuity of political ideas in eighteenth-century Ireland. The leading patriot spokesman of the 1780s, and the most famous radical of the 1790s, acknowledge their debt to predecessors in the 1690s, the 1720s and the 1740s. In reality, however, neither comment can be taken wholly at face value. In the case of Grattan's invocation of Molyneux and Swift, serious doubts have been raised as to whether the great patriot actually spoke these words in 1782, or whether they represent an embellishment added to later printed versions of the speech.[3]

---

[1] *The Speeches of the Right Hon. Henry Grattan*, ed. Daniel Owen Madden (Dublin 1874), p. 70. [2] Bartlett ed. *Tone*, p. 490, Journal for 7 March 1796. [3] Gerard O'Brien, 'The Grattan mystique', *Eighteenth-Century Ireland*, 1 (1986); W.J. McCormack, 'Vision and revision in the

As for Tone, the very first name in his pantheon strikes a false note. Rory O'More, descendant of a midlands Gaelic family, helped to bring about the alliance of Gaelic Irish and Old English that took place at the outbreak of civil war in 1641. Yet he was not self-evidently a central figure either in the politics of his own day or in any subsequent grand narrative of Irish history. His inclusion, in fact, seems to be evidence primarily of the desultory nature of Tone's reading in Irish history.[4] As for Swift and Molyneux, Tone's musings on the pantheon must be set against the account given in his autobiography of his first explorations of Irish political affairs. There he recalled how a realization that 'the radical vice of our government' was the influence of England 'was to me a great discovery, though I might have found it in Swift and Molyneux'.[5] By his own admission, in other words, the sense of a historical tradition followed rather than inspired his political commitment.

The problems of continuity and of the influence of one generation of political authors on the next raised by these two examples are not isolated ones. Gerard O'Brien's reassessment of Grattan's speech is only one of a series of recent studies that have cast doubt on the whole notion of a coherent tradition of patriot thought, carried forward from the first systematic public assertion of Irish constitutional rights in the 1690s to the apparent triumph of 1782, and subsequently helping to inspire the democratic republicanism of the 1790s. The issues raised by these studies have been of two main kinds. In the first place there has been a concern to restore what were previously seen as the leading bearers of such a tradition to their contemporary context. One consequence has been to demonstrate how untypical most actually were of the society in whose name they claimed to speak. We now know, for example, that Molyneux's intervention in the debate on the threatened Woollen Act was regarded by most of his contemporaries as both dangerously radical and damaging to Irish interests. It was only in the 1720s, against the background of a new set of constitutional conflicts, that his work began to be more widely cited. Indeed its emergence in the late eighteenth century as a central text in the patriot canon seems to have come via America rather than by direct transmission within Ireland.[6] In the same way Swift's celebrated interventions, in the *Drapier's Letters* and elsewhere, left him isolated among more cautious and pragmatic contemporaries.[7] Patrick McNally, in a particularly striking piece of reassessment, has argued that the supposedly

---

study of eighteenth-century Irish parliamentary rhetoric', *Eighteenth-Century Ireland*, 2 (1985). **4** One likely source is Thomas Leland's widely read history, first published in 1773, which contrasts 'Roger Moore', presented as a noble-minded victim of circumstance, with Sir Phelim O'Neill, whom Leland depicts as a cynical adventurer seeking to restore a fortune dissipated by his own extravagance. See Thomas Leland, *The History of Ireland* (Dublin 1814), vol. 3, pp. 93-4, 99. **5** Bartlett ed. *Tone*, p. 30. **6** Patrick Kelly, 'William Molyneux and the spirit of liberty in eighteenth-century Ireland', *Eighteenth-Century Ireland*, 3 (1988). **7** Neil Langley York, *Neither Kingdom nor Colony: The Irish Quest for Constitutional Rights 1698-*

ubiquitous rhetoric of competing 'Irish' and 'English' interests, given such prominence in accounts of the 1720s, in fact masked distinctly asymmetrical perceptions. It was above all English office holders in Ireland, and in particular English ecclesiastics, who insisted on imposing such a definition on what most others involved saw as specific and limited disagreements.[8]

A second tendency of recent research has been to emphasize the extent to which patriot rhetoric could mask vested interests and the pursuit of political power. The parliament of 1692 has long been recognized as a turning point in Anglo-Irish relations, when Irish MPs apparently rose up in protest against the failure to extend to Ireland the constitutional liberties recently defined or reasserted in England. But this revolt, it is now clear, arose, not just out of constitutional aspirations, but out of the personal ambitions of disappointed office seekers combined with practical grievances connected with the post-war settlement. By 1695 a judicious redistribution of places, combined with a tougher anti-Catholic policy, had prepared the ground for a compromise settlement in which the extravagant constitutional rhetoric of three years earlier was quietly abandoned by all but a militant few.[9] The Money Bill dispute of 1753-6, similarly, involved a transparent attempt by a powerful parliamentary faction, threatened with displacement, to gain popular support by presenting itself as engaged in the defence of Irish interests against English encroachment.[10] During 1769-72 the efforts of a new lord lieutenant, Townshend, to reduce the government's dependence on local 'undertakers' provoked an even more blatant resort to patriot rhetoric.[11] Gerard O'Brien, once again going further than others in the field, has sought to reinterpret patriot politics even in the 1780s and 1790s primarily in terms of the pursuit of office and advantage.[12]

In the light of this work the sensible historian thinks twice before referring to a patriot tradition in eighteenth-century Ireland. To do so is to risk imposing a retrospective unanimity and continuity where none in fact existed, while taking at face value the self-serving rhetoric of unsuccessful place hunters. At the same time there remains the danger that this necessary work of dismantling a simplistic myth of ideological continuity will be carried too far. If the brightest stars in the patriot tradition were hailed as such only from the safe distance of retrospect, this still means that those who invoked them felt a need to look

---

1800 (Washington, D.C. 1994), p. 48. **8** Patrick McNally, '"Irish and English interests": national conflict within the Church of Ireland episcopate in the reign of George I', *Irish Historical Studies*, 29 (1995). **9** J.I. McGuire, 'The Irish parliament of 1692', in T. Bartlett & D.W. Hayton (eds), *Penal Era and Golden Age* (Belfast 1979). **10** J.L. McCracken, 'The conflict between the Irish administration and parliament 1753-6', *Irish Historical Studies*, 3 (1942); Declan O'Donovan, 'The money bill dispute of 1753', in Bartlett & Hayton (eds), *Penal Era and Golden Age*. **11** Thomas Bartlett, 'The Townshend viceroyalty', in Bartlett & Hayton (eds), *Penal Era and Golden Age*. **12** Gerard O'Brien, *Anglo-Irish Politics in the Age of Grattan and Pitt* (Dublin 1987).

back in time for inspiration or example. If a patriot stance frequently cloaked self-interest, the arguments and imagery that sustained that stance had nevertheless to come from somewhere. Even within the more realistic context established by recent writing, in other words, there are still questions to be asked about the carrying forward from one period to the next of formulae and reference points, the development over time of a repertoire of arguments and precedents, and the interaction of alternative lines of thought.

From this starting point the chapter that follows examines the theory, as opposed to the practice, of eighteenth-century Irish patriot politics. It begins by looking at some examples of writing from what was to become the canon of patriot literature. The aim here is to examine both continuity and its opposite: the recurrence across time of particular themes or ideas, but also the different directions that could be taken in upholding the same broad political case. The second half of the essay suggests that a similar analysis can fruitfully be applied to the opposite, and much less studied, end of the ideological spectrum, where a variety of writers challenged or criticized the assertions, aims and methods of patriot theorists and agitators. A final section attempts to show that a discussion of this kind, focussing on ideas and modes of argument, is not only of importance in itself, for what it reveals of the basis, character and quality of Irish political thinking, but can also contribute to our understanding of practical political outcomes.

II

The relevance of an analysis that concentrates on the transmission of specific arguments and ideas is immediately apparent in any discussion of the origins of eighteenth-century patriot thinking. An intricate web of personal and literary connections links the first major assertion of Irish constitutional rights in the post-Revolution era to a number of less celebrated predecessors. On one reading, indeed, the chain of influences stretches back to the fifteenth century. On the eve of the parliament of 1692, Bishop Anthony Dopping published a version of the same *Modus Tenendi Parliamentum* whose discovery in the possession of Sir Christopher Preston, arrested in connection with an alleged conspiracy, had caused a brief flurry of excitement in 1418.[13] The details of this 'conspiracy' remain obscure. But it has been argued that the roots of eighteenth-century Irish patriotism can be traced back to a movement of self-assertion by those who thought of themselves as the English inhabitants of the late medieval colony, culminating in the celebrated declaration by the parliament of 1460 that 'the land of Ireland is and at all times has been corporate of itself, by the ancient

---

13 Art Cosgrove (ed.), *New History of Ireland*, vol. 2: *Medieval Ireland 1169-1534* (Oxford 1987), pp. 550-1.

laws and customs used in the same, free of the burden of any special law of the realm of England'.[14]

Where seventeenth-century authors are concerned, the links with the writings of the 1690s are more clear cut. The *Modus Tenendi Parliamentum* had come into Dopping's hands as part of a bequest from Sir William Domville, a former attorney general of Ireland. Domville himself had earlier used it as one of the sources for the 'disquisition' which he drew up, at the request of the convention summoned to manage the transition to restored monarchy in 1660, to counter the claim of the English parliament to legislate for Ireland. Later the document was passed by Dopping's son, Samuel, to his uncle, William Molyneux, who used it in his *Case of Ireland*. In this work Molyneux also drew on Domville's 'disquisition'. In addition both Domville and Molyneux drew, without acknowledgement, on an earlier document setting out the case for Irish legislative independence, drawn up on behalf of the opposition to Wentworth in the parliament of 1640-1.[15]

Beside this familiar catalogue of well defined influences and continuities it is also necessary to note a significant silence. The Irish parliamentary session of October-November 1692, as already mentioned, is generally seen as an important moment in the history of Protestant political self-assertion. Outraged by the lenient terms of the Treaty of Limerick, and by irregularities in the disposal of forfeited estates, members rejected the package of legislation prepared for them by the privy council. Instead they asserted their 'sole right' to control financial legislation and allegedly talked of removing Poynings' Law and of 'freeing themselves from the yoke of England'.[16] These demands were very close to those that had been made only three years earlier by James II's Irish parliament, whose members had forced their reluctant king to accept a bill denying the right of the English parliament to legislate for Ireland and had also pressed for the repeal of Poynings' Law.[17] The correspondence is hardly surprising: members of both assemblies were presumably aware of and influenced

---

14 James Lydon, 'Ireland and the English crown 1171-1541', *Irish Historical Studies*, 29 (1995), 281-94. **15** These connections may be traced in Aidan Clarke, 'Colonial constitutional attitudes in Ireland 1640-60', *Royal Irish Academy Proceedings*, sect. C, 90 (1990); J.G. Simms, *William Molyneux of Dublin: A Life of the Seventeenth-Century Political Writer and Scientist* (Dublin 1982); Patrick Kelly, 'The Other "Molyneux Problem": The Origins of *The Case of Ireland, Stated* (1698)' in Jane Ohlmeyer (ed.), *Political Thought in Seventeenth-Century Ireland* (Cambridge 2000); C.E.J. Caldicott, 'Patrick Darcy, An Argument', *Camden Miscellany*, 31 (1992). The most striking potential continuity is the frequent suggestion that Molyneux, reaching across barriers of religion and political allegiance, drew on the work of the Old English lawyer Patrick Darcy. However this is rejected by Kelly, who questions whether the 'declaration' of the early 1640s, which Molyneux clearly borrowed from, was really Darcy's work, while pointing out that there is no evidence that Molyneux also made use of Darcy's *Argument*, written in 1641 and published two years later. **16** McGuire, 'Irish parliament of 1692'. **17** J.G. Simms, *The Jacobite Parliament of 1689* (Dundalk 1966).

by the debates of 1640-1 and 1659-60. But it is also not surprising, given the composition and other measures of the Jacobite parliament, that the resemblance went unacknowledged. In fact the assembly of 1692 declared the proceedings of its Jacobite predecessor void, and had its records burned. Even sixty years later Charles Lucas, anticipating a term that was to be popularized by Charles Gavan Duffy a century and a half later, described the 1692 assembly as 'that patriot parliament', but was silent on its Jacobite predecessor.[18] It was not until 1782 that Henry Grattan, at the safer distance of a century, was able to separate the latter assembly's assertion of Irish rights from its moves towards the imposition of Catholic ascendancy, reminding his fellow MPs that before they had entered the field under James' banner Irish Catholics had 'extorted from him a magna charta, a British constitution'.[19]

The most celebrated outcome of this web of earlier influences, interacting with the novel political circumstances of the 1690s and after, was Molyneux's *The Case of Ireland being Bound by English Acts of Parliament Stated*. Published in 1698 as a protest against the proposed prohibition, by an act of the English parliament, of Irish woollen exports, this is generally regarded as the founding text of eighteenth-century Irish patriotism. As such it has been extensively analyzed.[20] Here it is necessary to note only some points relating to its place in the evolution of a repetoire of patriot argument.

The most significant feature of Molyneux's work, from this point of view, is the extent to which it rests the case for Irish constitutional liberties on a chain of precedent and entitlement extending into the medieval past. At the centre of Molyneux's argument was the agreement supposedly concluded, shortly after the first English intervention in the island, between Henry II and the rulers of Gaelic Ireland. The analysis was not wholly unhistorical: Molyneux accepted that 'the barbarous people of the island at that time' had almost certainly been intimidated by the army Henry had brought with him. At the same time he insisted that what had taken place was 'an entire and voluntary submission of all the ecclesiastical and civil states of Ireland', who in exchange 'had large concessions made them of the like laws and liberties with the people of England'.[21] In addition Molyneux emphasized three other moments in medieval constitutional history which were to figure prominently in subsequent writing. The first was in 1177, when Henry II made his son, John, lord of Ireland. By this means,

---

18 Charles Lucas, *The Rights and Privileges of Parliaments Asserted upon Constitutional Principles* (Dublin 1770), p. 45. **19** Speech on the Catholic question, 20 Feb. 1782 (Grattan, *Speeches*, Madden ed. p. 53). **20** Patrick Kelly, 'The other Molyneux problem'; Simms, *William Molyneux*; J.R. Hill, 'Ireland without union: Molyneux and his legacy', in John Robertson (ed), *A Union for Empire: Political Thought and the British Union of 1707* (Cambridge 1995); T.O. McLoughlin, *Contesting Ireland: Irish Voices against England in the Eighteenth Century* (Dublin 1999), pp. 41-64. **21** William Molyneux, *The Case of Ireland*, J.G. Simms ed. (Dublin 1977), p. 31.

Molyneux argued, the island became 'an absolute kingdom, separate and wholly independent on England'; indeed, if John had not subsequently succeeded his childless elder brother Richard as king of England, the two would have become wholly separate.[22] Secondly there was the *Modus Tenendi Parliamentum*, which Molyneux followed Dopping in tracing to the reign of Henry II.[23] Finally there was the 'Magna Carta' granted to Ireland by Henry III in 1216.[24]

These arguments from historical and legal precedent were supplemented by appeals to general political principle. At one point Molyneux compared the agreement between Henry II and the Irish with the 'original compact' between the king and people of England which had figured so prominently in the recent English debate on the Revolution.[25] Elsewhere he appealed to 'that universal law of nature, that ought to prevail throughout the whole world', of being governed only by laws to which consent had been given in parliament.[26] Most famously, there was his declaration that the subordination of Ireland to English law was contrary to 'reason and the common rights of all mankind'.

> All men are by nature in a state of equality, in respect of jurisdiction or dominion: This I take to be a principle in itself so evident, that it stands in need of little proof. 'Tis not to be conceived that creatures of the same species and rank, promiscuously born to all the same advantages of nature, and the use of the same faculties, should be subordinate and subject one to another; These to this or that of the same kind. On this equality in nature is founded that right which all men claim, of being freed from all subjection to positive laws, till by their own consent they give up their freedom, by entering into civil societies for the common benefit of all the members thereof. And on this consent depends the obligation of all human laws.[27]

The third sentence here was taken directly, though without acknowedgement, from Locke's *Second Treatise*, and the whole passage was a clear paraphrase of Locke's arguments.[28]

Molyneux's assertion of universal rights has generally been seen as more significant than his pedantic and tendentious marshalling of legal precedent and

---

[22] Ibid., p. 115. [23] Ibid., pp. 40-5. Modern historians are divided on the origins of the *Modus*, seeing it either as a copy, adapted to Irish circumstances, of an English original from the reign of Edward II, or as an text of Irish origin dating from the late fourteenth century. See Cosgrove (ed.), *New History of Ireland*, vol. 2, pp. 550-1. [24] Molyneux, *Case of Ireland*, pp. 50-1. [25] Ibid., p. 46. [26] Ibid., pp. 52-3. See also ibid., p. 93, where Molyneux argues that, even if it could be shown that Ireland had in the past submitted to English legislation, this would not invalidate the right, 'founded on such immutable laws of nature and reason', of being governed only by laws to which one has given consent. [27] Ibid., pp. 116-17. [28] John Locke, *Two Treatises of Government*, Peter Laslett ed. (Cambridge 1988), p. 269.

historical texts.[29] Yet it is important not to take his comments out of context. In the first place it is necessary to distinguish between the different general principles to which Molyneux appeals. His reference to the original compact certainly aligned him with Whig interpretations of the Revolution. But the term was nevertheless broadly enough accepted to have been endorsed by the Convention Parliament. As such it was considerably less subversive, in its associations and implications, than Locke's doctrines of equality and consent, to which Molyneux appealed only quite briefly, and without acknowledgement. At the end of his *Case*, moreover, Molyneux appealed to a third, again much less potentially dangerous, theory of government, when he called for the preservation of the 'noble Gothick constitution', once in operation all over Europe but now surviving only in King William's dominions of Great Britain, Ireland and Holland and, to a limited extent, in the kingdom of Poland.

A second reason for caution lies in the structure of *The Case of Ireland*. Molyneux develops his arguments, not as a statement of political faith, but as a highly formal chain of reasoning. Separate and sometimes mutually incompatible arguments succeed one another in an elaborate series of fall back positions. A celebrated example concerns the claim that England governed Ireland by right of conquest. First, Molyneux denied that there had been any such conquest: the Irish chiefs had voluntarily accepted Henry II as their lord. Next he insisted that conquest did not in any case grant the conqueror unlimited rights. Finally he offered his notorious assertion that the aboriginal Irish were by this time largely extinct, so that even if rights of conquest did exist the people of Ireland were the descendants of the conquerors not the conquered. In part this style of argument reflected contemporary intellectual fashions: precisely the same willingness to argue simultaneously along a series of parallel or even contradictory lines was also evident, as was noted in an earlier chapter, among defenders of the legitimacy of the Revolution.[30] But it may also be seen as reflecting the uncertainties of an author called on to articulate urgent political aspirations within a constitutional framework that had recently been radically redefined, and on the basis of a mixed and as yet undeveloped body of ideas. Either way the main point is that what Molyneux passed on to his eighteenth-century successors was less a fixed political position than an indication of several different ways in which the argument for Irish constitutional rights could potentially be developed.

Of these, the one in which the clearest continuities can be detected is the appeal to history and precedent. Jonathan Swift, the next major figure in what was to become the patriot canon, was not attracted to this style of argument. The fourth and most analytical of the *Drapier's Letters* referred back to the ear-

---

29 For example, Simms, *William Molyneux*, p. 108   30 See for example above, pp. 32. See also John Kenyon, *Revolution Principles: The Politics of Party 1689-1720* (Cambridge 1977), pp. 22-4.

lier rejection of the English parliament's claim to legislative authority by 'the famous Mr Molineaux, an English gentleman born here', but made no attempt to imitate Molyneux's careful marshalling of precedents and statutes. At one point indeed Swift renounced explicitly the attempt to ground Irish claims on history, noting that monarchs, 'even later than the days of Queen Elizabeth', had used their prerogative to override the law, so that 'it is only of late times that prerogative hath been fixed and ascertained'.[31] This indifference to the details of historical argument, however, was unusual. The third major author in the patriot canon, Charles Lucas, by contrast, ransacked legal and historical sources and elaborated constitutional arguments with the unrestrained enthusiasm of a typical autodictat. His response to his initial clash with the oligarchic corporation of Dublin was to try to present a transcript of the charter of the city of Dublin, with a dedication, to the king.[32] As his campaign broadened to include an attack on the Irish political establishment in general, the appeal to history continued. To demonstrate the limits of the power of the House of Lords he drew on ancient 'British, Saxon or English councils'. To define the balance of power between king and people he offered a history of English charters relating to the liberty of the subject, and the text of magna carta. To demonstrate that these texts were relevant to Ireland he looked back, as Molyneux had done, to 'the original compact' made between Henry II and the people of Ireland and confirmed by John.[33] He also followed Moyneux in emphasizing the possibility that if John had not subsequently succeeded Richard as king of England, the two crowns might have become separated.[34]

By 1770, when he published one of his last pamphlets, attacking Townshend's attempt to override the parliamentary opposition, Lucas took the medieval part of his case as read:

> I shall not at present trouble your excellency to look back into the ancient records, since Henry the Second's establishing the *Modus Tenendi Parlementum* and the general constitution of England in this kingdom, by the common consent of the then powers of the kingdom.[35]

But this was only to clear the way for an argument resting on the constitutional history of more recent centuries, beginning with the original provisions of Poynings' Law and the circumstances in which it had been passed and going on to examine its operation and modification in the sixteenth century, before concluding with a review of the arguments employed in the sole right controversy of 1692.

---

31 Jonathan Swift, *The Drapier's Letters and Other Works 1724-5*, ed. Herbert Davis (Oxford 1941), pp. 54-5, 62. **32** Charles Lucas, *A Letter to the Free-Citizens of the City of Dublin*, 2nd edn (Dublin 1749), pp. 31-2. **33** Charles Lucas, *A Nineteenth Address to the Free Citizens and Freeholders of the City of Dublin* (Dublin 1749), pp. 13-14. **34** Lucas, *Nineteenth Address*, p. 14; Molyneux, *Case of Ireland*, p. 115. **35** Lucas, *The Rights and Privileges of Parliament*, p. 7.

Other authors of the period made similar use of precedents derived from the historical record to support Irish constitutional claims. A defence of the parliamentary opposition in 1754 went no further back than the parliament of 1692, and some subsequent resolutions from 1703 and 1713, to defend the claim that the Commons were entitled to examine the public accounts and direct how revenue should be spent.[36] A pamphlet supporting the rejection of the money bill of 1769, on the other hand, cited precedents from five parliaments between 1499 and 1661 to contradict the administration's argument that it was standard practice to open new parliaments with a finance bill transmitted from London, before moving on to the claim of the Irish Commons in 1692 to possess the 'sole right' of introducing such bills.[37] By the 1780s, as part of the general growth and elaboration of patriot doctrines, argument on the basis of the constitutional technicalities of a distant past had become commonplace. In some cases, as with Molyneux and Lucas, such argument was supported by a careful if tendentious marshalling of documents and citations. When Henry Flood in 1781 introduced a resolution to modify Poynings' Law, for example, he treated the Commons to a long explanation of the origins of the measure in the 1490s, and its use in the sixteenth century.[38] For others, however, the existence and legitimating authority of Ireland's ancient parliamentary constitution had become an article of faith, existing in a tissue of slogans and half understood references. Thus Sir Frederick Flood, intervening in another debate in the same session, referred proudly to 'the Modus Tenendi Parliamenta transmitted hither by Henry the 3rd', while a colleague, not to be outdone, reminded his hearers that 'we had our modus tenendi parliamenta sent us by our first English sovereign, Henry II'.[39]

The continued appeal of the Molyneux tradition of legal and historical argument is also evident in the elaborate orations, or at least the printed versions of these speeches,[40] with which Henry Grattan on two occasions, in April 1780 and February 1782, attempted unsuccessfully to move a declaration of Irish constitutional rights in the House of Commons. In particular Grattan followed Molyneux in citing a battery of medieval instruments supposedly upholding Ireland's claim to be governed by its own parliament: 'the original compact of Henry the Second', the charter granted by John, the confirmation of this grant under Henry III in 1216, as well as later instruments under Edward I and Henry VI.[41] He dealt with some of the same legal judgements and opinions for and

---

36 *The Proceedings of the Honourable House of Commons of Ireland, in Rejecting the Altered Money Bill on December 17, 1753 Vindicated*, 2nd edn (Dublin 1754), pp. 43-91.   37 *Observations on a Speech Delivered the 26th Day of December 1769, in the House of Lords in Ireland* (Dublin 1770).   38 *Parliamentary Register*, vol. 1, 153-60.   39 Ibid., pp. 165, 173. For the actual date of the *Modus*, see above, note 23.   40 Grattan, *Speeches*, pp. 38-51, 54-70. For reservations about the subsequent rewriting of Grattan's parliamentary speeches see O'Brien, 'The Grattan mystique'.   41 Grattan, *Speeches*, Madden ed. pp. 58-60.

against Ireland's legislative independence. He also followed Molyneux closely in dealing with the apparently formidable list of occasions on which the English parliament had in fact enacted legislation binding on Ireland. Like Molyneux Grattan argued that Ireland's claim to legislative autonomy was not compromised by the acceptance of English statutes that did not represent new legislation, but were merely declaratory of the common law, or whose extension to Ireland had been legitimized by the presence during their passage of representatives from the Irish parliament. Molyneux, writing in 1698, had also been able to argue that the more frequent examples of English pretensions to a power to legislate for Ireland that had occurred in the period since the Restoration of the monarchy in 1660 were too recent to establish a right: ' shall precedents only of thirty-seven years standing be urged against a nation, to deprive them of the rights and liberties which they enjoyed for five hundred years before'.[42] By 1782, however, the contested encroachments of 37 years had become the repeated practice of 120. In consequence Grattan, while echoing Molyneux's main point, was forced to put forward a rather more elastic definition of precedent. The 'ancient acts' that could be cited as including Ireland in their provisions were 'too few to amount to a usage', while more recent instances were not precedents, but 'practices which require to be supported by precedents'.[43]

In contrast to this high level of continuity and repetition of themes and arguments, other parts of the patriot case reveal the wide variety of grounds on which Irish constitutional claims could be based. Molyneux had referred to Lockeian notions of natural rights, to the original compact, and to the ancient constitution. Swift, too, referred in passing to 'Gothic liberties', and to ideas of the mixed constitution, where each estate had its own clearly defined powers.[44] For the most part, however, his approach to the defence of Irish political rights, like his approach to the Revolution, was resolutely untheoretical. Thus the fourth *Drapier's Letter* reduced the validity of Wood's patent to the level of a practical problem. Any king, Swift argued, had an undoubted right to declare war. But he could in practice do so only if parliament were prepared to provide the necessary resources. George I, similarly, was fully entitled to grant William Wood a patent to mint copper coin; but he could not require his subjects to use it in their commercial dealings. In the same way Swift's analysis of the relationship of Ireland and Great Britain began from common sense definitions rather than general theory: the concept of a depending kingdom was 'a modern term of art, unknown, as I have heard, to all ancient civilians, and writers upon government'.[45]

---

[42] Molyneux, *Case of Ireland*, p. 88.   [43] Grattan, *Speeches*, pp. 57-8.   [44] For example, Swift to Pope, 19 Jan. 1721 (*Swift Corr.* vol. 2, p. 372). The strongest expression of Swift's belief in the mixed constitution is *A Discourse of the Contests and Dissensions between the Nobles and Commons in Athens and Rome*, ed. F.H. Ellis (Oxford 1967).   [45] *Drapier's Letters*, ed. Wood, p. 62.

The other important element which Swift contributed to patriot thinking was a sharpening of what was to become the dominant model of the relationship between England and Ireland, the idea of sister kingdoms, linked by a shared sovereign but in all other respects equal and independent. Molyneux had already made the case that Ireland was 'a complete kingdom within itself', acknowledged as such in fundamental constitutional instruments, and equipped with the legal and parliamentary institutions appropriate to that status.[46] Swift developed the point in a characteristically sweeping manner, arguing that under the statute of 1541 creating the kingdom of Ireland, 'we have, indeed, obliged ourselves to have the same king with them; and consequently they are obliged to have the same king with us'. That this should be so was not in fact self-evident and Swift himself seemed to recognize as much when he went on to offer a rather lame appeal to common sense: '... the law was made by our own parliament, and our ancestors then were not such fools ... [as] to bring themselves under I know not what dependence'. But he nevertheless concluded with an audacious exposition of the underlying principle:

> I declare, next under God, I depend only on the king my sovereign, and on the laws of my own country. And I am so far from depending upon the people of England, that, if they should ever rebel against my sovereign (which God forbid) I would be ready at the first command from his majesty to take arms against them; as some of my countrymen did against theirs at Preston. And if such a rebellion should prove so successful as to fix the Pretender on the Throne of England, I would venture to transgress that statute so far, as to lose every drop of my blood, to hinder him from being king of Ireland.[47]

In terms of political theory this was arguably no more than a logical development of the ideas advanced by Molyneux a quarter of a century earlier. In terms of practical politics, on the other hand, it represented a highly provocative raising of the stakes.

In contrast to Swift's pragmatic, common sense approach to the assertion of Irish constitutional rights Lucas was more prepared to frame his arguments in terms of doctrine and principle. Two main sets of general ideas can be detected. The first is the conventional notion of the balanced constitution: a 'body politic' is 'a fictitious body of men, bearing close analogy to the body natural', in which 'the head and members must be kept within their proper spheres, strictly, and in their several stations obliged to watch over and regulate the motions and minister to the exigiencies of each other'.[48] The second is 'the original compact

---

[46] Molyneux, *Case of Ireland*, pp. 115-16. [47] Ibid. p. 62. [48] Charles Lucas, *The Complaints of Dublin, Humbly Offered to his Excellency, William, Earl of Harrington* (no place, 1747), pp. 3-4.

between the governors and governed'. This was interpreted as implying a strict reciprocity of obligation and allegiance: 'it is as inconsistent with the subject's allegiance to suffer the king or his ministers to violate or encroach upon the sacred rights and privileges of the people, as for the people to oppose and invade the legal prerogatives of the prince'.[49] Lucas' heavy dependence on medieval precedent meant that he saw the Revolution as a reassertion of popular liberties that had existed for centuries. But his tone and language developed the implications of Revolution whiggery to the full. The king, in Lucas' version of the British and Irish constitutions, was the 'supreme magistrate', whose power 'is in no instance absolute or unlimited, his office being only fiduciary and executive, subject to the directive, if not the coercive, power of the laws'.[50]

Two further features give Lucas' thought a more distinctive twist. The first is his willingness to extend the same insistence on the need for checks and balances, and on the contractual nature of government, to the workings of parliament. The Commons, Lucas insisted, are 'but servants to their constituents, from whom they are entitled to receive wages'.[51] It followed that

> freedom and power; if they should be continued so long as to forget whence and for what purposes they derive their authority; if instead of receiving a compensation from their constituents for attendance and services they should bribe or otherwise unjustly influence their voices in elections; if they then should forget or disregard the fundamental laws of the institution, and so dissolve the original compact implied between the representative and the represented, by the very act of deputation or election ... the source of the enlivening spirit of the civil constitution must be poisoned ...

It thus became both the king, 'justly tenacious of the prerogative granted him for the good of his subjects, as well as his own security and honour', and the people themselves, to 'ever be watchful, if not look on these their delegates with a jealous eye'.[52]

This vehemence is understandable, given the manner in which the Irish Commons had supported Lucas's opponents in the battle over the composition of Dublin's municipal government. Yet his willingness to see parliament as the corruptible servant of the people, and his extension to its authority of the notion of a conditional and reciprocal contract, was nevertheless a bold step. Swift too had made his contempt for the general run of Irish MPs quite clear in his letters, and in his vicious poem 'The Legion Club'. Yet the *Drapier's Letters* had sidestepped the issue of what was to happen if parliament failed to defend the nation's

---

[49] Lucas, *Nineteenth Address*, p. 8. [50] Ibid., p. 7. [51] Ibid., p. 10. [52] Lucas, *Complaints of Dublin*, pp. 7-8.

liberties: other measures, Swift conceded, had passed by means of corruption, but Wood's halfpence would not succeed because those who accepted sinecures as bribes would know that salaries paid in the new coin would be worthless.[53] Lucas' stance is significantly more radical, looking forward to the years immediately following the triumph of 1782, when the right of the people to call their representatives to order became a central cause of conflict between the Volunteer movement and their former patriot allies within the political elite.[54]

A second distinctive feature of Lucas's thought was his willingness to consider the implications for his arguments of the ethnic and, by implication, religious divisions within Ireland. Molyneux, as mentioned earlier, had argued briefly that the aboriginal Irish were largely extinct, so that even the poorer, Gaelic-speaking Catholic inhabitants were the descendants of English immigrants. With this exception, he largely ignored the enormous discontinuity between the Gaelic chiefs who had received Henry II's original grant of English laws and liberties and those descendants of mid-Tudor or later immigrants who now claimed to have inherited them. Swift had addressed the Draper's fourth letter to 'the whole people of Ireland', while making clear that in fact this meant the Protestant people whose ancestors 'reduced this kingdom to the obedience of England'. Indeed one of his grievances was that the English of England 'look upon us as a sort of savage Irish, whom our ancestors conquered several hundred years ago'.[55] Lucas, by contrast, not only recognized that Henry II's original grant of English laws and liberties had been to the Gaelic Irish, but argued in outspoken language that 'the original compact was soon perfidiously broken' by measures denying the native Irish English law and liberty, which in turn had driven them into 'savage barbarisms'.[56] An acknowledgement that 'this nation has not been better treated by some of the ancient English governors than the Peruvians or Mexicans by the Spaniards' did not imply a rejection of the penal laws: Lucas made clear that as long as the pope continued to claim temporal power measures were necessary to compel Catholics to obedience. But in this respect his writing nevertheless once again looks forward to later developments, in this case to the more inclusive patriotism that was to be advocated, though also fiercely resisted, in the 1780s and 1790s.[57]

Grattan, as already noted, remained close to Molyneux in his reliance on historical and legal argument. At the same time there was a clear difference in tone and underlying assumptions. Molyneux had cast his work as a statement of the Irish case submitted to the judgement of the English parliament. Grattan com-

---

53 *Drapier's Letters*, ed. Wood, pp. 58-9. 54 Peter Smyth, 'The Volunteers and parliament', in Bartlett & Hayton (eds), *Penal Era and Golden Age*. 55 *Drapier's Letters*, ed. Wood, pp. 55, 64. For a less literal minded reading of Swift's meaning, see above, p. 98ff. 56 Lucas, *Nineteenth Address*, pp. 18-19. 57 Sean Murphy, 'Charles Lucas, Catholicism and nationalism', *Eighteenth-Century Ireland*, 8 (1993).

menced his second speech with a declaration that it was for England to prove its claim to make laws for Ireland. The various arguments by which it might seek to do so were then brusquely rebutted. The opinions of revered legal authorities, Blackstone and Coke, were rejected on the grounds that they were, as English judges, partial and dependent. Finally the suggestion that England's claim might rest on force and right of conquest, rather than law or principle, was met by a reference to the Volunteers, 'the soul of the country armed'. The immediate context for this sharpness was of course the American war. 'Before you decide on the practicability of being slaves for ever', Grattan urged his fellow MPs, 'look to America.'[58] Grattan himself, however, rested his assertion of Ireland's right to defend its constitutional liberties primarily on a radical version of the doctrines of the Revolution. On this basis, in fact, he suddenly abandoned a detailed dissection of the historical and legal precedents offered for English legislative authority to argue that precedent was in any case irrelevant. 'The reign of Henry the Eighth was a precedent against the privilege of parliament; forced loans had their precedents; ship money had its precedent.' The indefeasible rights of the British subject, however, had been 'sufficient against precedent ... to form a petition of right, a declaration of right, a revolution, cancel the oath of allegiance, depose James, establish William, royalize the house of Hanover'.[59] At this point ideas closer to those developed by Swift and Lucas were grafted onto the framework of legal argument established by Molyneux.

Taken as a representative sample of patriot argument, then, the work of Molyneux, Swift, Lucas and Grattan provides examples of both continuity and discontinuity. The former is most evident in the deployment, extending backwards beyond Molyneux to his mid-seventeenth-century predecessors, of a historically-based definition of Irish rights. But there are also other common themes: the original compact, the precedent of 1688, the mixed constitution. At the same time it is also important to note the marked variations, reflecting differences in personality and intellectual allegiance, in the way in which the same basic case was argued. Thus we may contrast Molyneux's faith in law and formal reason, Swift's reliance on robust common sense, Lucas's more explicit political theory, assembled with an autodictat's earnestness, Grattan's combination of earlier historical and legal arguments with an appeal to the assumptions of the new Whig ideology of the 1780s.

All of this work, finally, can usefully be contrasted with the *Letters of Orellana, an Irish Helot,* published in 1785 by the future United Irishman William Drennan. In the interval since Grattan's speeches of 1782 a great deal had taken place. Restrictions on Irish trade had been lifted in 1779. In 1782 Poynings' Law had been modified, and the British parliament had dropped its claim to legislate for Ireland. But a further agitation for reform of the electoral

---

[58] Grattan, *Speeches,* pp. 67, 50. [59] Ibid., pp. 61-2.

system in 1783-4 had failed. These developments are clearly reflected in the *Letters of Orellana*, published as part of a last attempt to revive the reform movement. In particular their influence can be perceived in Drennan's forceful critique of what had been achieved by the 'constitution of 1782'. Without a reform of the electoral system, the vindication of the exclusive rights of the Irish parliament was no more than 'a transference of arbitrary power from despotism abroad to aristocracy at home'. There was also personal criticism of former patriot leaders who had failed to support the continued agitation. Drennan criticized both Grattan, for having accepted the £50,000 bestowed on him by parliament ('I believe him to be great even with his wages; but his best friends would have thought him greater without it'), and the veteran aristocratic reformer Lord Charlemont, for advocating patience and perseverance ('Resolutions. resolutions. Shall we never have done with resolutions?').[60]

More important than these expressions of impatience with former patriot heroes was Drennan's abandonment of what had been a standard part of Irish constitutional debate, the glorification of the British system of government. Molyneux, Swift and Lucas had all based their arguments partly on the Irish claim to participate in the rights and liberties of Englishmen. Drennan, however, went out of his way to condemn the 'sanctified veil of mystery' thrown over the constitution, leading to an uncritical acceptance of 'the supposed perfection of this complex sort of being called king, lord and commons'. The world was too young, he insisted, for any plan of government to be accepted as perfect. More specifically Drennan rejected the proposition, up to this time generally accepted both by supporters and by opponents of the political establishment, that the particular virtue of the British system of mixed monarchy was the achievement of a mutually restraining equilibrium between the different estates of crown, aristocracy and democracy. Those who sought to preserve liberty by means of such a system of checks and balances showed themselves, in Drennan's scornful phrase, 'more conversant in the constitution of a clock than that of a commonwealth'. Instead his appeal was to a very different idea of liberty, conceived of in terms of universal and inherent rights established and upheld by the popular will.

> The science of politics, not less demonstrative than others, has its first principles and self-evident truths, which are axioms in their nature, the source from whence all reasoning must spring, and distinguished by the name of constitutional rights.

The only solid foundation for freedom was thus 'constitutional rights, enforced by the controlling energy and momentum of the mighty mass to which those

60 William Drennan, *Letters of Orellana, an Irish Helot* (Dublin 1785), pp. 19, 17, 45-6.

rights belong'.[61] In practice, as Drennan made clear a few years later, this meant universal suffrage and the annual election of parliaments.[62]

The *Letters of Orellana* was a young man's book. It was also an effort to maximize support for a new radical initiative. It is not surprising, on either count, that the rejection of a whole tradition of political thought based on the merits of the balanced constitution was not sustained throughout. On the contrary a later part of the *Letters*, cast in the form of a proposed address to George III, constituted a marked retreat. Here Drennan, echoing Molesworth and Brooke, wrote of a constitution inherited from the 'feudal barbarism' of early Europe and preserved uniquely in Britain by 'their insular situation, the spirit of their ancestors, the succession of fortunate circumstances, and the restorative virtue of revolutions'. The result was 'a pyramid of matchless workmanship, founded on the broad base of democracy, and ascending with due gradation, until the image of the sovereign is exalted upon its height and terminates its elevation'. The real grievance, in this version, was the illegitimate influence of the aristocracy over elections, threatening to destroy the balance between different estates.[63]

The inconsistencies in Drennan's polemic highlight the complexity of the whole issue of continuity and discontinuity in relation to the radical politics of the last years of the eighteenth century. At first sight his 'pyramid of matchless workmanship' and his appeal to the 'mighty mass' represent, not just less and more radical programmes of reform, but two wholly different political vocabularies. If the first looked back to arguments developed by Molesworth, Lucas and others, the latter seemed to look instead to the other side of the Atlantic, where circumstances had forced growing numbers of Americans to abandon the language of British constitutionalism altogether and develop instead an appeal to inherent and equally distributed human rights. Yet the discontinuity is not necessarily as complete as this contrast would suggest. Even in the proposed address to the king, Drennan's reference to 'the restorative virtue of revolutions', presented as regularly needed to combat the tendency to decay inherent in all human institutions, highlighted the underlying radicalism of his vision. And indeed, looked at from the point of view of practical politics rather than theory, the leap from a mixed system of government, regulated by a very strong version of the rights of the people, to a rejection of the whole concept of balance in favour of reliance on the popular will was not in fact so very great. Drennan's waverings between the two may thus be seen as illustrating two alternative ideologies of opposition, one old and one new, available to critics of the late eighteenth-century political order in Ireland. But they also provide a glimpse of the manner in which one of these both contributed to and was partially absorbed into the other.

61 *Letters of Orellana*, pp. 8-12. 62 *The Trial of William Drennan*, J.F. Larkin ed. (Dublin 1991), pp. 131-3. 63 *Letters of Orellana*, pp. 54-8.

III

From the arguments of Molyneux, Swift, Lucas and Grattan we may turn to their opposite. The second part of this essay examines some critiques of patriot political positions, and of the writings of leading patriot spokesmen, produced at different times between the 1740s and the 1780s. The authors concerned should not in any sense be seen as members of a self-conscious school of political writing. Their work deals mainly with specific issues; they neither cite one another directly nor show significant signs of borrowing from one another's writings. Yet for all this an analysis of their arguments reveals not just what was often an effective critique of patriot argument, but the elements of a quite coherent alternative vision of the practice and principles of political life.

The type of reasoned anti-patriot argument with which we are concerned here must be distinguished from mere personalized insult or accusations of rabble rousing. The transition from the latter to the former in fact mirrored the changing character of the debate on Irish constitutional rights. Charles Lucas, an independent minor professional delivering a radical challenge from outside the political establishment, encountered much straightforward abuse. One critic denounced him as 'our modern Massienello', while others mocked his humble origins.[64] Critics of the opposition to the lord lieutenant during the Money Bill dispute of 1753-6 could not use the same charge of seeking to rise above one's proper station. Instead pro-government pamphlets presented the opposition as disappointed place seekers, and mocked the alcohol-fuelled excesses of political banquets where 'the high patriot toasts commence not till after the ninth or tenth bumper'.[65] As early as 1749, however, Sir Richard Cox, writing under the pseudonym Anthony Litten, felt it necessary to meet Lucas's challenge with a more carefully reasoned, if still deeply hostile, critique of his writings.[66] By the 1770s and 1780s, as patriot politics gained ground not just in popular opinion but among sections of the middle classes and gentry, the need for argument rather than invective appears to have been generally recognized.

The motives of those who attempted to provide such argument varied. Cox, for example, was a government supporter in 1749, but he had earlier been in opposition and was to be one of the most irreconcilable opponents of the administration during the Money Bill dispute. He was also the grandson of the

---

64 James Taylor, *Lucas Detected; or a Vindication of the Sheriffs and Commons of the City of Dublin* (Dublin 1749), pp. 12-13; 'Anthony Litten' [Sir Richard Cox], *The Cork Surgeon's Antidote Against the Dublin Apothecary's Poison for the Citizens of Dublin, Numbers 1-7* (Dublin 1749), Letter 1, p. 9; Letter 3, p. 4; T. Taylor, *Lucas Refuted, or Liberty Supported* (Dublin 1749), pp. 10-11.   **65** Thomas Shuttle, *A Letter to the Freehold Farmers of Ireland* (Dublin 1755), pp.13-15. See also *Advice to the Patriot Club of the County of Antrim on the Present State of Affairs in Ireland* (Dublin 1756), pp. 13-14; *A Dialogue between Dick – and Tom – Esqs. Relating to the Present Divisions in I—d* (Dublin 1754), pp. 11-12.   **66** Cox, *The Cork Surgeon's Antidote*.

author of *Hibernia Anglicana*, who had himself at one stage planned to write a reply to Molyneux.[67] Other pro-government authors were clearly paid for their work. 'A candidate author' in 1755 mockingly offered his services to the beleaguered Primate Stone, using the epigraph 'The labourer is worthy of his hire'.[68] Townshend reported to London in 1770 on his efforts to find authors to convince 'the general sense of the public' of the factious nature of the opposition to his administration.[69] Grattan's son was later to claim that Frederick Jebb had thanked his father for the annuity of £300 he had received for his reply to Grattan's *Observations on the Mutiny Bill*, 'but he admitted it was no answer whatsoever'.[70] As with the patriots themselves, however, there is room both for an analysis that probes individual and collective motives and vested interests, and for one that focusses primarily on the ideas and arguments being developed. (There is also at least the possibility that Grattan junior's malicious anecdote reflected a recognition that Jebb had in fact produced quite a sharp critique of some of his father's positions.)

One theme that can be picked out from this developing body of more thoughtful anti-patriot writing is its approach to history. Legal and historical precedent, as we have already seen, played a central role in the thought of Molyneux, Lucas and Grattan, as well as of less able imitators and followers. A possible response to such argument was to reply in kind. In 1770, for example, George Macartney, a County Antrim landowner who was chief secretary under Lord Townshend during 1769-72, collaborated with Richard Jackson, MP for Coleraine, in a closely reasoned analysis of the ostensible basis of the opposition being offered to Townshend's administration. MPs had been induced to reject a money bill on the grounds that such measures should always be initiated from within the House of Commons. Macartney and Jackson responded to the historical arguments offered with an alternative set of citations, and in one instance a different reading of the parliamentary record, to show that it was in fact customary to open a new parliament with a money bill transmitted from London. The Commons' stand in 1692 was thus an isolated instance, repudiated by the opinions of both the British and Irish judges at the time, and nullified by the consistent practice since that date. Their conclusion was one of which, if made in support of the opposite side, either Molyneux or Grattan would have been proud, appealing to

> what the continued wisdom and experience of not less than the long period of two hundred and eighty four years had confirmed, what

---

67 S.J. Connolly, *Religion, Law and Power: The Making of Protestant Ireland* (Oxford, 1992), p. 83, n. 28. **68** *A Candidate Author's Letter to the P****te* (Dublin 1755). **69** Quoted in Thomas Bartlett, 'The Townshend Viceroyalty' in Bartlett & Hayton (eds), *Penal Era and Golden Age*, p. 99, n. 27. **70** *Memoirs of the Life and Times of the Right Honourable Henry Grattan* (London 1839), vol. 2, p. 192.

twelve successive reigns had sanctified, what every historian had recorded, what the C–mm–ns first desired, and the Cr—n approved, and what the Cr—n now supports legally, when the C–mmns would against law overturn it.[71]

In this case, however, the debate was on a very specific point of constitutional practice. The more frequent response to appeals to history as a foundation of Irish constitutional claims was to question the relevance of precedents and formulae from the distant past. Thus Cox mocked Lucas' dependence on 'ancient grants, moduses etc. ... musty old records hardly legible'. Nor was this just a philistine sneer. The reason why it was nonsense to go back to the remote past to investigate the question of Ireland's dependency on England was that 'in truth, in ancient times it is hard to trace anything like a settled constitution in either country'. Instead prerogative and liberty had fluctuated according as the king was weak or strong, 'until the Glorious Revolution was effected and a real constitution was formed in Britain'. This relativism allowed Cox effectively to undercut Lucas' appeal to Magna Carta by drawing attention to certain features, such as the declaration that barons could seize the lands of the king until he had amended any abuses complained of, that made it a document wholly of its time. Molyneux himself was likewise restored to a limiting historical context. His book had been condemned 'and the authority of the British parliament was asserted, and by the operation of their and our laws, we are in fact become absolutely dependent for all we have'. Molyneux's assertion that England had no more right to bind Ireland than to bind Scotland likewise demonstrated the irrelevance of his arguments to the present time.[72]

Other anti-patriot authors took a similar line. A supporter of the administration during the controversy over the money bill of 1769, for example, echoed Cox by arguing that even if the acceptance of money bills framed by the administration could be established as an uninterrupted usage only since 1695, these precedents had greater weight than earlier ones, since the constitution had been fixed on a firm basis only with the Revolution.[73] A few years later William Knox, having discussed the charters granted to Ireland by Henry II and John, explicitly warned against interpreting these in eighteenth-century terms. Because parliament in the present day possessed 'high, perhaps boundless jurisdiction', there was a tendency to assume the same had always been the case. However,

---

71 *A Comparative State of the Two Rejected Money Bills in 1692 and 1769, with Some Observations on Poynings Act ... by a Barrister* (Dublin 1770), pp. 16-25, 91. For the authorship of this pamphlet see Peter Roebuck (ed.), *Macartney of Lisanoure 1737-1806* (Belfast 1983), p. 320, n.26.
72 [Cox], *The Cork Surgeon's Antidote*, Letter 3, pp. 5-6; Letter 2, pp. 10-11; Letter 1, pp. 8-9; Letter 4, pp. 10-13.   73 *An Answer to Observations on a Speech Delivered the 26th Day of December 1769* (Dublin 1770), p. 15.

this was not so. 'The doctrine in former ages was that all power was in the king; the doctrine now is, that all power is derived from the people.' One consequence was that the grants made to Ireland had not required the consent of the English parliament. Another was that the people of Ireland, having accepted the laws of England, were now bound by whatever laws had subsequently been made by English parliaments, whether or not they were represented there.[74]

From this insistence on historical context, Knox proceeded to his alternative reading of the Irish past. Like Molyneux he took as his starting point the proposition that the people of twelfth-century Ireland had not been conquered, but had submitted to Henry II in exchange for guarantees of constitutional rights: 'they stipulated for a common right with their invaders, not only to all the privileges they should enjoy in Ireland, but to a community of rights and privileges with them in their own country, England'. For Knox, however, this founding charter was the basis, not of a separate Irish political entity, but rather of a political union. For three centuries thereafter, as was demonstrated in the statutes of successive English parliaments, 'England and Ireland were deemed by the king and parliament and people of England to be incorporated, and the inhabitants of the two islands to be one people, and equally entitled to the same immunities, and subject to the same restraints'. What undermined this union was partly the growth of a spirit of monopoly and commercial rivalry within England, but also 'the vanity of Henry VIII in taking the title of king of Ireland, and by consequence erecting the island into a kingdom'. Knox concluded with an appeal for the Irish to follow the example of Scotland and Wales, and 'absorb their local legislature in that by which the whole empire is governed'.[75]

Knox's rewriting of Ireland's history was also revisionist in another sense. Molyneux had assumed a continuity from the liberties guaranteed to the twelfth-century Gaelic princes to those claimed by Irish Protestants of his own day, without enquring into the means by which one had displaced the other. Lucas had offered an emotive account of the reduction of the native Irish to 'slavery and wretchedness', but had made this part of a catalogue of shared grievances: 'the native Irish were treated like slaves, and barbarous enemies to the crown; and ... soon after the English-Irish shared the like fate'.[76] Knox likewise denounced the erection of the Pale, and the exclusion of the native Irish from English law, as a 'public and notorious violation of the great charter of Henry'. These 'iniquities', however, had been the work of the Irish parliament and of the ancestors of the current Protestant population:

> The descendants of the Laceys, the Fitzgeralds, the Cavennaghs, the Courcys and many more who may find themselves injured by the recital

---

[74] [William Knox], *Considerations on the State of Ireland* (Dublin 1778), pp. 29-32. [75] Ibid., pp. 14, 37, 55, 59. [76] Lucas, *Nineteenth Address*, p. 19. [77] Knox, *Considerations*, pp. 20-1, 28.

of the injustice done to those they take to have been their ancestors by those they call English, ought to change the subject of their complaint, and lament that *their* ancestors were capable of such cruelty and injustice to *their* countrymen; neither the government or people of England were instrumental in the wrong.

More radically still, he went on to condemn the later replacement of descent by religion as a mark of distinction: '... although the Reformation did not take place in England for 350 years after Henry's invasion of Ireland, yet the Protestants of Ireland are weak enough to stigmatize the whole body of the Roman Catholics as descendants of the ancient Irish, and as such are unwilling to allow them a community of rights and privileges with themselves.'[77] These judgements had no strict connection in logic with the argument for a union. But it seems clear that in Knox's mind a rebuttal of the claim of the Protestant Irish to represent a people whose historic claims had been trampled on contributed to the task of undermining their constitutional pretensions.

A second recurrent theme in anti-patriot writing is a rejection of abstract reasoning in favour of common sense and practical experience. Government, one of Lucas' critics proclaimed, tended to descend, like estates, from one generation to the next: '... the reason is obvious, when we reflect, that they who are, from their infancy, brought up to any one thing, are, by far, more competent judges, than they who have had only speculative views, and gain their ideas by bare conception.'[78] Jebb, thirty years later, framed what was almost certainly a criticism of Grattan in very similar terms:

> Impressions concerning our people, and particularly our glorious Volunteers, must not be permitted to be taken from the paintings of a man who views our political concerns through the medium of intemperate zeal, and who, impracticable himself, would give to our politics the same inflexibility which characterizes his own mind. Eager to accomplish the freedom of Ireland, he seeks it in extremes, and, in the severity of an unaccommodating spirit, he loses the very end he would die to obtain.[79]

Charles Francis Sheridan took a similar view. Government, in the nature of things, could approach only within a certain distance of the ideal. Theoretical ideas of perfection could, given the excited state of the public mind, be dangerous. The particular error to which the political theorist, as opposed to the

---

[78] Taylor, *Lucas Refuted*, p. 4.   [79] Frederick Jebb, *Considerations Submitted to the People of Ireland ... in Answer to a Pamphlet Lately Entitled 'Observations on the Mutiny Bill etc.'* (Dublin 1781), p.7.

'good practical politician', was prone was that of 'carrying just reasoning, upon true premises, farther than the nature of things will warrant' so that his 'fine spung theory ... must necessarily evaporate in empty speculation'.[80]

In practical terms the appeal from abstract reasoning to common sense implied a call to avoid becoming entangled in purely theoretical issues. Since every man knew the kingdom was dependent, Cox demanded, 'what matters then, whether it be so by original force or consent? We find we are now thriving apace, and therefore whether our dependancy be antiently constitutional or not, it agrees with us.'[81] Macartney and Jackson, reproducing for their readers a version of the former's speech to the House of Commons in 1769, sought to present the custom of opening each parliament with the passage of a money bill transmitted from England as 'a point of form, a punctilio, a ceremony, a courtesy which an affectionate younger sister has always paid to her older, from her tenderest years, a civility of prescription which establishes no new claim, abrogates no old pretension'.[82] In the same spirit, Jebb and Sheridan opposed demands in 1781 that Ireland should follow up its victory over free trade by insisting that the recent Mutiny Act should be amended so as to limit its duration. A perpetual mutiny act, Grattan had argued, would make it possible for the crown at some future date to invade Irish liberties. Jebb and Sheridan's challenge was not so much to the plausibility of this concern as to the efficacy of a proposed solution depending on formal guarantees abstracted from a realistic political context. Any attempt by the crown to employ the army to override Irish rights, Jebb pointed out, would be quickly checked by the British parliament, aware of the implications for its own liberties. If on the other hand the British parliament connived at such an invasion, then 'all will be reduced to the question of force between the two nations, where parchment barriers will little avail either'. Sheridan likewise derided the notion that an army that would let itself be used to trample on constitutional liberties would desist simply because an Irish mutiny act had expired.[83]

For the same reasons Jebb and Sheridan wrote against the other main patriot demand, that the repeal of British laws restricting Irish commerce should be followed up by a parliamentary declaration of Ireland's legislative independence. What was important, Sheridan insisted, was that the laws that had formerly bound Ireland had been repealed. To claim that, without the declaration demanded, Ireland's freedom was not complete was the equivalent of asserting that a country that had once been invaded could not be free until it had a

---

80 Charles Francis Sheridan, *A Review of the Three Great National Questions Relative to the Declaration of Right, Poynings's Law and the Mutiny Bill* (Dublin 1781), pp. 20-24. 81 Cox, *Cork Surgeon's Antidote*, Letter 4, p. 4. 82 *A Comparative State of the two Rejected Money Bills*, p. 75. 83 Jebb, *Considerations Submitted to the People of Ireland*, p. 48; Sheridan, *A Review of the Three Great National Questions*, pp. 118-22.

formal guarantee that it would never be attacked again. In any case such a declaration, made unilaterally by Ireland, would add nothing to its security. The Irish should therefore rest content 'with the practical enjoyment of a free legislature', leaving the people of Great Britain to enjoy the illusion, if they chose, of the supremacy of their parliament.[84] Jebb took the same line. Now that Ireland had been granted a free trade, she should not 'add to her calamity by an unreasonable demand of the redress of speculative grievances'.[85]

These arguments against 'speculative views' were reinforced by appeals to consider the practical realities of the Anglo-Irish connection. Early writers tended to emphasize the inescapable inequality of power between the two kingdoms. The pointlessness and danger of antagonizing a powerful England formed a major theme of Cox's attack on Lucas. Only a madman 'would provoke a nation able without much labour to reduce us to our primitive nothing, to exert that power they have in order to convince us that we are dependent'. In these circumstances agitation on constitutional issues was 'snarling without teeth'. Molyneux's *Case of Ireland* and the claim to a 'sole right' in 1692 had both been damaging to Irish interests. Instead Cox advocated a graceful surrender to the inevitable. To represent dependency as 'the free choice of Ireland puts her into the most amiable light, of using her liberty so as not to abuse it'. But to search the historical record as Lucas had done, in order to prove that Ireland ought to be independent, was only to confess that she was dependent by compulsion, 'and puts upon us the badges of slaves'.[86] Similar prudential arguments were offered by a supporter of Townshend's administration. Where patriot authors had generally argued for Ireland's superior status, as a kingdom, over the American colonies, this pamphleteer pointed instead to its weaker strategic position:

> Is it not an absolute illusion to compare us with the colonies? ... Have we the same connections with the people of England which the colonies have, to induce them to espouse us? Are we at as great a distance from England as they are? Could we retain in our hands millions of the money of England until we compelled the doing of that which we would wish to have done?[87]

Macartney, likewise, could not resist adding to his image of harmless domestic courtesies the warning that 'an older sister, however affectionate, may become jealous of her younger for some omission, perhaps an unimportant one, and construe that omission to be an injury, a premeditated injury'.[88]

---

[84] Sheridan, *A Review of the Three Great National Questions*, p. 49. [85] [Jebb], *Considerations Submitted to the People of Ireland*, p. 71. [86] [Cox], *Cork Surgeon's Antidote*, Letter 2, pp. 10, 7, 13-14; Letter 3, pp. 5-6. [87] *Some Questions upon the Legislative Constitution of Ireland* (Dublin 1770), p. 18. [88] *A Comparative State of the two Rejected Money Bills*, p. 75.

As patriot opinion grew in extent and self confidence, such a tone was likely to prove increasingly counterproductive. Instead critics of patriot positions came over time to prefer a less confrontational approach that nevertheless highlighted some of the practical contradictions behind the rhetoric of linked but equal kingdoms. 'This appendancy of Ireland to the crown of a greater country,' Jebb pointed out, 'in which country too the executive authority of both kingdoms, with its pomp and patronage, resides, does necessarily create, without any malicious intent, a comparative inferiority.'[89] When it came to regulating the size and composition of the army, Sheridan likewise argued, 'the comparative inferiority of Ireland, in point of wealth, strength and population,' would have 'given an air of ridicule to any act of her parliament tending to secure the balance of power in the constitution of both countries, a duty the parliament of Great Britian was so much better able to fulfill.'[90] Even in Irish domestic affairs, moreover, the executive had behind it the financial resources of Great Britain, reducing the power which parliament could hope to exercise over it.[91] However, it was left to the explicitly unionist William Knox to throw down the most direct challenge: 'can you hope to be deemed a dependence of the British crown only for the purpose of being protected by the English fleets and armies, and enjoying the advantage of the treaties and alliances procured by England, and be considered by her as an independent people in all other respects?'[92]

For some authors, like William Knox, these inescapable practicalities of the relationship between Ireland and England (or, as Irish writers far less frequently expressed it, Great Britain) pointed to a legislative union as the only rational arangement. Others, however, sought to bring abstract constitutional speculation down to earth without surrendering the notion of Ireland as a distinct political entity. For them a recurrent theme was that the true relationship between Ireland and Britain was something that should not be defined too precisely. There was no more dangerous undertaking, Cox insisted, than meddling with the dependency of Ireland on Britain: 'it is the hardest thing imaginable, to steer so exactly, that a man shall not run upon a rock, one side or the other'.[93] 'What the nature of our dependence upon England is', John Monck Mason confessed in 1758, 'I really do not know; and must, at the same time, declare that I never wish to be better informed of it … Never did any subject require to be treated with this cautious reserve, more than the mysterious connection between this and its sister kingdom.'[94] 'That connection', Sheridan agreed, 'must ever appear a species of problem, being the only instance in the annals of mankind where two distinct and separate kingdoms under one common sov-

---

89 Jebb, *Considerations Submitted to the People of Ireland*, p. 4. **90** Sheridan, *A Review of the Three Great National Questions*, p. 92. **91** Ibid., p. 63. **92** Knox, *Considerations on the State of Ireland*, p. 7. **93** [Cox], *Cork Surgeon's Antidote*, Letter 2, p. 5. **94** J.M. Mason, *Remarks upon Poynings's Law and the Manner of Passing Bills in the P–t of I–d* (Dublin 1758), pp. 9-10.

ereign could with reciprocal advantage enjoy the same degree of liberty.'[95] The argument against 'just reason' carried to extremes was thus not merely that it ignored political reality, but that it sought to impose a precise definition on what was in fact best left ambiguous.

IV

An appeal to the mysterious character of the Anglo-Irish connection may seem a feeble conclusion. But in fact this argument identified precisely one of the central weaknesses of the patriot case as it came to be elaborated during the eighteenth century. To see this it is necessary to look briefly at the way in which political ideas interacted with political realities.

At the centre of the patriot case was the notion of what would later be described as dual monarchy. Ireland and England (later Great Britain) were sister kingdoms, sharing a monarchy under whom each enjoyed equal rights. On this basis Molyneux rejected any comparison between Ireland, a kingdom, and the colonies of north America. Swift, likewise, had distinguished between Ireland's allegiance to the king and its complete independence of the English parliament, ramming the message home in his theatrical proclamation of the willingness of the Irish, if necessary, to take up arms for the former against the latter. Grattan was equally uncompromising. 'Parliament', he proclaimed in 1782, 'is exclusive legislature ... Like that of England, our legislature is composed of king, Lords and Commons; but the word king is exclusive, the word Lords exclusive, and the word Commons exclusive; when you say you are governed by a king, you mean one king, when you say you are governed by a parliament, you mean one parliament.'[96]

The existence under the same ruler of two separate kingdoms, each with its own laws and institutions, was not an inherently unworkable arrangement. Early modern Europe contained numerous examples of multiple or composite monarchies.[97] In most such cases, however, legal and representative institutions had developed piecemeal over time in order to reflect and defend specific local privileges and exemptions within what was generally recognized as a system of divided power and overlapping jurisdictions. Ireland was different. Its status as a separate but dependent kingdom dated back to 1541 (although Molyneux and Lucas, citing Henry II's grant to John, put it more than three centuries earlier). But it was only in the 1690s that Irish Protestants, newly secure in their own kingdom and seizing the opportunities for constitutional self assertion created

---

[95] Sheridan, *A Review of the Three Great National Questions*, pp. 83-4.   [96] Grattan, *Speeches*, p. 60.   [97] J.H. Elliott, 'A Europe of composite monarchies', *Past and Present*, 137 (1992).

by the Revolution, had made their bid for equality. In consequence their demands, despite the appeals to history on which they claimed to rest, did not in fact grow out of a gradually developed body of customary practice, leading to a pragmatic and empirically tested allocation of central and local power. Rather they were the absolute and non-negotiable claims implied by a theoretical claim to equality. In particular the role envisaged for the Irish parliament was not that of a defender of sectional or regional liberties, similar to the Hungarian diet or the *parlements* of France. Instead when Irish Protestants framed their demand for representation they turned instinctively to the parliament of Great Britain as the model on which to base their constitutional aspirations. They did so, moreover, at a time when the British doctrine of the absolute supremacy of parliament was assuming its final form. The result was that they committed themselves to an ideal of a sovereign, omnicompetent legislature wholly inappropriate to Ireland's actual political position.

There was also a more concrete problem. At the centre of the dual monarchy model was, inevitably, the monarchy itself, the one link between two sister kingdoms. But monarchy was not a static institution. In the sixteenth and seventeenth centuries it had been possible to argue that Ireland and England were each ruled, separately, by the same person. By the eighteenth century, however, despite the evasions that had characterized the Revolution settlement, real power in England had quite clearly passed from crown to parliament. In 1768 Thomas Pownall, former governor of Massachusetts, correctly identified this change as the underlying cause of the growing conflict between Great Britain and its North American colonies, whose inhabitants found that they were no longer subject to royal government, but to a parliament in which they had no representation.[98] In Ireland the point was most clearly spelt out during the debates on the union in 1799. The notion that Ireland should be ruled by its king-in-parliament, one government supporter pointed out, was meaningless, since in practice the king did nothing without the advice of his ministers, who were 'the servants of a parliament exclusively British'.[99] However, the essential point had been made half a century earlier by Cox, in his critique of Lucas. The king of Great Britain was the supreme executive power; the means of exerting that power, on the other hand, depended wholly on parliament. Hence dependence on the crown of Great Britain could only mean dependence on its people, through their representatives in parliament.[100]

By contrast the patriot position required that the changes that had taken place in the formal structures, and even more in the practical workings, of the British political system should be wholly ignored. The extent to which this was so was

---

[98] Thomas Pownall, *The Administration of the Colonies* (1768, facs. reprint New York 1993), pp. 119-47. [99] Quoted in R.B. McDowell, *Irish Public Opinion 1750-1800* (London 1944), pp. 247-8. [100] Cox, *Cork Surgeon's Antidote*, Letter 3, p. 6.

dramatically illustrated by Charles Francis Sheridan when, in his earlier role as an opposition writer, he published his celebrated refutation of Blackstone's doctrine of the absolute supremacy of the British parliament. 'The parliament of Great Britain', Sheridan argued, 'cannot of right exercise any act of authority over the people of other communities, who have not entrusted them with any power.' It was true that a 'strong presiding power' was essential to preserve the prosperity and security of the empire. But this was provided by the king.

> Linked together by one common relation to the supreme executive power, a power which can contract alliances in which the whole empire is included; which can declare war, in the name of the whole empire; and can make peace, which the whole empire is bound to observe. A power which can superintend and protect the separate interests of each community in the empire; which can put a negative on every act of the legislature of any one state, calculated only to procure a partial advantage to that state, at the expense of the general good of the whole.

By this means, Sheridan concluded triumphantly, the British constitution provided the means by which 'separate and distant states, forming one empire, may each of them enjoy the same degree of liberty, yet the unity of the empire be preserved'.[101] But his argument depended entirely on what was by this time mere legal fiction: that what was done in the name of the king of Great Britain reflected his decisons rather than those of the current ministry.

The practical consequences of this wilful blindness became evident in the settlement of 1782 and its aftermath. At their moment of triumph in 1782 Grattan and Charlemont rejected proposals by the new Whig ministry for a constitutional treaty between the two kingdoms. Instead they insisted on the immediate amendment of Poynings' Law, and the repeal of the declaratory act. Pitt's attempt three years later to make a commercial treaty the basis of a new constitutional relationship was frustrated by the refusal of a large parliamentary grouping to accept the necessity for any form of joint regulation, even in matters of imperial trade.[102] Irish intransigence reached a peak in 1789, when parliament insisted that it was for it alone to decide when and on what terms the prince of Wales should assume the regency during the incapacity of George III, despite warnings that this was to call into question the one remaining link, a

---

101 Charles Francis Sheridan, *Observations on the Doctrine laid down by Sir William Blackstone Respecting the Extent of the Power of the British Parliament, Particularly with Relation to Ireland*, 2nd edn (London 1779), p. 62   102 For a review of the main issues see J.C. Beckett, 'Anglo-Irish constitutional relations in the later eighteenth century' in idem, *Confrontations* (London 1972), pp. 123-41; R.B. McDowell, *Ireland in the Age of Imperialism and Revolution 1760-1801* (Oxford 1979), chap. 6; James Kelly, *Prelude to Union: Anglo-Irish Politics in the 1780s* (Dublin 1992).

shared monarchy, holding the two kingdoms together. It was against this background that English ministers began to think that the only long term solution to what they now saw as the problem of Anglo-Irish relations was a legislative union.[103] Parliament, Grattan had said, implied exclusive legislature. William Pitt, in 1799-1800, took him at his word.

It is in this context that one can best appreciate the significance of the critique of the patriot argument discussed in this paper. It would be wrong to suggest that the authors of that critique, any more than the patriots themselves, appreciated the full importance of the issues at stake. Their writing remained closely tied both to the specific Irish case and to particular issues within that case; their whole approach discouraged generalized speculation. Within these limits, however, their arguments were both shrewd and well directed. Their representation of the actual functioning of Irish politics, in terms of the distribution of patronage and the balance of power between parliament and executive, was more accurate than much patriot rhetoric. They took realistic account of the differences in size and wealth between the two kingdoms. They showed an awareness of the implications for Anglo-Irish relations of the transfer of power from king to parliament that had been initiated by the Revolution. In all of these respects, moreover, they brought to Irish political writing a distinctive mode of analysis, characterized by a critical approach to historical argument and an emphasis on practice over abstract principle. These characteristics entitle their work to be recognized as a significant part of the complex and varied pattern of eighteenth-century Irish political thought. Applied to the specific area of Anglo-Irish relations, in the form of an insistence that some things were best not too explicitly defined, their approach may also have represented the only realistic way in which a separate Irish parliament and administrative system could have hoped to survive the crisis of the late eighteenth century.

---

[103] The fullest survey of thinking on the question is James Kelly, 'The origins of the act of union: an examination of unionist opinion in Britain and Ireland 1650-1800', *Irish Historical Studies*, 25 (1987).

The harp without the crown: nationalism and republicanism in the 1790s[1]

IAN McBRIDE

I

The boundaries of Irish political debate were extended spectacularly during the political and social ferment of the 1790s, as the ideological buttresses of the Protestant Ascendancy, which had dominated Ireland for a century, were subjected to a sustained assault. The 'patriot' conception of the British state as a composite monarchy, linking co-equal jurisdictions under a single crown, was discredited, as revolutionary separatism became thinkable for the first time. More fundamental still, perhaps, the formal exclusion of Catholics from political life was widely attacked, and a new, non-sectarian vision of Irish nationhood was popularized. Finally, the theoretical underpinnings of the social hierarchy were dissolved as radical propagandists mobilized hundreds of thousands of Irish men and women from the middling and lower orders in a massive underground conspiracy against the Dublin Castle administration. Although this revolutionary challenge was repulsed by military force in 1798, the mental world of Irish people was permanently altered, and the language and iconography of the United Irishmen would have a profound impact on future republican movements.[2]

The Irish radicals of the late eighteenth century were conscious that they lived in an age of revolution which had seen the birth of new republics in North America and Europe, and the political vocabularies they employed bore a close resemblance to those found elsewhere: the myth of an ancient constitution, classical republicanism, natural rights theory, Enlightenment rationalism and the rights of man. Any attempt to describe Irish republicanism therefore involves a confrontation with many of the questions which have puzzled British, American or French historians. To what extent where United Irish pamphleteers and journalists operating within inherited conventions? How far were older frameworks of thought overwhelmed by new democratic and uni-

---

[1] I am grateful to James Quinn and Jim Smyth for comments on some of the issues raised in this essay. [2] For political conflict in the 1790s see N.J. Curtin, *The United Irishmen: Popular Politics in Ulster and Dublin, 1791-98* (Oxford 1994); Kevin Whelan, *The Tree of Liberty: Radicalism, Catholicism and the Construction of Irish Identity 1760-1830* (Cork 1996).

versalist notions? To draw up a balance sheet of change and continuity presents a challenge for early modern historians, most of whom subscribe to a methodological approach which situates individual texts within broader 'languages' that have evolved over a longer period of time.[3] The decade of the 1790s constitutes a rupture with established patterns of political thought and organization which divides the modern period from the *ancien régime*. Part of our role as historians of political discourse is to de-familiarize political concepts such as liberty, nationality, and sovereignty, by restoring them to the vocabularies which first gave them meaning; but this task becomes problematic when we reach the age of the American and French Revolutions and the principles of representative democracy which have become such fundamental assumptions of the Western nation-state.

In addition to these general difficulties, there are further complications arising from Ireland's unusual position as a metropolitan colony of Great Britain. The constitutional claims advanced for the kingdom of Ireland habitually rested on its historic parliamentary institutions and traditions, but the semi-autonomous parliament at College Green occupied an increasingly anomalous place within the unitary British state which had taken shape during the revolution of 1688-9, the union of 1707, and the American war of 1775-83. Irish patriotism, though it both borrowed from and contributed to American and Scottish discussions of the imperial system, had no exact parallel. Beyond these constitutional peculiarities there lay the social, cultural and ethnic fractures which had resulted from the conquests and settlements of the Stuart period. Although the century which followed the Williamite wars has usually been associated with Protestant varieties of patriotism, older Jacobite modes of Irish self-assertion were never entirely eradicated. An ethnocentric version of the story of Ireland, described by Tom Garvin as an 'ideology of dispossession and repossession',[4] could still be detected among the remnants of the Catholic gentry and among the urban and rural middle classes; in the last two decades of the century these impulses would find a popular voice in Defenderism.[5] Although Irish political culture – for Protestant, Catholic and Dissenter alike – was predominantly an English-speaking one, it was inflected in different ways by the origin-myths of the Gaelic, Old English and New English communities. Finally, and most obviously, there was the exceptional religious composition of the Irish population. Following the removal of the old Catholic elite, more

---

3 For the two most influential models see James Tully (ed.), *Meaning and Context: Quentin Skinner and his Critics* (Cambridge 1988) and J.G.A. Pocock, *Virtue, Commerce and History: Essays on Political Thought and History, Chiefly in the Eighteenth Century* (Cambridge 1985). 4 Tom Garvin, 'Nationalism and separatism in Ireland, 1760-1993: a comparative perspective' in J. Bermanendi, R. Maiz and X. Nuñez (eds), *Nationalism in Europe Past and Present* (Universidad de Santiago de Compostela 1994), p. 89.

relaxed attitudes to denominational differences would eventually develop, but the continuing rejection of the state religion by three quarters of the total population served as a reminder of Ireland's unstable past, and its continuing refusal to conform to European norms.

Before I attempt to elucidate some of these themes, some words of caution concerning the corpus of primary material may be in order. The first issue concerns the largely derivative nature of Irish political writing in the last quarter of the eighteenth century. With the arresting exception of Edmund Burke, none of the Irish writers of this period made a major contribution to European political thought – and Burke, the son of an Irish Catholic convert who made a career as an English Whig, is very much the exception that proves the rule. Radical publicists did not attempt to set out systematic expositions of Irish republicanism; we should not expect to discover that their political commitments were underpinned by a consistent theoretical position or that they wrestled with the conceptual distinctions which have vexed intellectual historians. Pamphleteers such as Wolfe Tone wrote in response to immediate events and in pursuit of specific objectives. As his biographers have pointed out, Tone explicitly eschewed a theoretical approach: 'I confess I dislike abstract reasoning on practical subjects ... When I feel a grievance pinch me sorely, I look neither for the major nor minor of a proposition or syllogism, but merely for the proximate cause and the possibility of removing it.'[6]

Secondly, we must not forget the legal and political constraints imposed on public discourse at a time of international war and domestic unrest. In December 1792 an address to the Volunteers adopted by the Dublin Society of United Irishmen led to the arrest and ultimate conviction of Archibald Hamilton Rowan on a charge of seditious libel; by the end of 1794 the same publication had provided the basis for the prosecution of the author, William Drennan, and of the proprietors of the *Northern Star* newspaper. Another United Irishman, the notorious Napper Tandy, fled the country after he was charged with distributing a paper, 'Common-Sense', which had violently denounced the Beresford and Foster families.[7] This legal crackdown on Irish disaffection was part of the wider government reaction which produced the English treason trials and, most

---

5 Kevin Whelan, 'An underground gentry? Catholic middlemen in eighteenth-century Ireland' in idem, *The Tree of Liberty*, pp. 3-58; Breandán Ó Buachalla, 'Irish Jacobitism and Irish nationalism: the literary evidence' in Michael O'Dea and Kevin Whelan (eds), *Nations and Nationalisms: France, Britain, Ireland and the Eighteenth-Century Context* (Oxford 1995), pp.103-16; Thomas Bartlett, 'Select documents XXXVIII: Defenders and Defenderism in 1795', *Irish Historical Studies*, 24 (1985), 373-94.   6 'Reply to a Pamphlet Entitled "The Protestant Interest in Ireland Ascertained"' in Thomas Bartlett (ed.), *Life of Theobald Wolfe Tone* (Dublin 1998), p. 322.   7 The handbill was written by John Keogh. Another, and greater, charge was that Tandy had administered a Defender oath.

notoriously, the trial and transportation of a group of Scottish radicals between 1792 and 1794. It was against this background that William Drennan published a letter to the new lord lieutenant, Earl Fitzwilliam, which denied that the north of Ireland was infected with 'French principles' and protested that the inhabitants were instead 'most obstinately attached to the principles of Locke'. This passage, and others like it, has been cited as evidence that the United Irishmen were 'deeply immersed in British radical Whig culture', and few would disagree with this verdict.[8] At the same time, it should be recalled that Drennan had dropped out of the movement following his trial, and that he hoped that Fitzwilliam's arrival would reactivate the broader constitutional campaign for reform. Even Drennan, moreover, justified his invocation of Locke and Blackstone by arguing that no Whig could object to such impeccable authorities on the constitution.[9] Similarly, the deployment of the United States as a political paradigm must be treated with caution: in England, Paine and other radicals raised the American example to offset the loyalist concentration on the violence and anarchy of revolutionary France.[10] Such tactical considerations complicate the relationship between the public writings of the United Irishmen and their private views, raising questions about the ways in which radical texts were read by their intended audience.

We must also appreciate that the aspirations and methods of Irish radicals were not static, but responded to a cycle of confrontation and polarization that began with the conservative backlash of 1792-3. Throughout the decade, political discourse became more closely tied to the threatened or actual use of force. As government action took its toll and older leaders dropped out of the conspiracy, the balance within the republican ranks shifted towards younger men who had not played a part in the reform campaigns of 1778-85, and whose political education was more straightforwardly Paineite. After the outbreak of war, political dissent in Ireland was viewed in the context of a protracted international conflict, and a spiral of violence at home intensified. These years witnessed the emergence of a mass public and new forms of mobilization; concomitantly a popular style of journalism was pioneered, and radicals experimented with a variety of literary forms and media. As Mark Philp has shown in a careful analysis of the English reformers, radical argument in the 1790s is best regarded as tactical, innovative and provisional.[11] Again, this shifting political context presents problems for historians of political thought, who must be sensitive to rhetorical techniques and generic forms as well as political maxims.

---

8 Curtin, *United Irishmen*, p. 36.   9 Drennan to Samuel McTier, [30 Oct. 1792], in D. A. Chart (ed.), *The Drennan Letters, 1776-1819* (Belfast 1931), p. 93.   10 Mark Philp, 'The role of America in the "debate on France", 1791-5: Thomas Paine's insertion', *Utilitas*, 5 (1993), 221-37.   11 Mark Philp, 'The fragmented ideology of reform' in idem (ed.), *The French Revolution and British Popular Politics* (Cambridge 1991), pp. 50-77.

For our purposes here it may help to distinguish three broad stages of activity in the 1790s, whilst allowing for some overlap between them. The first was the moral-force, constitutional, phase of the United Irishmen, when the chief task was the reinvigoration of the parliamentary reform movement and the conversion of Protestant radicals to Catholic emancipation, goals which demanded a fundamental rethinking of conventional definitions of the Irish nation. During this phase of activity, which culminated in the Dungannon Convention of February 1793, the two most significant political writers were Wolfe Tone, author of the classic *Argument on Behalf of the Catholics of Ireland* (1791) and Drennan, who composed most of the addresses issued by the Dublin Society of United Irishmen. Whilst it would be misleading to draw a rigid line between the constitutional and insurrectionary phases of the movement, political circumstances were altered dramatically by the internationalization of the French Revolution and the outbreak of war in 1793. The wartime measures adopted by the London and Dublin governments made it clear that the public goals of the radical societies – the revival of Volunteering and the summoning of conventions on the Dungannon model – could no longer be realised.

A second phase of radical journalism was related to popular politicization, particularly in Ulster and Dublin, and to the cementing of an alliance between the United Irishmen and the Defenders. Thanks to Nancy Curtin and Louis Cullen, we now know that a plebeian stratum of organisation can be traced back as far as 1792, when radical activists such as Thomas Russell, Samuel Neilson and Henry Joy McCracken were already touring the northern countryside and establishing links with prominent Catholics like the Teelings, Bernard Coile and James Coigly.[12] In the turn towards a mass insurrectionary strategy, however, the repressive measures of 1793-4, which closed down the channels of constitutional agitation, and the recall of the pro-Catholic viceroy Fitzwilliam in 1795 were important landmarks. The chief vehicle for radical politics during these years was the *Northern Star*, whose contributors included William Sampson, Thomas Russell, and a number of Presbyterian clergymen such as James Porter, William Steel Dickson, and Thomas Ledlie Birch. In their attempts to communicate with a constituency which had little experience of political debate, the United Irishmen highlighted the tangible benefits which would follow from parliamentary reform, with the abolition or reduction of tithes, church rates, hearth-money, excise taxes and the county cess all high on the agenda.[13]

---

[12] N.J. Curtin, 'The transformation of the United Irishmen into a revolutionary mass organization, 1794-6', *Irish Historical Studies*, 24 (1985), 463-92; L. M. Cullen, 'The internal politics of the United Irishmen' in David Dickson, Dáire Keogh and Kevin Whelan (eds), *The United Irishmen: Republicanism, Radicalism and Rebellion* (Dublin 1993), pp. 176-96. [13] See, for example, *The Oppression of Tithe Exemplified; or, A Review of the Late Contest between Conscientious Scruple and Ecclesiastical Exaction* (Belfast 1797).

Finally, the arrival of a French invasion fleet in Bantry Bay at the end of 1796 signalled the beginning of a third stage, characterized by physical confrontation, terror and counter-terror. Over the next two years the United Irishmen established their supremacy over large areas of Ulster, as radicals immobilized the magistracy and the courts, infiltrated the militia, and organized nocturnal arms raids. In the north, civil war smouldered as the government tried to break the republican organization with a combination of military action, legal prosecution, and infiltration. The centre of the conspiracy shifted to Dublin, and the 'system' was spread through the Leinster counties. While loyalists and republicans attempted to intimidate each other by displays of physical strength, political debate was reduced to a commentary on the practical struggle, most notably the subject of state repression. Increasingly, United Irish literature operated on a crude, emotive level. But these years, whilst they produced little theoretical reflection, would be crucial in shaping the republican legacy. It is against this shifting background of republican mobilization that we must examine the changing configuration of 'nation', 'republic' and 'people' in United Irish thought.

II

On 16 August 1789, the newly founded Whig Club published a set of resolutions denouncing the increasing influence of the crown over both houses of the Irish Parliament and defending 'the constitution of the realm, as settled by the revolution in Great Britain and Ireland in 1688, and re-established in 1782'.[14] Although a more vigorous branch soon appeared in the north, the Whig Club followed the leadership of Grattan and Charlemont, and its creed may be viewed as a recapitulation of the old patriot tradition: its chief aim was the restriction of ministerial patronage. Two months later a new association was founded, however, which would quickly eclipse the conservative patriotism of the Whigs. The manifesto of the Society of United Irishmen of Belfast, published in October 1791, set out three simple principles, beginning with a blunt diagnosis of the Anglo-Irish relationship. '*We have no national government*', they began, 'we are ruled by Englishmen, and the servants of Englishmen, whose object is the interest of another country, whose instrument is corruption, and whose strength is the weakness of Ireland.' The weight of English influence in the Irish government was so great, they claimed, that it had disturbed the balance which was essential to 'the preservation of our liberties, and the extension

---

14 Quoted in Neil Longley York, *Neither Kingdom nor Nation: The Irish Quest for Constitutional Rights, 1698-1800* (Washington, D.C. 1994), pp. 200-1.

of our commerce'. This situation could only be rectified by one measure, 'AN EQUAL REPRESENTATION OF ALL THE PEOPLE IN PARLIAMENT'. Although the United Irishmen raised conventional grievances concerning the corrupting effects of government patronage, these were merely symptoms of a disease in the constitution which called for 'a complete and radical reform'. Finally, this endeavour required 'a cordial union among *all the people of Ireland*', and hence the radicals urged that 'no reform is practicable, efficacious, or just, which shall not include Irishmen of every religious persuasion'.[15]

Each of these statements, drafted by Wolfe Tone, had been anticipated by the radical fringe of the old reform movement, and the United Irish programme was in many ways a crystallization of ideas that had been widely floated in the 1780s. Never before, however, had these arguments been advanced with such confidence and directness. The turning point, of course, was the debate on the French Revolution. As we shall see, the republican vocabulary adopted by the French and translated by Thomas Paine entailed major ideological innovations. Just as important as the revolutionary doctrine of the rights of man, however, was the euphoric rhetoric generated by events on the Continent. The United Irishmen were living in an age of reform, 'when unjust governments are falling in every quarter of Europe' and, equally importantly, 'religious persecution is compelled to abjure her tyranny over conscience'.[16] The revolution had apparently swept away a whole world of disabling customs and prejudices, and radicals in Ireland as elsewhere caught the mood of utopian promise which offered an end to despotism and superstition.[17] To understand the political discourse of the 1790s we need to measure the extent to which older constitutionalist lines of argument were dropped in favour of Paineite rationalism and natural rights; but we must also be alert to the language of reason, light and nature, to the celebration of innovation, the growing confidence in human perfectibility, and the belief that European civilization was being regenerated.

The patriot tradition represented by the Whig Club continued to operate within the framework of the British constitution. In their demand for a 'national government', by contrast, the United Irishmen were moving towards a concept of representative democracy, grounded on popular sovereignty, which broke with the anglocentric discourse of the Whig tradition. 1789, declared Samuel Neilson in the *Northern Star*, was the most glorious of all revolutions: whereas the English revolution was merely 'local', the French, 'like the dew of heaven, inspires all Europe, and will extend the blessing of liberty to all mankind as citizens of the world, the creatures of one Supreme Being'.[18] Events in Paris generated new terminology and new symbolism – the Bastille,

---

15 'Declaration and Resolutions of the Society of United Irishmen of Belfast' reprinted in Bartlett (ed.), *Life of Theobald Wolfe Tone*, pp. 298-99. **16** Ibid., p. 298. **17** See, for example, 'Aristides', *Northern Star*, 3 Nov. 1792. **18** *Northern Star*, 7 Nov. 1792.

the cap of liberty, the opposing labels of aristocrat and democrat, the title of 'citizen' and the cropped hairstyle of the republican. The continuing recourse to French rhetoric and imagery implied the abandonment not only of 1688 but also of its Irish counterpart, 1782. Thus Tone, whose *Argument on Behalf of the Catholics* (1791) captured some of the immediacy and indignation of Paine's prose, described the 'revolution' of 1782 as 'the most bungling, imperfect business that ever threw ridicule on a lofty epithet'.[19]

While Tone suggested that the lessons of 1641 and 1688 were no longer applicable in the 'days of illumination', other reformers went further still, demanding that Protestants rethink the very premises on which their historical self-understanding was founded. Like Tone's *Argument*, William Todd Jones' *Letter to the Societies of United Irishmen of the Town of Belfast* (1792) was designed to dispel the reservations entertained by many Ulster Presbyterians on the emancipation issue. In reaction to apprehensions that enfranchised Catholics would attempt to overturn the land settlement, Jones pointed out that many opulent Catholics had taken leasehold interests in the old forfeited estates. More controversially, he embarked on a rehabilitation of the 'Patriot' parliament of 1689, defending the moderate ambitions of the Court of Claims and commending the Jacobites for asserting the legislative independence of the kingdom of Ireland.[20] The infamous act of attainder, he contended, was a fabricated pretext for the forfeiture of Catholic estates under William III and the introduction of the penal code. Indeed the whole corpus of Protestant atrocity literature was challenged in an attack on 'those gossiping old women Goody King and Goody Story, who assert the apparitions at Portadown bridge, and the screeches of murdered Protestants for a fortnight together, in the black water'.[21] Protestant presuppositions about the superiority of the English common law and the reformed religion were inverted, as Jones located the connecting thread of Irish history in the expropriation of Catholic land, the proscription of Catholic worship, and the oppression of the Catholic common people. In sum, he concluded that

> ... the Irish were a nation tyrannized over, and harassed, from the usurpation of Henry the 2d. and the robberies of Strongbow, to the

---

[19] 'An Argument on Behalf of the Catholics of Ireland', reprinted in Bartlett (ed.), *Life of Theobald Wolfe Tone*, p. 281. Satirical attacks on British constitutional and legal structures later formed the basis of two of the most widely read United Irish works, William Sampson's *Review of the Lion of Old England* (Belfast 1794) and his *A Faithful Report of the Trial of Hurdy Gurdy* (Belfast 1794), the former written in collaboration with Thomas Russell. [20] William Todd Jones, *Letter to the Societies of United Irishmen of the Town of Belfast*, 3rd edn (Dublin 1792), esp. pp. 6-7. [21] Idem, *Reply to an Anonymous Writer from Belfast, signed Portia* (Dublin [1792]), pp. 10, 24.

period of Reformation: and that religious animosity restoring exhausted vigour to national aversion, the Irish catholics have endured a constant, unremitting, and hideous persecution, on account of religion, as well as for their lands, from the era of Elizabeth.[22]

In other ways, too, Whig anglocentrism was rapidly being superseded. While many of the arguments employed by the United Irishmen had Lockeian or classical-republican antecedents, the French Revolution, and the debate sparked off by Burke's impassioned defence of the old order, hastened the development of a more sharply focused theory of representative government. The choice, defined by Paine, between the egalitarian regimes of America and France and the hereditary systems of the Old World, was dramatized by the European war which radicals continued to see in fundamentally ideological terms. Locke was still cited as the orthodox exponent of contractual government, but his writings were now reread in the light of Paine's democratic convictions.[23] Whereas Locke had confined the right of resistance to a desperate appeal to heaven under a tyrannical ruler, Paine's citizens reserved the right to remodel their government as they saw fit. The accelerated pace of political argument was evident in the columns of the *Northern Star*, which emphasized popular sovereignty and the rights of man rather than constitutional balance, the elimination of corruption and executive influence. Although occasional references to the ancient constitution appeared in its columns – particularly in 1792/3 – the suasive force of precedent was generally relegated in favour of universal rights.

In his repudiation of the hereditary system Paine had abandoned the mixed or balanced constitution favoured by most reformers: monarchy and aristocracy were incompatible with the conviction that each generation must consent to its own constitutional arrangements. It is well known that most English radicals chose not to follow Paine this far, but what about their Irish counterparts? At first the French Revolution could be assimilated to conventional categories without much damage. In 1790, for example, the Belfast Constitutional Society, a mysterious forerunner of the United Irishmen, congratulated France on adopting 'a republican system of government' and expressed the hope that enlightened citizens of every country would imitate their example.[24] Yet these sentiments were offered *before* the abolition of the monarchy, at a time when

---

[22] Ibid., p. 23.   [23] 'Seditious Extracts from John Locke's *Essay on the Human Understanding*', *Northern Star*, 14 July 1792. For Paine generally see Gregory Claeys, *Thomas Paine: Social and Political Thought* (Boston 1989); for his reception in Ireland see David Dickson, 'Paine and Ireland' in Dickson, Keogh and Whelan (eds), *United Irishmen*, pp. 135-50.   [24] 'Belfast Constitutional Compact', 1 Oct. 1790 (National Archives of Ireland, Rebellion Papers 620/19/12).

republicanism obviously retained its older 'commonwealth' significations. At the end of December 1792, however, following the declaration of the French republic and the trial of Louis XVI, the *Northern Star* dropped the crown from its emblem: above the harp there was now placed a sunburst, the masonic symbol of enlightenment. At the same time William Drennan confided to his sister in Belfast that he was 'a real republican', though he was willing to conform with the moderates for tactical reasons.[25] Following the execution of Louis XVI on 21 January 1793, his more cautious sister, Martha McTier, contrasted the debauched behaviour of the French with the true principles of a republic, which she took to be 'simplicity of manners and virtue', and spoke wistfully of the days when the New Light Dissenters of Belfast 'made no scruple of declaring their partiality for that form of government, without its ever being supposed that they had a wish to overturn their own'.[26] Henceforward the term 'republican' was increasingly reserved for the partisans of the regicidal French, yet it never quite lost its eighteenth-century ambiguity. As late as 1797, Arthur O'Connor tested the boundary between real Whiggery and sedition when he declared that 'if to place the liberties of my country on its true republican basis be treason, then I do glory in being a traitor'.[27]

Officially, of course, the objects of the United Irishmen were limited to parliamentary reform and Catholic emancipation. While the Dungannon Convention of 1793 backed this programme, it also affirmed attachment to 'the form and original principles of the British Constitution' and disapproved of 'republican forms of government, as applied to this kingdom'.[28] Yet it seems likely that the private preferences of the radical reformers, particularly the younger generation, were hostile to the maintenance of both monarchy and aristocracy. In examining their public discourse we must attend not only to what they said, but to what they omitted to say. Unlike moderate reformers, the United Irishmen often declined to affirm the constitutionality of their aims by invoking the Revolution principles of 1688; later versions of their test or oath were regarded as republican because they called for an equal representation of the people but made no mention of parliament. And while the United Irish leadership publicly disavowed revolutionary aims, the anonymous handbills that swept the countryside from 1794 were less coy in their denunciations of kingcraft.[29] In any case, the programme of manhood suffrage and annual parliaments announced by the United Irishmen would have rendered the hereditary elements in the constitution inoperative, and by challenging ministerial

[25] Drennan to Martha McTier, 24 Dec. 1792 (PRONI, Drennan Papers, T.765/364). [26] McTier to Drennan, 8 Feb. 1793 (PRONI Drennan Papers, T.765/389). [27] Arthur O'Connor, 'Address to the Electors of the County of Antrim' (National Archives, Dublin, Rebellion Papers 620/26/123). [28] For a general account see the *Belfast News-Letter*, 22 Feb. 1793. [29] For a curious example see 'The Children's Catechism' [handbill, Belfast, 1794],

patronage would have dissolved the last substantive link between the two kingdoms. Similarly, the idea of a constitutional convention, while it conjured up the relatively comforting precedents of 1689 and 1782, had more troubling American and French connotations, and had always been at odds with the Anglo-Saxon parliamentary tradition.

These implicit challenges to the Anglo-Irish connection raise the question of how far, or in what sense, we may classify the United Irishmen as nationalists. Until recently academic historians have taken care to differentiate the late eighteenth-century radicals from later varieties of nationalism by contrasting their cosmopolitan, Enlightenment assumptions with the romantic, particularist views of the Young Ireland movement or the Gaelic revival. While R.B. McDowell conceded that Georgian Ireland participated in the romantic enthusiasm for Gothic and Gaelic matters, he insisted that 'no attempt was made to use the Irish language and its literature as a basis for a national culture distinct from that of England'.[30] Individual radicals such as William James McNeven and William Sampson were familiar with Gaeldom, but more concerned with classical antiquity, British constitutional history and French revolutionary theory.[31] More recently, Tom Dunne, in a study of Irish popular culture, has dismissed the notion that the interest of a few liberal Protestants in 'assimilating suitable drawing-room versions of Gaelic literature to contemporary romantic modes' carried political implications.[32] Finally, in the most sophisticated discussion of this question, Joep Leerssen has argued that Irish patriotism was a 'remarkably a-historicist' creed, confined to the world after 1688, and that the adoption of the Gaelic past was 'a purely literary affair'.[33] Although Leerssen's focus was on the Anglo-Irish patriotism of Molyneux, Swift, Grattan and Flood rather than that of Tone or Drennan, he sees the act of union as the decisive turning-point in shifting Irish political argument away from constitutional terms towards Gaelic heritage.[34] There was no continuity, in his view, between the patriotism of the pre-union period and that of the Young Irelanders.

This long-established picture has been subject to challenge since the appearance of Mary Helen Thuente's *The Harp Re-Strung* (1994), an important study which has stimulated a new interest in the cultural aspects of Irish radicalism in the late eighteenth century. Pointing to the welter of ballads produced by the United Irishmen, their support for the Belfast Harp Festival in 1792, and the publication of the Gaelic magazine *Bolg an tSolair* (1795), Thuente has argued that Irish literary nationalism originated with the United Irishmen, rather than

---

discussed below. **30** R.B. McDowell, *Irish Public Opinion, 1750-1800* (London 1944), pp. 23-4. **31** Ibid., p. 210. **32** Tom Dunne, 'Popular ballads, revolutionary rhetoric and politicisation' in Hugh Gough and David Dickson (eds), *Ireland and the French Revolution* (Dublin 1990), p. 143. **33** Joep Th. Leerssen, 'Anglo-Irish patriotism and its European context: notes towards a reassessment', *Eighteenth-Century Ireland*, 3 (1988), 22-23. **34** Ibid., p. 24.

Thomas Moore or the Young Ireland poets. She marshals an impressive amount of evidence to show that Irish antiquities, music and language all featured in United Irish literature, that the first republicans were involved in the revival of Irish music, and that they promoted the study of the Irish language. At the core of her study is the previously neglected corpus of poems and songs published in the *Northern Star*, the *Press*, and the republican songbook, *Paddy's Resource* (1795). United Irish verse glorified not only Ireland's history and culture but also its martial traditions. Typical of these battle calls was 'Tara', a poem published in the *Northern Star* for 18 April 1796, which celebrated the 'seat of ancient heroes' whose 'mighty deeds' included the use of 'arms to overthrow' the 'invading foe'.[35] As Thuente shows, United Irish propaganda generated 'what have become the stereotypical images of Irish nationalism: bards, harps, shamrocks, green flags, political martyrs, and blood sacrifice'.[36]

Since Thuente's thesis has gained widespread acceptance, it is important that several reservations be registered. As a preliminary argument, it is worth noting that the connections drawn between cultural and political activities are not as straightforward as she suggests. Thuente remarks, for example, that all four organizers of the Belfast Harp Festival of 1792 – Dr James McDonnell, Henry Joy, Robert Bradshaw and Robert Simms – had close connections with the United Irishmen.[37] On closer examination, however, we find that McDonnell, while certainly a friend of Tone, Russell and the McCrackens, was a political conservative; and that Joy took the opposite side to his cousins, the McCrackens, in the political debates of the 1790s. Edmund Bunting, the collector and transcriber of ancient Irish music, is another example of a Gaelic enthusiast who remained a moderate in politics. The 'Athens of the north', it should be remembered, was a small town of 20,000 inhabitants, led by a close-knit elite, and events such as the Harp Festival should not be exclusively identified with one strand of opinion. Elsewhere, Thuente observes that Francis Dobbs, the author of *The Patriot King; or, Irish Chief* (1773, 1775), was 'a member of the family of United Irishman William Sampson's mother', but omits to mention that he broke with the parliamentary reform movement in 1783. Finally, as she herself notes, the antiquarian William Hamilton became so notorious as a clerical magistrate after 1796 that he was assassinated by republicans.[38] Plainly, there was no simple correlation between the fashion for Gaelic antiquity and radical political commitments.

Moving to a more theoretical level, the boasts made by patriots on behalf of their cultural heritage also deserve closer scrutiny. Throughout the eighteenth century, both Protestant and Catholic intellectuals had appealed to the

---

[35] Mary Helen Thuente, *The Harp Re-Strung: The United Irishmen and the Rise of Irish Literary Nationalism* (New York 1994), pp. 96-7. [36] Ibid., p. 3. [37] Ibid., p. 8. [38] Ibid., pp. 34, 37-8.

remote Gaelic past to promote their political objectives, and it is not surprising to find that in the 1790s bold claims were made for the island of saints and scholars.[39] The preface of the Gaelic magazine, *Bolg an tSolair*, celebrated the Irish language as 'the mother tongue of all the languages in the West', and asserted that 'no nation ever encouraged poets and music more than the ancient Irish'.[40] On 23 October 1793 the *Northern Star* announced that the Belfast Society for Promoting Knowledge, to which many United Irishmen belonged, would 'revive and encourage all communications concerning the antiquities of Ireland' and would publish Edward Bunting's collection as 'new and decisive proof of the existence of a high degree of civilization among our ancestors, at a period when the greatest part of Europe was buried in the deepest barbarity and ignorance'.[41] From these statements it seems that the United Irishmen (among others) were interested less in recovering the *particular* features of the Gaelic past, than in demonstrating that it met *universal* standards of civility, refinement and politeness. What is missing from these declarations is the nineteenth-century argument, so central to Young Ireland propaganda, that Ireland's right to separate nationhood was grounded in cultural difference.

Although, in this area as in others, the 1790s was a period of fluidity and experimentation, the United Irishmen continued to imagine the Irish nation in civic and territorial terms rather than as an ethnic or cultural entity. This distinction bears some resemblance to the contrast between patriotism and nationalism drawn by Maurizio Viroli. The language of patriotism, he maintains, was used 'to strengthen or invoke love of the political institutions and the way of life that sustain the common liberty of a people', whereas the language of nationalism arose in late eighteenth-century Europe 'to defend or reinforce the cultural, linguistic, and ethnic oneness and homogeneity of a people'. Thus patriots defended the nation against tyranny, oppression, and corruption, whilst nationalists were concerned with the threat posed by 'cultural contamination, heterogeneity, racial impurity, and social, political, and intellectual disunion'. This is not to say that patriots had no interest in cultural and linguistic forms or in their ethnic origins, but only that these remained minor themes compared to political liberty and the legal and constitutional forms necessary to preserve it.[42] Whether we describe this distinction, as Viroli does, as one between patri-

---

39 For an excellent general survey see Joep Leerssen, *Mere Irish and Fíor-Ghael: Studies in the Idea of Irish Nationality, its Development and Literary Expression Prior to the Nineteenth Century*, 2nd edn (Cork 1996), pp. 294-376. **40** Thuente, *Harp Re-Strung*, p. 9. **41** Ibid., p. 34. **42** Maurizio Viroli, *For Love of Country: An Essay on Patriotism and Nationalism* (Oxford 1995), esp. pp. 1-2. Cf. John Hutchinson's definition of nationalism as 'a belief that humanity is divided into culturally distinctive communities which should be politically autonomous', in 'Irish Nationalism' in D. George Boyce and Alan O'Day (eds), *The Making of Modern Irish History: Revisionism and the Revisionist Controversy* (London 1996), p. 109.

ots and nationalists, or think in terms of different varieties of nationalism, is in many ways unimportant. Whereas the Young Irelanders imagined the nation *primarily* as an organic entity whose genius had been distilled in its language, their eighteenth-century predecessors imagined the nation *primarily* as a community of laws and institutions.

Behind the demand for 'national government', then, there lay a complex set of political notions. What is clear, is that Irish political discourse in the 1790s gave the Ireland/England polarity a sharper definition than had previously existed. This trend can be seen in the writings of Tone as early as his *Spanish War!* pamphlet (1790), which dared to ask why Ireland should continue to fight Great Britain's battles. Although he repeated the classic view of the Anglo-Irish connection as a dual monarchy, his call for Ireland to assert its 'rank among the primary nations of the earth', like his demand for an independent foreign policy, a navy and a national flag, pointed to outright separatism.[43] It is also present in the *Argument on Behalf of the Catholics*, where Tone wrote that there was 'no one position, moral, physical, or political that I hear with such extreme exacerbation of mind as [that] which denies to my country the possibility of independent existence'.[44] On the basis of the above survey the United Irishmen might be described as republicans and separatists, if only in an ulterior sense; the evidence for categorizing them as nationalists is less clear. On the one hand, as I have stressed, they made no attempt to articulate an explicit doctrine of cultural particularism; on the other, they certainly appealed to feelings of collective belonging – ethnic, confessional, and social – and in the process they constructed an image of England as alien, oppressive, and an historic enemy of Ireland. As we shall see, the sense of conflict between England and Ireland, as distinct from the older antithesis of court and country, would mutate further in the inflammatory propaganda of 1796-8.

III

Nothing emerges more forcefully from the intensive research carried out over the last twenty years than the impressive levels of politicization achieved in Ireland during the 1790s. Older accounts often explained the mass support for the United Irish programme by reference to agrarian grievances and sectarian animosity, while the rebellion itself was viewed as a defensive reaction to the

---

43 [T.W. Tone] *Spanish War! An Enquiry how far Ireland is Bound, of Right, to Embark in the Impending Contest on the Side of Great-Britain?* (Dublin 1790), pp. 31, 42. 44 [Tone], 'Argument on Behalf of the Catholics', p. 291. In this passage Tone hoped that someday 'it will be found that we are as competent to our own government, regulation *and defence*, as any state in Europe'.

brutality of the Orange Order and the forces of the Crown. In sharp contrast, the current generation of '98 scholars have portrayed the rebellion as the culmination of a sophisticated insurrectionary conspiracy based on a widespread awareness of democratic principles. The social roots of the rebellion, it has been argued, stretch back into the 1750s and 1760s, when the beginnings of sustained commercial and agricultural growth laid the foundations for the expansion of the middling sorts in both urban and rural society; at the same time the appearance of the Whiteboys signalled the beginnings of agrarian insurgency among farmers and craftsmen adversely effected by shifts in the new market economy.[45] But if these factors created the social conditions for politicization, it was the unprecedented explosion of print culture, at first in the northern province, and then in Leinster and Munster, that converted discontent into disaffection.[46]

The creation of a mass base for the United Irish conspiracy prompts questions about the social dimensions of republican thought, and the extent to which Irish Jacobinism had moved away from liberal notions of political economy towards a 'proto-socialist' position.[47] Until very recently the majority of historians viewed the United Irishmen as essentially bourgeois revolutionaries – politically radical but socially conservative. Proponents of this view have cited the well-known disclaimer of the Dublin Society of United Irishmen, that '[b]y liberty we never understood unlimited freedom, nor by equality the levelling of property, or the destruction of subordination'.[48] That the United Irishmen were opposed to social revolution was apparently confirmed by William James MacNeven's testimony to the Irish government in the aftermath of the rising. A radical reform, he maintained, would not have produced a redistribution of property, though it would have led to the abolition of tithes and hearth money, lower indirect taxes, the abolition of excise laws, and reform of the legal process. Having examined the views of Emmet, O'Connor, Drennan and Tone, R.B. McDowell was able to conclude that Irish radicals 'accepted the current orthodoxies of political economy'; while they hoped that increased prosperity and lower taxation would bring benefits for the poor they did not

---

45 L.M. Cullen, 'The 1798 rebellion in its eighteenth-century context' in P.J. Corish (ed.), *Radicals, Rebels and Establishments* (Belfast 1985), pp. 91-113. **46** The best discussions are Curtin, *United Irishmen*, chs. 7-8 and Kevin Whelan, 'The republic in the village: The United Irishmen, the Enlightenment and popular culture' in *Tree of Liberty*, pp. 59-96. See also Gillian O'Brien, '"Spirit, impartiality and independence": the *Northern Star*, 1792-1797', *Eighteenth-Century Ireland*, 13 (1998), 7-23. **47** For a balanced review of the evidence on this question, see James Quinn, 'The United Irishmen and Social Reform', *Irish Historical Studies*, 31 (1998), 188-201. **48** 'Address to the Volunteers', 14 September 1792, reprinted in *Society of the United Irishmen of Dublin* [proceedings] (Dublin 1794), p. 46. For later reassurances that reform would not threaten the rights of property see *A Letter on the State of Parties, and on the Subject of Reform, Addressed to the People. By a Friend to Ireland* (Belfast 1796), pp. 7, 12.

envisage significant modification of existing economic relationships.[49] Both Elliott and Curtin, who have located the Irish radicals of the 1790s within the classical republican and Lockeian traditions, have confirmed this judgement.[50]

As scholarly research has come to focus on popular politicization, however, a more complex picture has emerged. In a pioneering article published in 1980, James Donnelly assembled new evidence derived from pamphlets and handbills to show that local United Irish leaders, in an effort to attract recruits, had fuelled expectations that loyalist estates would be confiscated and redistributed. Even if the radicals rejected a systematic redistribution of property, he argued, it was natural that their relentless assault on the landed gentry and the clergy should arouse plebeian expectations of a new agrarian system.[51] The 'social-radical' character of United Irish ideology has been accentuated in Jim Smyth's *Men of No Property*, which counters the moderate views expressed by MacNeven, Emmet and Drennan with the populism of Russell, McCracken, Hope and Coigly. As Smyth observes, the later 1790s produced a small number of radical tracts, including the anonymous *Union Doctrine; or Poor Man's Catechism* [1796?] which echoed the proposals made in part two of Paine's *Rights of Man* for a welfare system financed by a programme of graduated taxation.[52]

A fuller understanding of the social-radical tracts requires a consideration of their intended contribution to popular mobilization. To begin with, it is worth stressing the sheer scale of the propaganda enterprise undertaken by Irish Jacobins in the 1790s. One key weapon was the pamphlet, now published in greater numbers than ever before. Following the appearance of Tone's *Argument on Behalf of the Catholics* (1791), 10,000 copies were quickly struck off in Belfast and distributed throughout the north.[53] Impressive as they were, these figures were eclipsed by Thomas Paine's *Rights of Man*, published in two parts in February 1791 and February 1792. Part One went through seven editions in 1791 and was serialized in three Dublin newspapers and the *Belfast News-Letter*.[54] Prominent United Irishmen such as O'Connor, Russell and Sampson also produced pamphlets, while the Belfast and Dublin societies published their resolutions and addresses. More important still were the radical newspapers, foremost among them the *Northern Star* of Belfast, published twice weekly at the price of two pence. Finally, thousands of handbills were sold for a penny or dis-

---

[49] McDowell, *Irish Public Opinion*, p. 202.   [50] Marianne Elliott, *Partners in Revolution: The United Irishmen and France* (New Haven 1982), pp. 27-8; Curtin, *United Irishmen*, p. 283. A comparison with Smyth, cited below, will reveal that the difference is largely one of emphasis.   [51] J.S. Donnelly, Jr., 'Propagating the cause of the United Irishmen', *Studies*, 69 (1980), 21.   [52] Jim Smyth, *The Men of No Property: Irish Radicals and Popular Politics in the Late Eighteenth Century* (London 1992), p. 167.   [53] Thomas Addis Emmet, 'Part of an essay towards the history of Ireland' in William James MacNeven, *Pieces of Irish History* (New York 1807), p. 16.   [54] Dickson, 'Paine and Ireland', p. 138.

tributed free in bales throughout the countryside. For the first time Irish political writers were addressing the labouring population, often in a colloquial idiom, often resorting to crude, scurrilous satire.[55]

In embarking upon this new propaganda venture, radical publicists were not operating in a vacuum. Their intended audience already possessed a diverse literature, which comprised popular devotional works, catechisms, last dying speeches, chivalric romances, ballads, almanacs, prophecies, historical works such as Ashton's *Battle of Aughrim* and Mitchelburne's *Siege of Londonderry*, and crime stories such as *Irish Rogues and Rapparees* and the *History of Redmond O'Hanlon*. The main supplier of this popular readership in the small towns and countryside, described by J.R.R. Adams as 'literate, but not learned', was the chapman, the itinerant trader who sold cheap items at fairs and markets or simply from door to door.[56] Whilst significant elements of this material, such as the religious and historical works, can be labelled 'Protestant' or 'Catholic', it was for the most part a shared culture.[57] Just as the United Irish system colonized or absorbed pre-existing clubs, Volunteer companies and Masonic lodges, so their polemicists harnessed these conventional forms of popular literature. As we have already seen, the variety of media utilized by the radicals included political songs and ballads which tapped into oral folk traditions; they also employed adaptations or parodies of the creed and the catechism, whose question-and-answer formula was suited to the entrenchment of a core doctrine in a culture which was making the transition to literacy.[58] Like the chapbooks, many radical publications bore the hallmarks of oral literature; they were designed to be read – and reread – aloud.[59] One Presbyterian clergyman claimed that James Porter's *Billy Bluff* (1796) was virtually memorized by the entire peasantry of his district.[60]

The ideological character of this literary outpouring may be described loosely as Paineite. The United Irishmen sought to familiarize their readers with the principle of popular sovereignty, with conceptions of natural and civil rights, universal suffrage and representative government, and with the American and French constitutions – though we can also locate more traditional ideas

---

55 For levels of literacy see Niall Ó Ciosáin, *Print and Popular Culture in Ireland, 1750-1850* (Basingstoke 1997), ch. 2; Graeme Kirkham, 'Literacy in North-West Ulster 1680-1860' in Mary Daly and David Dickson (eds), *The Origins of Popular Literacy in Ireland: Language Change and Educational Development 1700-1920* (Dublin 1990), pp. 73-96. 56 See J.R.R. Adams, *The Printed Word and the Common Man: Popular Culture in Ulster 1700-1900* (Belfast 1987). The quotation is from p. 21. 57 Ibid., p. 6. 58 For mock creeds, see 'Cread' (Rebellion Papers 620/41/112); 'A POLITICAL CREED', appended to [James Porter], *Billy Bluff and Squire Firebrand or, A Sample of the Times, as it Periodically Appeared in the Northern Star* (Belfast 1797). For catechisms see below. 59 On reading aloud, see Ó Ciosáin, *Print and Popular Culture*, pp. 186-191. 60 Henry Montgomery, 'Outlines of the history of Presbyterianism in Ireland', *Irish Unitarian and Bible Christian*, 2 (1847), 331.

from the biblical millenarianism of Presbyterian Covenanters to the Catholic motifs of dispossession and repossession. There are particular difficulties, however, in analyzing this literature, specifically designed for an uneducated audience. 'I never liked kings and Paine has said of them what I always suspected', wrote Mrs McTier; 'truth seems to dart from him in such plain and pregnant terms, that he, or *she* who runs may read'.[61] The sense of empowerment that came from reading Paine was connected to his ability to articulate, with a new directness, conclusions which seemed to have been obvious all along. 'Time and time again', as James Boulton comments, 'Paine makes statements which appear commonplace in a context of political theory; they prove to be revolutionary in their implications.'[62] In attempting to recover the social meaning of such texts we need to consider not just what the United Irishmen were *saying*, but what they hoped to achieve by saying it. In order to mobilize farmers, shopkeepers, artisans, and mechanics behind a democratic political programme, it was first necessary to undermine the ties of deference which had underpinned the social hierarchy.

The nature of this enterprise was plain to alarmed conservatives, whose surviving correspondence abounds with comments on the subversive effects of the new lower-class literature. Dublin Castle was informed that the handbills disseminated by the United Irishmen in 'every village, fair, and market' were 'studiously framed so as to operate on vulgar minds through the medium of their ruling passions'; that they were designed to teach the people that they were 'the most wretched, abused, oppressed people under the canopy of heaven' and that all their miseries could be attributed to one political cause, 'the radically bad government under which they lived'.[63] Around the time of the Dungannon Convention of 1793, the liberal Ulster MP George Knox reported that the north was 'completely innoculated by Paine who persuades every man to think himself a legislator and to throw off all respect for his superiors'.[64] What emerges again and again from loyalist sources is the connection between the novel doctrines of the Irish Jacobins and the social composition of their readership. Thomas Addis Emmet described the same process of literary enfranchisement rather more positively, when he spoke of the United Irish method of 'making every man a politician'.[65] Their task, in other words, was to fashion an accessible, democratic language of politics which would enable the common people to become citizens in what Mark Philp has called a 'republic of political discourse'.[66]

---

[61] McTier to Drennan, 28 Oct. 1792 (PRONI Drennan Papers, T.765/345). [62] James T. Boulton, *The Language of Politics in the Age of Wilkes and Burke* (London 1963), p. 136. [63] Quoted in Donnelly, 'Propagating the cause', 9. [64] George Knox to the duke of Abercorn, 14 Feb. 1793 (PRONI Abercorn Papers, T.2541/1131/4/12). [65] Emmet, 'Part of an essay towards the history of Ireland', p. 77. [66] Mark Philp, *Paine* (Oxford 1989), p. 115.

Perhaps the most immediately striking feature of the republican onslaught on the old order is the new virulence with which the authority of kings, aristocrats and priests was assailed. In calling into question established social structures, popular writers such as the Revd James Porter, author of the satirical classic *Billy Bluff* and several of the songs in *Paddy's Resource*, deployed the weapons of ridicule and transgression to devastating effect. A more primitive example of this festive idiom can be found in 'The Children's Catechism', a handbill printed at Belfast in 1794 and circulated among 'the common people' for the purpose, according to one moderate reformer, of 'bringing regal government into contempt'.[67] George III, casually described as 'a German *Bastard*', was indeed one target, as the pugnacious author revealed the absurdity of 'ten millions of people setting up *one*, perhaps the meanest, of themselves to govern them', and scorned the language of servility generated by royal government. But this carnivalesque critique of government also extended to parliament, defined as a 'collection of animals – some to play cards, some to loll and sleep' who devised 'schemes of taxation to reduce the poor man's daily pay' in order to prosecute their destructive war against the innocent French.[68] Especially prominent among United Irish targets were magistrates and clergymen of the established church.[69] These two offices, often combined in a single person, embodied state authority at the parochial level, both in a practical sense, as the representatives of civil and ecclesiastical authority in the localities, and in a symbolic sense, as the chief actors in the ritualistic expression of paternalism and deference. A recurrent trope in Paineite literature focused on the conjuror's tricks involved in magisterial and clerical imposture, the absurd dress, ridiculous titles and cheap theatre which could no longer fool labouring men who had learned to think for themselves.

In their efforts to marshal the artisan and middling classes in support of reform and the French cause, it was not sufficient to stimulate contempt for social and political authority; the United Irishmen had also to convince their adherents that social and economic distress could be attributed to the monopolization of political power by the landed elite and by their own lack of representation. To this end the old analysis of court corruption was broadened out to encompass plebeian grievances. One example is the handbill signed 'Common Sense', written by John Keogh, the leader of the Catholic Committee, and addressed to the Presbyterians of the northern province.[70] His simple message was that economic difficulties were the products of excessive taxation,

---

67 'The Children's Catechism' [Belfast 1794]. A copy of this handbill is preserved in the Joy Papers in the Linenhall Library, Belfast. **68** See also Thomas Russell, *A Letter to the People of Ireland, on the Present Situation of the Country* (Belfast 1796), pp. 15-16. **69** For examples see Curtin, *United Irishmen*, ch. 7. **70** [John Keogh], 'Common Sense', handbill dated Sept. 1792. There is a copy in PRO(L) H.O. 100/38/5.

exacted to support the ruinous and unjust wars by which dynastic states preserved their wealth and power: 'You are taxed to pay placemen, taxed for German generals, taxed for prostitutes, taxed by tithes, taxed to bribe those who restrict your commerce and manufactures, even taxed to bribe the very men who vote away your money in taxes.' And to bring the message home to his audience, the Dissenters of the Ulster borderlands, Keogh launched a personal attack on the Beresfords, a prominent Ascendancy family: 'observe one of them at the head of the revenue, his son council to the Commissioners, another Taster of Wines, his daughter married to the head of the treasury, his noble relation by adoption and connection at the head of the law, his brother a bishop in the high road to the primacy, the head of the church'. Ireland was being governed by a junta, whose dependants filled the revenue, the law, the army, and the church, and the whole rotten structure fed on the industry of the common people.

The vision which these handbills sought to create was of a world turned upside down, where the lazy robbed the industrious, the clergy twisted a religion of love and charity into a vehicle for military aggression, where the defence of the country was taken out of the hands of the brave Volunteers and entrusted to foreign oppressors, where virtuous reformers were imprisoned and transported while magistrates connived at the violent expulsion of Catholics from County Armagh. The cure for all of these ills was reform, which would end grievous taxes and unjust tithes, and allow commerce and manufactures to flourish. To achieve this goal, however, Irishmen must unite. Thus 'Common Sense' pointed out that those who fomented divisions between Presbyterians and Catholics were 'the very men and their dependants who thus fleece both, tax them and tithe them, and wish to set them by the ears, that they may continue their depredations'. Similarly 'One of the People', the author of a handbill distributed through Armagh, Down and Louth in 1794, urged his readers to 'let the Presbyterian embrace the Catholic with cordiality; let religious distinctions no longer exist; as we all acknowledge one God and common father let us live together like children of the same family'.[71]

In assessing the social radicalism of the United Irishmen the question of whether or not their ideas can be categorized as proto-socialist is perhaps beside the point. In an age when the vocabulary of social categorization was in flux, the older terms, 'ranks' and 'orders', were giving way to a concern with occupation and income levels as opposed to inherited status.[72] Radical writers opted for a binary vision of society which directed collective grievances against the landed elite. Thus Paine found 'two distinct classes of men in the nation, those

---

[71] A copy of this handbill, printed at Newry in 1794, can be found in the Joy Papers, Linenhall Library, Belfast.   [72] P.J. Corfield, 'Class by name and number in eighteenth-century Britain', *History*, 72 (1987), 38–61.

who pay taxes, and those who receive and live upon the taxes', while Thomas Spence denounced the 'grand, voluptuous nobility and gentry' who lived on the wealth generated by 'the toil of the labouring classes'.[73] This polarity of rich and poor was echoed by some Irish radicals, including Thomas Russell, who explained that 'the rich men (those whose wealth arises from commerce excepted) derive their wealth from the labours of the poor'.[74] With very few exceptions, radicals attributed social and economic problems to deficiencies in the political system rather than an unequal distribution of wealth. As 'The Children's Catechism' put it, the vast parasitic network of patronage, the system of 'slavery, priestcraft, kingcraft, and aristocracy', had to be destroyed before Irishmen, could 'enjoy the blessings of God in an earthly Paradise'. And yet Smyth's broader criticism, that historians have often exaggerated the social conservatism of the United Irish movement, is a persuasive one. The notable feature about Irish radicalism in the 1790s is not that it echoed the older Walpoleian opposition but that it was enlarged to accommodate plebeian aspirations.[75]

IV

To conclude this discussion, I would like to turn briefly to the law-and-order debate which intensified after Hoche's failed expedition to Ireland at the close of 1796. During the next two years, the regular forces stationed in Ireland were reinforced, the yeomanry was raised, the powers of the magistracy were increased, radicals were arrested, imprisoned and disarmed, and parts of the country were placed under effective military rule. Among the radical responses was James Porter's *Wind and Weather* (1797), a bizarre send-up of the jeremiad sermons preached on national days of thanksgiving, which sought to reassure the disaffected that the French would come again.[76] More audacious still was William Sampson's *Advice to the Rich* (1796), which advised the 'men of property' to study the examples of 'American loyalists, French émigrées, or the Stadholderian refugees'.[77] Turning the alarmist reaction of the magistrates on its head, Sampson sought to win over the undecided by establishing the scale of

---

73 Ibid., p. 53. **74** Thomas Russell, *A Letter to the People of Ireland, on the Present Situation of the Country* (Belfast 1796), p. 17. **75** In this respect the United Irishmen look forward to the English radicalism of the post-1815 period. See Gareth Stedman Jones, 'Rethinking Chartism' in idem, *Languages of Class: Studies in English Working Class History 1832-1982* (Cambridge 1983), pp. 90-178. **76** James Porter, *Wind and Weather. A Sermon on the Late Providential Storm which Dispersed the French Fleet off Bantry Bay. Preached to the Congregation of Gray-Abbey, on Thursday the 16th February, being the Fast Day Appointed by Government for Thanksgiving* (Belfast 1797). **77** [William Sampson], *Advice to the Rich: in a series of Letters, Originally Published in the Northern Star* (Belfast 1796), pp. 9, 20.

discontent and persuading them that their future lay with the radical movement. How could property be secure when nine-tenths of the people, both soldier and citizen, were believed to be 'traitors' by the government? Was it really wise, he asked, to arrest and imprison those bold reformers who alone could control the revolution when 'the dreaded tumult arises, and the popular thunder rolls'?[78] What future was there for an Irish landed class which was both despised and distrusted by the English and hated by their own people?[79] In a rather unconvincing effort to calm fears of social upheaval, Sampson promised that the revolution would not lead to an equalization of property and that those clergy who did not prove 'enemies to their country' would receive compensation for the disestablishment of the church.[80]

Scattered throughout Sampson's tract were graphic references to the imprisoned, the transported, the hanged, and the poor exiles of Armagh. The theme of state coercion was also the focal point of one of the best known tracts of the later 1790s, *The Appeal of the People of Ulster to their Countrymen* (1797).[81] Published in both the *Northern Star* and the *Press*, the *Appeal* was also printed separately in Belfast and distributed as far afield as Kilkenny, Dublin, Wexford and Wicklow. It presented a grim picture of Ulster under martial law, no doubt intended as a warning for the people of the south: 'Our best citizens are entombed in Bastilles, or hurried on board tenders, our wives and our children are become the daily victims of an unconstrained and licentious foreign soldiery'.[82] In response to accusations that the United Irishmen had instituted a system of terror, the author admitted that a few assassinations had taken place, but explained that the people had been provoked by 'a system of premeditated persecution', and that in any case the victims had been notorious magistrates.[83] Moreover, it was argued, the fine words of the law-and-order party had to be set beside the reality of the Armagh outrages, where magistrates had turned a blind eye to Orange brutality.[84] The images of sons watching as their fathers were torn from their families and illegally imprisoned, and pregnant women dragged from their beds and thrown into the street to watch their houses burned, were typical of the florid rhetoric which formed the staple diet of the inflammatory *Press*.

It is in this context that we should return to the literary invocations of the Irish past considered by Thuente. Although, as I have argued, Thuente has exaggerated the ideological continuities between United Irish literature and the romanticism of the Young Ireland movement, it is undeniable that 'the lurid

---

[78] Ibid., p. 8, 28. [79] Ibid., p. 17. [80] Ibid., p. 25. [81] *The Appeal of the People of Ulster to their Countrymen, and to the Empire at Large* [Belfast, April 14, 1797], also published in *Northern Star*, 14 April 1797, the *Press*, 13 March 1798, and in *Truth Unmasked: or, Food for the Liberty* ([Dublin? 1797]), pp. 3-9. For the geographical distribution see Smyth, *Men of No Property*, p. 161. [82] *Appeal of the People of Ulster*, p. 1. [83] Ibid., p. 1 [84] Ibid., p. 2

and sentimental mode' that characterized Arthur O'Connor's *Press* anticipated the rhetoric of nineteenth-century nationalism.[85] Given the military situation in the north, there was perhaps little surprise in the motifs of martyrdom and resurrection which figure in William Drennan's 'The Wake of William Orr', one of many elegies written after the execution of a popular United Irishman. What is surprising, however, is the identification of Orr's death with 'Warfare of six hundred years!/ Epochs mark'd by blood and tears' – a reference to internal dissensions to be sure, but one with an implicit anti-English edge.[86] Thomas Russell's 'The Fatal Battle of Aughrim', an imitation of Smollett's famous 1746 poem 'The Tears of Scotland', mourned the loss of Ireland's freedom in 1691 and the 'warriors sunk on Aughrim's plains'.[87] Of course, the heroic warriors recruited from Ireland's past were valued as defenders of their *patria* rather than their faith. Moreover, not all United Irishmen were comfortable with literary Jacobitism, as Robert Simms made clear when he informed Russell that the restoration of James II would have set back the cause of liberty by a century.[88] Nevertheless, some Protestant radicals had momentarily identified with the struggles of an older Irish nation, a nation that was *de facto* Catholic, and in doing so they facilitated the attempts of later generations of nationalists to assimilate the 1798 rebellion to an unbroken tradition of resistance to British rule.

V

While Curtin, Whelan and others have explored the mechanisms of mass politicization, which underpinned the rebellion of 1798, one glaring problem still remains: what happened to the ideology of radical populism after the United Irish defeat? During the early decades of the nineteenth century, Irish politics apparently slumped back into the orthodox patterns of landlord influence, agrarian unrest and a Catholic crusade which, if radical in its methods, was deliberately constitutionalist in its objectives. An attenuated Presbyterian populism survived in the north-east, as evidenced by the sporadic reprinting of *Billy Bluff*, though opposition to Anglican landlordism was now carefully differentiated from national separatism.[89] It is tempting to suggest that a reverse trend

---

85 Thuente, *Harp Re-Strung*, p. 115. **86** Drennan, 'The Wake of William Orr' in the *Press*, 13 Jan. 1798, reprinted in Thuente, *Harp Re-Strung*, pp. 241-2. Cf. Drennan to McTier, 29 Sept. 1797, in Chart (ed.), *Drennan Letters*, p. 262: 'It is six hundred years in our annals of slaughter/ Since the robbers of England came over yon water'. The *Press* for 23 Nov. 1797 contained another elegy on Orr by William Hamilton Drummond. **87** Thuente, *Harp Re-Strung*, pp. 119-20. **88** Robert Simms to [Thomas] Russell, 10 Aug. 1797 (TCD Sirr Papers, 868/2, f. 309v). **89** A Belfast edition published in 1840 claimed to be the thirteenth; further Belfast editions appeared in 1868 and 1879. For the context see Ian McBride, 'Memory and

occurred in the south, as communal insurgency shed the vestiges of Paineite ideology. Memories of '98 seem to have resurfaced during outbursts of agrarian unrest, but their precise form will remain unclear until an up-to-date study is made of the Ribbonmen and other underground networks. What knowledge we have suggests that United Irish iconography, passed on in abridged editions of *Paddy's Resource*, was now subsumed within the specifically Catholic ideology of dispossession and repossession.[90]

One by-product of United Irish proselytizing was the stimulation of conservative attempts to reach a mass audience. The preoccupation of magistrates with book clubs and the public reading of newspapers continued into the early nineteenth century as a series of government inquiries reported on the causes of popular disturbance, culminating in the recommendation that a national system of education be established. At the same time the three main churches, likewise preoccupied with the perceived problem of social order, became interested in the extension and regulation of popular literacy. A year after the rebellion, the Anglican minister and former United Irishman Whitley Stokes called for the replacement of chapbooks with self-help literature and the dissemination of the scriptures in the Irish language.[91] Strikingly, he suggested that efforts to restore social harmony would only succeed if the authorities adopted the tactics of the United Irishmen by promising to better the condition of the poor.[92] The mass-scale distribution of bibles and religious tracts was already underway, as a host of voluntary associations, beginning with the Association for Discountenancing Vice, sprang up. Often such moralistic works were aimed explicitly at the lower classes, written in plain language, and published in chapbook form. Ironically, then, one manifestation of the United Irishmen's legacy was provided by the Irish Society for Promoting the Education of the Native Irish (1818) and its many competitors.[93]

The resumption of sectarian postures under the pressure of the Second Reformation brings us back to the basic task of measuring change against continuity. Over the last ten years opinion on this question has shifted markedly. In the 1970s and 1980s, historians like Tom Dunne suggested that the ideals of the French Revolution were assimilated to traditional cultural and religious orientations, such as the Jacobite hope of foreign deliverance from an alien, Protestant usurper. 'At most', he concluded, radicalism 'added a new layer of rhetoric and explanation to the long-established concerns of Ireland's colonial culture.'[94] In contrast, a number of bicentenary publications have emphasized

---

forgetting: Ulster Presbyterians and 1798' in Thomas Bartlett, Dáire Keogh and Kevin Whelan (eds), *The 1798 Rebellion* (Dublin forthcoming). **90** For later editions of *Paddy's Resource* see Thuente, *Harp Re-Strung*, p. 234. **91** Whitley Stokes, *Projects for Re-Establishing the Internal Peace and Tranquillity of Ireland* (Dublin 1799), pp. 41–3. **92** Ibid., p. 49. **93** Ó Ciosáin, *Print and Popular Culture*, esp. ch. 11. **94** Dunne, 'Popular ballads, revolutionary

the transformative impact of Jacobin ideology, and instructed us to accent 'the forward-looking, democratic dimension' of United Irish thinking.[95] In part, the rise of a 'post-revisionist' interpretation can be explained by the more extensive exploration of source material, as historians have moved away from the moderate statements of reformist intellectuals such as Emmet and MacNeven towards the ephemeral propaganda of the handbill. In part, the difference is a theoretical one: whereas Dunne sought to correct the anachronism of a crude nationalist approach, the post-revisionists, influenced by literary models of colonialism, have endeavoured to restore to centre-stage the theme of resistance to British rule.

In this essay I have focused on two of the more 'forward-looking' aspects of republican thought, whilst trying not to lose sight of the many tensions – cosmopolitan/historical, secular/sectarian, civic/ethnic – within it. In both their cultural and social outlook, United Irish polemicists moved beyond the real Whig framework of the Volunteer movement, but we should resist the temptation to proclaim them as romantic nationalists or as socialists *avant la lettre*. A romantic *rhetoric*, anticipating blood-and-soil constructions of Irishness, certainly co-existed with an enlightenment *ideology* focused on citizenship. For the United Irishmen, however, the rhetoric of nationalism was always subordinated to the pursuit of their republican goals; in this respect they differ from subsequent separatists, for whom the republic supplied the means for the goal of national liberation. In their populism, too, the radicals of the 1790s occupy an awkward, transitional position; here we find an incipient economic liberalism, complicated but never directly confronted by a barrage of proposals for altering the existing system of property relations. It is instructive to note that while Arthur O'Connor's *Press* has provided some of the best evidence for both Thuente's literary nationalism and Smyth's social-radicalism, neither feature in his *The State of Ireland* (1798), the one attempt to define Irish Jacobinism at a theoretical level.[96]

One way forward, perhaps, is for a more sensitive exploration of the ways in which printed material was appropriated or reworked as it entered a popular culture which was only partially literate and partially English-speaking. Recent work by Niall Ó Ciosáin explores the ways in which English-language texts were read as they passed into a predominantly oral culture which transmitted its own understanding of history through the medium of Irish.[97] Magistrates, whose

politicisation', p. 141. **95** Kevin Whelan, 'Reinterpreting the 1798 rebellion in County Wexford' in Dáire Keogh and Nicholas Furlong (eds), *The Mighty Wave: The 1798 Rebellion in Wexford* (Dublin 1996), p. 34. **96** Arthur O'Connor, *The State of Ireland*, ed. James Livesey (Dublin 1998). **97** Ó Ciosáin, *Print and Popular Culture*; see also Tom Dunne, 'Subaltern voices? Poetry in Irish, popular insurgency and the 1798 rebellion', *Eighteenth-Century Life*,

comments naturally reflected the assumptions of the governing classes, insisted that the lower orders were not interested in reform and emancipation, but in the abolition of tithes and the reduction of rents. Another common perception was expressed by the solicitor general, John Toler, when he reported from Tyrone that the people interpreted the United Irish programme to mean that 'they are to have the country to themselves'.[98] How were hints about the redistribution of land received in Catholic Ireland, where the survival of an 'underground gentry' served as a reminder of the seventeenth-century confiscations? How was the anti-clericalism of Tom Paine received in Presbyterian Ulster, where theological objections to the alliance of church and state were deep-seated?[99] In recovering the meaning of texts, particularly texts designed for mass consumption, the way in which they are read is also important.

In the meantime, we should not be surprised that the republicanism of the United Irishmen continues to give rise to conflicting interpretations. This was a period when political conflict intensified rapidly, against the background of the war with revolutionary France. From the anti-militia riots of 1793, known in Wexford as the first rebellion,[100] the strains imposed by the international struggle injected an unprecedented level of violence into Irish society. Its dynamic, improvised character makes the ideological experimentation of the 1790s a moving target. As Irish politics polarized, the radical creed incorporated new themes; it was broadened out to encompass new sources of discontent; and its emphasis and imagery shifted. While older oppositional paradigms were still present, republican discourse was pulled in new directions by revolutionary and universalist sentiments. We should resist the urge to impose a coherent pattern on this eclectic amalgam, and attempt instead to explore the practical context which led Irish writers to employ so many different, and sometimes conflicting, arguments. In this era of revolution, war and crisis, it was hardly surprising that Irish Jacobins seldom felt compelled to think through the inconsistencies and ambiguities in their position.

22 (Nov. 1998), 31-44. **98** Quoted in Quinn, 'United Irishmen and social reform', 194. **99** See I.R. McBride, *Scripture Politics: Ulster Presbyterians and Irish Radicalism in the Late Eighteenth Century* (Oxford 1998). **100** L.M. Cullen, 'The 1798 rebellion in Wexford: United Irishman organisation, membership, leadership' in Kevin Whelan and William Nolan (eds), *Wexford: History and Society* (Dublin 1987), p. 253.

Conservative Protestant political thought in late eighteenth-century Ireland

JAMES KELLY

I

The *raison d'être* of conservative Protestant political thought in late eighteenth-century Ireland was to provide the 'Protestant interest' with an ideological rationale to enable it to justify its dominant position in the Irish constitution. Since mainstream Protestant thinking during most of the eighteenth century aspired to the same end, though significantly it used different language to articulate it, it has frequently been implied that Irish Protestantism was ideologically static following the consolidation by the Protestant interest of its command of the political, economic and social structures of Ireland in the decades after 1690. As a consequence, both mainstream Protestantism and the ideological conservatism that emerged in the late eighteenth century have been neglected compared with the politically more marginal, but more restless, ideologies of Protestant patriotism and republicanism that sought to reconstitute political structures along more identifiably modern lines. This is in the process of being redressed, and recent explorations of Protestant commemorative practices, 'the making of Protestant Ireland', 'court ideology', and the origins of 'Protestant ascendancy' have illuminated a number of key aspects of Protestant identity.[1] Significantly, this work has shown that the tendency to portray mainstream Protestantism as procrustean or immutable is unsustainable. Quite the contrary; it presents an identity which, within the parameters of its largely conservative defining principles, continued to adapt to changing circumstances. Indicatively, the realization that state-sponsored and popular Williamite commemorative practices had become stale by the 1720s prompted the animation of the popular celebration of William of Orange's memory and the inaugura-

---

1 T.C. Barnard, 'The uses of 23 October 1641 and Irish Protestant celebrations', *English Historical Review*, 106 (1991), 889-920; Robert Eccleshall, 'Anglican political thought in the century after the revolution of 1688' in D.G. Boyce et al. (eds), *Political Thought in Ireland since the Seventeenth Century* (London 1993); James Kelly, '"The glorious and immortal memory": commemoration and Protestant identity 1660-1800', *Proceeedings of the Royal Irish Academy*, sect. C, 89 (1994), 25-52; J.G. McCoy, 'Court Ideology in Mid-Eighteenth-Century Ireland' (unpublished M.A. thesis, St Patrick's College, Maynooth, 1990); S.J. Connolly, *Religion, Law and Power: The Making of Protestant Ireland 1660-1760* (Oxford 1992);

tion of a raft of new commemorative occasions in the 1730s and 1740s.[2] Commemorative patterns underwent further change in the late eighteenth century, but the primary generator of new thinking then was the opposition to Catholic relief because the granting of civil and political rights to Catholics posed a direct threat to the constitution many Irish Protestants were committed to uphold.

Though recent work indicates that the threat posed by the appeal of Jacobitism to the Catholic population should not be under-estimated, the Protestant political establishment in Ireland operated free from serious ideological challenge between the 1690s and the mid-point of the eighteenth century, when the question of repealing the disabilities imposed upon Catholics began to be agitated. Even then, and for the best part of another quarter century, the prevailing consensus within Protestantism on the inadvisability of relieving Catholics ensured the rejection of all substantive proposals for Catholic relief on the grounds that Protestants could not relax their vigilance against such a restless and unforgiving enemy. This message lost much of its appeal in the reformist atmosphere of the late 1770s, when toleration became the watchword of the moment. However, support for a purely Protestant constitution remained strong, and once the legislative focus shifted from toleration to empowerment, those of a more conservative viewpoint not only regained the initiative within the Irish Protestant community, they reinforced their ideological message through the incubation of a political lexicon that reflected their determination to protect their privileged position. This process, which began in the mid-1780s, when the Church of Ireland was seen to be under attack, was expanded and advanced in the revolutionary environment of the 1790s when what has been termed 'neo-conservatism' became the most powerful tendency within Irish Protestantism.

Like their equivalents elsewhere, Irish Protestant opponents of political and constitutional change seemed engaged for much of the 1790s in a rearguard action to defend those values they esteemed against the alliance of Catholic and Protestant radicals that sought to recast the structure of their polity. Matters went badly for them at the outset as the British government insisted, against their advice, that Catholics should be enfranchised, but they were enabled subsequently to offer stouter resistance and, consequently, to

---

W.J. McCormack, *Ascendancy and Tradition in Anglo-Irish Literary History from 1789 to 1939* (Oxford 1985); Jacqueline Hill, 'The meaning and significance of "Protestant ascendancy"' in Lord Blake (ed.), *Ireland after the Union* (Oxford 1989); James Kelly, 'The genesis of Protestant ascendancy' in G. O'Brien (ed.), *Parliament, Politics and People* (Dublin 1989), pp. 93-127. **2** Kelly, 'The glorious and immortal memory', 37-42; idem, 'The emergence of political parading 1660-1800' in T.G. Fraser (ed.), *We'll Follow the Drum: The Irish Parading Tradition* (London forthcoming).

grow in number and influence as the fears generated by politically motivated disorder, social unrest and revolutionary intrigue at home and abroad brought many erstwhile liberals round to their way of thinking. Given this context, it was hardly surprising that the greatest crisis Irish Protestantism experienced in the whole of the eighteenth century – the 1798 rebellion – provided the occasion for a powerful re-statement of the threat Catholicism posed to the lives and liberties of Protestants and the necessity of preserving the Protestant constitution intact that resonated with conservatives in Britain as well as Ireland. This is highly significant because it served to give contemporary British conservatism, which had lacked ideological vitality since the demise of 'old Toryism' and the embrace by the British establishment of an increasingly tolerant attitude to Catholicism, direction and focus.[3] It also makes the explication of the history of conservative Protestant thought in Ireland more than ordinarily interesting because as well as illuminating the response of Irish Protestants to the repeal of the penal laws, it reveals the shared origins of British as well as Irish nineteenth-century Protestant conservatism.

In common with their British counterparts, opponents of constitutional, political and religious change in Ireland did not come to possess a distinctive nomenclature until the rhetoric of the ideology they developed was in place. It might be observed that because their objective was to preserve the constitutional status quo this was not a matter of major consequence. However, Irish Protestant conservatives did coin a term that defined the condition they sought to secure and that provided them with both a rallying cry and a name around which they could gather. This was 'Protestant ascendancy'. Use of this term in this essay will be confined to the ideological context out of which it derived, though it has long been used by historians and literary scholars in a broader and wider sense. The more semantically neutral term 'conservative' will be employed when describing and discussing the Protestant opponents of constitutional change that are its subject.

II

By the mid-eighteenth century Irish Protestants no longer felt obliged to pursue the security of the 'Protestant interest' with the intensity they had displayed in successive parliaments from 1695. However, they were as determined as ever to protect and perpetuate their political and religious liberties. A cursory examination of such seminal statements of Protestant opinion as William Molyneux's *The Case of Ireland being Bound by Acts of Parliament in England, Stated* (1698)

3 James Sack, *From Jacobite to Conservative: Reaction and Orthodoxy in Britain c.1760-1832* (Cambridge 1992), passim.

might suggest that Protestants were wont to appeal to the idea of an 'ancient constitution', specifically to the inauguration of parliamentary government by Henry II, in support of their defence of their rights, but in practice their constitutional horizon was dominated by the Glorious Revolution of 1688.

The deposing of James II remained an event of abiding consequence in the political thinking of Irish Protestants because, as well as liberating them from the experience of Catholic rule, it inaugurated a constitutional monarchy in which commoners participated with the monarchy and aristocracy in making law and in the practice of government. This was a deeply valued privilege because the normative practice elsewhere in Europe tended towards absolutism. Moreover, as Reed Browning and H.T. Dickinson have shown for England, and Gerard McCoy for Ireland, their acknowledgement of the importance of 1688 in securing these liberties appreciated from the 1730s with the elaboration of the argument that the 'modern constitution' established by the Glorious Revolution was 'infinitely better' than 'the ancient constitution' because it offered them 'real liberty'.[4] Influenced by this, Irish Protestants replicated their English counterparts and gloried in their 'balanced constitution' because, as Sir Richard Cox observed in 1748, it assured them 'liberty in its largest and clearest character'.[5] Some patriots and commonwealthmen argued logically that their liberties would be fuller if the commercial and constitutional restrictions imposed by the Westminster parliament were repealed, but mainstream opinion was little agitated by such concerns. Indeed, it resented the attempt by patriots to appropriate the moral imperative inherent in that appellation because those involved interpreted their own actions and behaviour as no less principled.[6] They were equally disapproving of the manoeuvres of the various undertakers and faction leaders who populated the mid-eighteenth-century political landscape, and who, by their self-interested actions, threatened the maintenance of political harmony in domestic politics and in Anglo-Irish relations.[7] At the same time, because factionalism, like patriotism, operated within the existing Protestant constitution and accepted its core principles, it did not pose a threat to the Protestant constitution and, therefore, it did not demand or elicit a specific ideological response.

The same could not be said, of course, of calls to enhance the social, religious, economic and political rights of Catholics because this appertained

---

[4] H.T. Dickinson, *Liberty and Property: Political Ideology in Eighteenth-Century Britain* (London 1977); Reed Browning, *Political and Constitutional Ideas of the Court Whigs* (London 1982), p. 54; McCoy, 'Court Ideology', pp. 35-6. [5] Richard Cox, *A Charge Delivered to the Grand Jury ... of Cork on Twelfth of July 1748* (Dublin 1748), p. 8; McCoy, 'Court Ideology', pp. 29-34 passim; Browning, *Court Whigs*, p. 160. [6] James Kelly, *Henry Flood: Patriots and Politics in Eighteenth-Century Ireland* (Dublin 1998), pp. 68-9. [7] See, generally, R.E. Burns, *Irish Parliamentary Politics in the Eighteenth Century* (Washington 1989-90).

directly to the 'Protestantism' of the Irish constitution. The concern of Irish Protestants on this point derived in part from the fact that the Protestant population was, as Archbishop Synge observed (albeit with reference to the dioceses of Tuam and Ardagh) in 1745, 'but a handful in comparison of the Papists that surround them'. But of weightier and more consequential import was their perception, informed by their understanding of Catholic doctrine and history, that Catholicism posed a threat to their lives as well as to their liberties.[8] Doctrinally, this conviction derived from the belief that 'Popery', as Roman Catholicism was routinely labelled, was not just a religion. Rather it was, one concerned commentator observed in 1749, 'a complicated system, mixed up with many doctrines of a political nature, that are dangerous to civil governments and societies'. By extension, because the Catholic church

> avows the lawfulness of breaking faith and the solemnest oaths made to Protestant princes and makes a merit of dethroning them and murdering their innocent subjects, it becomes all Protestants to look about them and to guard their lives and fortunes against a body of such insidious enemies, till they shall publicly disavow principles and tenets so dangerous to all civil societies.[9]

The author of this caution was not optimistic this would ever occur. For this reason, he concluded with John Whitcombe, the bishop of Clonfert, that because 'Popery and tyranny are inseparable' and because Catholics would, if given the opportunity, institute a 'court of inquisition ... for extirpating the Protestant religion', Irish Protestants had no alternative but to introduce 'penal laws ... against them ... for the defence of the government against their dangerous principles and practices'.[10]

Since these sentiments were expressed at the height of a Jacobite invasion scare, one might surmise that they were sectional and not representative, but this is not so. The opinion voiced by Archbishop Synge as to the seditious intentions of 'Romish priests' was shared across the Protestant community at the mid-point of the eighteenth century. Even the benign Bishop Berkeley recommended that Catholics should be required to take an oath denying the pope's power to depose Protestant princes in order to bind them to the state.[11] Catholics and Protestants differed so passionately on their interpretation of

---

8 Archbishop of Tuam to clergy of dioceses of Tuam and Ardagh, in *Faulkner's Dublin Journal*, 15 Oct. 1745. **9** *The Axe Laid to the Root or Reasons Humbly Offered for Putting the Popish Clergy under Some Better Regulation* (Dublin 1749), p. 22. **10** Ibid.; Bishop of Clonfert to clergy of his diocese in *Faulkner's Dublin Journal*, 12 Oct. 1745. **11** *The Axe Laid to the Root*, p. 14; McCoy, 'Court Ideology', p. 66; Patrick Kelly, 'Berkeley and Ireland', *Etudes Irlandaises*, 11 (1986), 20.

Christianity, and in the ideological and political implications of their beliefs that most Protestants found it impossible to conceive of Roman Catholicism as just a rival religion whose adherents could be won over to righteousness by conversion. It was a religion, of course. But it was also a dangerous and seditious belief system that would, if allowed to operate free of restriction, endeavour to ensure the eradication of Protestant liberties, the Protestant religion and Protestant lives.[12]

These fears were reinforced by the belief, widely promulgated, that each Catholic bishop swore on his consecration 'to persecute heretics, schismatics and rebels to the pope, to the utmost of his power'.[13] They received greater ideological reinforcement, however, from the conclusion that throughout history Catholics had routinely sought to effect the extirpation of heresy through massacre. The Revd Edward Young articulated this perception vividly in 1763 when he maintained that in 'the annals of every age, since the first establishment of papal usurpation, the records of every country where it has gained firm footing, are stained with the bloody marks of its tyranny'.[14] The event that predisposed Protestants to dwell on this in the Irish context was the 1641 rebellion when, according to modern estimates, 3-4,000 Protestants fell victim to Catholic assailants. As far as eighteenth-century Irish Protestants were concerned the number of fatalities was dramatically higher, and they asserted this belief annually by holding commemorative services during which an account was read attributing the 'many thousands' of Protestant casualties to the malice of 'malignant and rebellious Papists and ... Popish clergy'.[15] This partial as well as partisan interpretation was largely shaped by Sir John Temple's seminal *History of the Irish Rebellion*, which informed generations of preachers whose annual 23 October sermons offer critical insight into what Robert Eccleshall has termed 'Anglican political thought'.[16] Indeed, it was on one such occasion that Robert Young articulated his analysis of the 'bloody' intentions of Catholics cited above. Similarly apocalyptic sentiments linking events in Ireland in 1641 with the duke of Alba's 'Council of Blood' (1567-73), the St Bartholomew's day massacre (1572), the gunpowder plot (1605) and the expulsion from Spain of the Moriscoes (1609) were advanced by others on comparable occasions.[17]

---

12 McCoy, 'Court Ideology', pp. 62-72. **13** Benjamin Bacon, *A Sermon Preach'd at St Andrew's, Dublin before the Honourable House of Commons, on Sunday 23 October 1743* (Dublin 1743), p. 2, cited in McCoy, 'Court Ideology', p. 58. **14** Edward Young, *A Sermon Preached in Christ-Church, Dublin, on Sunday October 23, 1763* (Dublin 1763), p. 5, cited in McCoy, 'Court Ideology', p. 52. **15** See Kelly, 'The glorious and immortal memory', 27 and passim; Barnard, 'The uses of 23 October 1641'. **16** The most penetrating analyses of 23 October sermons are provided by Barnard, 'The uses of 23 October' and Eccleshall, 'Anglican political thought'. **17** Kelly, 'The glorious and immortal memory'; McCoy, 'Court Ideology', pp. 50-2.

The reiteration of this point and the publication of the sermons in which it was made ensured that eighteenth-century Irish Protestants did not allow the 1641 rising to pass into history. Any prospect of this happening was diminished further by the integration into this chronicle of Catholic vengefulness of current instances of persecution such as occurred at Thorn in Polish Prussia in the 1720s and at Salzburg in 1732.[18] The mensuration of the communal acceptance of any belief in the early modern period is problematic. But the continuing appeal of Temple's *History* (Irish editions were published in 1713, 1714, 1724, 1746 and 1766[19]); the healthy market for atrocity literature such as John Lockman's *History of the Cuel Sufferings of the Protestants*;[20] the emotive refutation of such attempts as were made by Catholics to offer a more temperate analysis of 1641;[21] and panics engendered in 1726, 1739, 1743, 1745 and 1762 by rumours of impending massacres emphasize that Protestants remained strongly persuaded of the malignity of Catholic intentions towards them.[22]

The genuine fear to which this attests both informed and reinforced Protestant perceptions that their constitutional liberties would be eroded should Catholics be permitted to effect the repeal or modification of the corpus of anti-Catholic legislation implemented by the Irish parliament between 1695 and 1728. Their conviction on this point was affirmed by the belief that the promotion and protection of religion was intrinsic to the maintenance of both political and social order, and that this demanded a Protestant constitution that embraced church and state. The Revd Edward Maurice put this well when he informed his eminent audience at Christ Church cathedral on 23 October 1755 that 'a constitution without a leading establishment in religion is not perfect', and it was a matter of some satisfaction to him that the Church of Ireland was, as he put it, 'interwoven with the constitution of our country'.[23] This was how Protestants in Britain as well as Ireland believed it should be. An as yet small

---

18 Gerald McCoy, 'Patriots, Protestants and Papists' in *Bullán*, 1 (1994), 107-08; Colin Haydon, '"I love my King and my country, but a Roman Catholic I hate": anti-Catholicism, xenophobia and national identity in eighteenth-century England' in Tony Claydon and Ian McBride (eds), *Protestantism and National Identity: Britain and Ireland c.1650-c.1850* (Cambridge 1998), pp.33-52. **19** Thomas Bartlett, *The Fall and Rise of the Irish Nation: The Catholic Question 1690-1830* (Dublin 1992), p. 7. **20** John Lockman, *A History of the Cruel Sufferings of the Protestants and Others by Popish Persecutions* (Dublin 1753). **21** Eoin Magennis, 'A beleaguered Protestant: Walter Harris and the writing of *Fiction Unmasked*', *Eighteenth-Century Ireland*, 13 (1998), 86-111. **22** Patrick Fagan, *An Irish Priest in Penal Times: The Chequered Career of Sylvester Lloyd* (Dublin 1993), pp. 81-3; Devonshire to ——, 21 Sept. 1739 (PRO(L) S.P. 63/402); M.B. Buckley, *Life and Writings of Arthur O'Leary* (Dublin 1868), pp. 45-6; W.P. Burke, *The Irish Priests in the Penal Times* (Waterford 1914), p. 292; Lauder to Bandon, 10 Apr. 1762 (TCD Crosbie Papers, Ms 3821/248). **23** Edward Maurice, *A Sermon Preached in Christ-church, Dublin, on Thursday 23 October 1755* ... (Dublin 1755), p. 24, cited in McCoy, 'Court Ideology', pp. 46-7.

number were prepared to agree, as the English Catholic, William Fermor, discovered, 'that a toleration of all religions might ... be a just measure in a free country'. As this suggests, a distinction can be drawn between those who were prepared to allow Catholics religious toleration, if they took an oath of allegiance to the state, and those who were not willing to acquiesce in any relaxation of the penal laws either because they were uncompromisingly anti-Catholic or because they deemed it incompatible with the Protestant character of the state. However, even the most liberal were prepared to do so only in so far as it was compatible with the maintenance of 'a church establishment', and 'it was universally thought a prudent measure to admit none to places of state who were not of the established church'.[24]

In the second half of the eighteenth century, Irish Protestants generally were less accommodating than their English *confrères* on this point.[25] As far as a majority was concerned, and this conviction was held most firmly by those of a conservative orientation, the Church of Ireland was both an integral and an indivisible component of the constitution and it was their duty to support it. Inevitably, the emergence of the question of relieving Catholics from the penal laws posed immediate and challenging questions. For conservatives in particular, there was agreement that it was their responsibility to ensure that whatever changes were made did not endanger their lives or liberties. This meant, in practice, that 'the Protestant constitution in church and state' had to be preserved secure and intact.

III

The conviction that their political and religious liberties derived from the fact that they possessed a 'Protestant constitution in church and state', and the large volume of existing commentary on the subject, equipped Protestants with ready arguments with which to resist demands for Catholic relief when these emerged during the mid-eighteenth century. Though the Catholic Committee, which was founded in 1756 to lobby for the amelioration of Catholic grievances, operated within the existing political system,[26] its very existence was a cause of unease as Walter Harris demonstrated when he maintained that Catholics should be content that they were allowed to practise their 'religion as free as any Protestant' though anti-Catholic laws remained on the statute book.[27] And

---

24 Fermor to Lord —, 9 Oct. 1789 (BL Dropmore Papers, Add. Mss 59264 ff 1-2). 25 For a perspective on the situation in England see Colin Haydon, *Anti-Catholicism in Eighteenth-Century England, c. 1714-80* (Manchester 1993). 26 Bartlett, *Fall and Rise*, passim; Maureen Wall, *Catholic Ireland in the Eighteenth Century*, ed. Gerard O'Brien (Dublin 1989). 27 Walter Harris, *Fiction Unmasked: Or an Answer to a Dialogue Lately Published* (Dublin 1752), p. 10.

the combined weight of traditional antipathy to Catholicism, reinforced by the fear generated by agrarian disorder in Munster in which conservatives reflexively identified French involvement, generated sufficient unease about Catholic revanchism to ensure that opposition was strong.[28] The relief measures proposed in the 1760s appertained to modest fiscal and leasehold matters. But the facts that successive proposals were denied; that otherwise radical political voices like Charles Lucas endorsed the calls made by Protestant corporations to have the customary quarter fees demanded as a condition of allowing Catholics to trade in towns given the sanction of law, on the grounds that it was in the interest of 'the Protestant religion' in towns corporate; and that a proposal to combat corruption on the corporation of Limerick was rejected in 1762 because it was contrary to the New Rules (1672), that were 'framed for the support of the Protestant interest', all emphasize the strength of the commitment to resist any dilution of Protestant privilege.[29]

Despite these successes in the 1760s, the readiness of a growing number of Protestants in the 1770s to accept that Catholics could be allowed greater economic freedom compatible with the security of their constitution necessitated the intensification of the rhetoric of Protestant opposition from those who continued to believe relief was ill-advised.[30] Thus Dublin Corporation condemned the proposal to grant freehold securities and long leases to Catholics made in 1772 as 'highly injurious to the Protestant interest' because it would 'give Papists a power over property' which they could use to establish an electoral influence. Grand juries also actively lobbied against proposals to allow Catholics 'to lend out money on mortgages' in 1774, but the intervention that struck the most forceful ideological note originated with the clergy of the diocese of Cloyne. Their commendation of Bishop Charles Agar for his 'support of the Protestant interest' encouraged him to lead the opposition to the bill in the House of Lords on the grounds that 'the interest of the Protestant religion would be materially injured' if it was ratified because it meant 'putting into the hands of the Papists a liberty which, with the blood of our ancestors, was strenuously withheld'. Agar also articulated the religiously inspired anxiety that if the bill became law it would discourage 'conversion from the errors of Popery', as well as allowing Catholics to exercise political influence indirectly.[31] The

---

28 McCoy, 'Court Ideology', pp. 77-9; Report of David Power, 1711 in *Galway Reader*, 4 (1953), 32-3; P.O'Connell, 'The plot against Fr Nicholas Sheehy', *Irish Ecclesiastical Record*, 108 (1967), 376; Richard Caulfeild (ed.), *The Council Book of the Corporation of Cork* (Guilford 1876), pp. 556-7; — to Chatham, 28 Dec. 1770 (PRO(L) Chatham Papers, 30/8/84 f. 89). 29 McCoy, 'Court Ideology', pp. 24-5; Bill for regulating the Corporation of Limerick, 1762 (PRO(L) P.C. 1/3058). 30 Doran to Burke, 18 Dec. 1769 in Hugh Fenning, 'Some problems of the Irish mission', *Collectanea Hibernica*, 8 (1965), 106-7. 31 McCoy, 'Court Ideology', p. 77; John Brady (ed.), *Catholics and Catholicism in the Eighteenth-Century Press* (Maynooth 1966), pp. 155, 164-5; *Finn's Leinster Journal*, 9 Apr. 1774.

latter claim was highly problematic. But the conviction that any breach of the 'barrier and defence against tyranny and oppression' provided by the penal laws 'would greatly weaken the Protestant interest' was firmly held, and both this measure and another to allow Catholics to take long leases on building ground were decisively rejected.[32] The Protestant community at large was so pleased with the outcome that 'thanks' were offered in Protestant churches in Dublin in May 1774:

> The PROTESTANT RELIGION, and her amiable sisters LIBERTY and PROPERTY return thanks to ALMIGHTY GOD for their late deliverance from the hands of POPERY and PERSECUTION.[33]

The strength of Protestant convictions on this is further evidenced by the response of the otherwise liberal *Freeman's Journal*, one of whose contributors maintained that Protestants ought not to sanction any enhancement in Catholic rights because, their professions of loyalty notwithstanding, they were determined 'to deprive Protestants of life or property ... when a safe opportunity offers'.[34]

The pervasiveness of such attitudes provides a ready explanation as to why the ratification in 1774 by the Westminster parliament of the Quebec Act, which provided for freedom of worship for the Catholics of French Canada, was greeted with such alarm by Protestants in Ireland as elsewhere in the empire. One commentator accused ministers of 'pav[ing] a direct road to arbitrary government'. Others alleged George III was facilitating the 'establishment of Popery'; while still others reminded their brethren of 1641 'when these barbarous and inhuman butchers unlocked the secrets of their breasts, and gratified their horrid thirst for human sacrifices' by spilling 'Protestant blood'.[35] Ongoing Whiteboy activity in Munster and Leinster gave such extreme claims credibility, and confirmed Protestants in their conviction that 'dreadful consequences' must result from giving power to a Papist'.[36] Significantly, Edmund Butler, the MP for County Kilkenny, was not challenged when he observed in the House of Commons in March 1778 that 'most who wish well to the Protestant interest do not choose to relax the laws relative to Popery'.[37]

It was more than a little ironic that Butler should venture this opinion at this moment, as a few months later MPs were fully occupied debating the most significant measure of Catholic relief proposed to date. The object of the 1778 relief bill was to allow Catholics to purchase land on the same terms as Protest-

---

[32] Brady (ed.), *Catholics in the Press*, pp. 155–61. [33] *Hibernian Journal*, 20 May 1774. [34] Brady (ed.), *Catholics in the Press*, p. 162. [35] *Hibernian Journal*, 29 June, 1, 22 July, 29 Aug. 1774. [36] Brady (ed.), *Catholics in the Press*, pp. 169–70; *Hibernian Journal*, 4 Sept. 1775. [37] Henry Cavendish's parliamentary diary, vol. 9, p. 57 (Library of Congress, Washington).

ants and to bequeath it unburdened by the controversial gavelling requirement. Inevitably, those who described themselves as the 'real friends' of 'our glorious constitution both in church and state' took a traditional line and vowed to resist any change. They contended that any interference with 'the Popery laws' must ensure that 'Popery ... gr[e]w stronger and more dangerous every year'. They also trotted out the familiar argument that, because Popery was 'idolatrous' and predisposed to commit 'the most horrid cruelties and massacres on the persons of Protestants', it was contrary to divine will as well as human logic to accord it toleration.[38] However, the political mood of the late 1770s was less disposed to indulge established perceptions on this point, as the contributions to the debate of George Ogle, who was to become one of the foremost political advocates of neo-conservatism from the mid-1780s, reveal. He responded initially by claiming that if the 1778 measure was approved it would be akin to 'burying the constitution by torchlight and the Protestant interest along with it'. This remained his position, but it is significant that rather than attack Popery, he enjoined Protestants to rally to the defence of their constitution in all its branches on the grounds that 'there is nothing ... sacred that has not been handed down by our ancestors' for which the bill did not possess major implications and he itemized 'the constitution ..., the Protestant interest, ... landed property ..., and the church and state of Ireland'. It was his considered opinion, indeed, that the bill was 'totally calculated to alter the constitution ..., to subvert the Protestant religion ..., [and] to take the landed property out of the hands of Protestants' – in sum, 'to subvert the civil and religious rights of church and state'.[39]

Ogle's arguments against Catholic relief were less beholden to traditional Protestant apprehensions of Catholic massacre and to religious concerns over conversion than had been the case a mere four years earlier because of the palpable diminution in interdenominational suspicion that took place in the late 1770s.[40] Many remained unconvinced, but the mood of toleration was strong and the readiness of the British government to favour Catholic relief facilitated a significant shift in Protestant opinion. Instead of simple opposition, patriots like Henry Flood and Lord Charlemont, who had previously resisted any dilution of the penal laws, professed themselves willing to allow Catholics civil and economic (but not political) rights. Even hard-liners were obliged to shift their position as George Ogle demonstrated. Though the standard bearer of opposition to the 1778 Catholic relief proposal, he took a position on religious toleration that was genuinely liberal compared with that taken by his equivalents up till then. The fact that he and others who opposed the 1778 legislation described

38 *Freeman's Journal*, 9, 25 June 1778. **39** Cavendish's parliamentary diary, vol. 10, p. 34, vol. 6, pp. 2, 65 **40** James Kelly, 'Inter-denominational relations and religious toleration in late eighteenth-century Ireland', *Eighteenth-Century Ireland*, 3 (1988), 41-2.

themselves as opposed to religious 'persecution, or any disobliging laws, except where absolutely necessary', attests to the extent of the shift in thinking that had taken place.[41]

The most crucial index of this is provided by the fact that the Catholic relief bill reached the statute book. The high standing in which the Capuchin advocate of religious toleration, Arthur O'Leary, was held in some Protestant circles is a further indication.[42] This was not to the liking of those who continued to hold that to grant Catholics civil rights in any sphere was incompatible with the interests of Protestants, but the tide was so strongly against them that they seemed to raise no more than a murmur of protest in 1782 when further relief measures were approved which effectively negated a swathe of anti-Catholic legislation appertaining to land, religion and education. This was due in part to Henry Grattan's clever alignment of the Volunteers behind the cause of Catholic relief. However, behind their apparent readiness to treat Catholics with some generosity, hard-liners were drawing firm lines, as Ogle indicated when he professed his preparedness 'to give the Papists every indulgence consistent with the safety of the established church'. On first glance, this does not appear particularly different from Henry Grattan's claim of 15 February 1782 that he was prepared 'to grant [Catholics] ... every privilege compatible with the Protestant ascendant', whereas Ogle and he differed fundamentally. Grattan was willing to contemplate that Ireland might evolve from '*a Protestant settlement*' to an 'IRISH NATION',[43] but Ogle had more in common with Lord Charlemont who opined that 'the House [of Commons] seems to be running mad on the subject of Popery'.[44] Significantly, the concerns voiced centred primarily on ensuring their exclusion from the political process. Thus John Fitzgibbon's concern that the security of the title of those landowners who held forfeited land should not be endangered prompted him to advance an amendment stating that the right of Catholics to 'have, hold and inherit ESTATES IN FEE SIMPLE' did not extend to lands in parliamentary boroughs. Henry Flood agreed. It was politic, he argued, 'to enbosom the Roman Catholics in the body of the state', but it was unwise to go 'beyond toleration' and 'to make a change in the state':

> Ninety years ago the question was whether Popery and arbitrary power should be established in the person of King James, or freedom and the

---

[41] Cavendish's Parl. diary, vol. 10, p. 34; *Freeman's Journal*, 9 June 1778. [42] James Kelly, '"A wild Capuchin of Cork": Fr Arthur O'Leary' in G. Moran (ed.), *Radical Priests* (Dublin 1998), pp. 74-92. [43] Bartlett, *Fall and Rise*, pp. 100-2; *The Parliamentary Register ... of the House of Commons of the Kingdom of Ireland* (17 vols, Dublin, 1782-1801), vol.1, pp. 196, 239, 247, 255; James Kelly, *Henry Grattan* (Dundalk 1993), p.17. [44] Charlemont to Flood, 1 Jan. 1782 (BL Flood Papers, Add. Mss 22930).

Protestant religion in the person of King William — four-fifths of the inhabitants of Ireland adhered to the cause of King James; they were defeated ... The laws that followed ... were not laws of persecution, but of political necessity ... What then is the consequence if you give [Roman Catholics] equal power with the Protestants? Can a Protestant constitution survive?[45]

As far as Flood was concerned the answer to this question was an unequivocal 'no' because, he pronounced, 'our constitution must be partial' if its essentially Protestant character was to be maintained.[46]

If Flood's observation suggested that many Protestants believed that further concessions could not safely be extended to Catholics, there were others who believed things had already gone too far. The reflection of the antiquarian Austin Cooper in 1784 on observing the refurbishment of a 'Popish chapel' in Dublin that 'Protestants' yet unborn would 'execrate' the 'inconsiderate toleration' currently being implemented because it portended 'the ruin of the Protestant interest' and, possibly, an early repetition of the crisis of the late 1680s, reveals this at an individual level.[47] The striking improvement in the political influence of those of a conservative outlook during the mid-1780s and the invigoration of conservative thinking during the second half of the decade indicate that this position did not want for supporters.

IV

The relative appeal of conservatism and liberalism to Irish Protestants was put to the test when the issue of parliamentary reform took political centre stage in 1783-4. The primary objectives of the coalition of interests that advocated reform was to correct the worst defects of the borough system and to increase the electorate. There was reasonable agreement on the first of these points, but the second exposed deep differences because it necessitated considering extending the franchise to Catholics. In view of the preference expressed by Henry Grattan in February 1782 for the emergence of an 'Irish nation', there was some limited support for the idea in liberal circles, but because the movement also attracted the support of known advocates of a purely 'Protestant constitution', such as George Ogle and Henry Flood, it was not destined to be achieved.[48] The resulting incapacity of reformers to negotiate what one of their number

45 *Parliamentary Register*, vol. 1, pp. 247, 253; Kelly, *Henry Flood*, pp. 304-5. 46 *Parliamentary Register*, vol. 1, p. 282. 47 Liam Price (ed.), *An Eighteenth-Century Antiquarian: Austin Cooper's Diaries* (Dublin 1942), pp. 112-13. 48 James Kelly, 'The parliamentary reform movement and the Catholic question 1782-85', *Archivium Hibernicum*, 43 (1988), 95-117.

termed 'the rock of religion and indulgence to Catholics' gratified conservatives who did not see any good reason to change the representative system. Their spirits were boosted by the decisive manner that MPs asserted the primacy of parliament by rejecting the plan of reform of the Grand National Congress of Volunteer delegates referred to them in late November 1783.[49] Moreover, when the reformers subsequently endeavoured to advance their cause by pursuing the orthodox route of petitioning, their opponents prevailed once more. This time they effectively deployed the traditional contention that their 'matchless constitution, … the envy of the world' was so perfectly balanced that to tamper with it was to tamper with perfection.[50] This was an influential argument, and its impact in conservative quarters was reinforced by the assertion that reform coupled with Catholic enfranchisement was 'purely calculated for the ruin of the current establishment in church and state'.[51]

There was plenty of scope here for the elaboration of a forceful conservative argument against tampering with the constitution, but no attempt was made to do this at this time. In truth, it was not needed. The comparative ease with which the case against reform prevailed in the political arena in 1783-84 mirrored the facility with which largely conservative politicians regained possession of the corridors of power.[52] However, the challenge posed by the demand for parliamentary reform had not long receded when another and, in the eyes of those who deemed the position of the Church of Ireland as integral to the Protestant constitution as an exclusively Protestant representative system, an equally formidable threat loomed. This proved a particularly critical moment because not alone had many of the most vocal opponents of Catholic relief already identified the security of their church as a matter of paramount importance, they now generated a response that was more ideologically impactive than was the case in the late 1770s and early 1780s when the matter of relieving Catholics of economic and religious disabilities was at issue. In the process they provided the coalition of laity and clergy resolutely opposed to further rights for Catholics with a new vocabulary that marked the formal emergence of late eighteenth-century neo-conservatism.

Irish Protestants were reflexively disposed to regard orchestrated rural discontent as a threat to their position,[53] and their reaction to the emergence in Munster in the mid-1780s of the agrarian movement known as the Rightboys was no different. The Rightboys' main goal was to regulate the tithes paid to the clergy of the Church of Ireland, but whereas previous attempts to bring this

---

49 *Parliamentary Register*, vol. 2, pp. 226-64.   **50** *A Reform of the Irish House of Commons Considered* (Dublin 1783), p. 29; *A Sermon Preached by the Rev Francis Turner A.B. on Sunday, 8th of August 1784* (Dublin 1784), pp. 13-4.   **51** Mentor, *The Alarm or an Address to the Nobility, Gentry and Clergy of Ireland* (Dublin 1783), pp. 3, 6.   **52** James Kelly, *Prelude to Union: Anglo-Irish politics in the 1780s* (Cork 1992), pp. 56-78.   **53** See footnote 28.

about in the 1760s and 1770s had met with a sternly uncompromising response,[54] there was a readiness within liberal circles to conclude that reform rather than repression was more appropriate on this occasion.[55] This was not to the satisfaction of conservatives, but they were slow to articulate a contrary case. Indeed, when George Ogle first raised the matter on the floor of the House of Commons on 6 February 1786, he was initially more agitated by the seizure by an errant Catholic of disputed lands in Connaught than he was by the actions of the Rightboys. Arising out of the conviction that Catholics aspired 'to restore every Popish proprietor to his own estate', this was an issue upon which conservatives were particularly prone to take alarm,[56] and Ogle captured their anxiety on this point vividly by warning the assembled members that 'when the landed property of the kingdom' was being threatened, as it was in this instance, then nothing less than 'the Protestant ascendancy was at stake'. The absence of an outcry suggests that most MPs concluded correctly that this was an isolated incident. The Rightboys were a more serious matter, and having informed MPs that it was their 'business ... to guard' what he interchangeably denominated 'the Protestant interest' and 'the Protestant ascendancy', Ogle pointed out that the Rightboys' 'resistance ... to the collection of tithes' tended 'to the utter overturning of the Protestant establishment in church and, consequently, in state'.[57] As far as Ogle was concerned, this was reason enough for parliament to authorize an appropriately coercive response, but, to the dismay of supporters of a Protestant constitution, when the administration formulated its response it embraced tithe commutation as well as counter-insurgency measures.[58]

This was utterly unacceptable to those who concurred with Ogle that the constitution in church and state was an indivisible whole. The future archbishop of Dublin, Euseby Cleaver, articulated their unease when he forecast the 'end to the Protestant interest' if 'parliament admit of any commutation of the tithes'. He was not short of allies. Expectedly, they were most numerous within the ranks of the church and its lay advocates, but a number of prominent conservative politicians were equally perturbed. The Speaker of the House of Commons, John Foster, pronounced himself 'decidedly against any commutation' on the grounds that it collided with his commitment 'to preserve the constitution against innovation'.[59] Taken aback by the intense feelings the issue gen-

---

[54] J.S.Donnelly, jr., 'The Whiteboy movement 1761-5', *Irish Historical Studies*, 21 (1978-9), 20-55; idem,'Irish agrarian rebellion: the Whiteboys of 1769-76', *Proceedings of the Royal Irish Academy*, Section C, 83 (1983), 293-331.   [55] James Kelly, 'The genesis of Protestant ascendancy', pp. 105-6.   [56] BL Lansdowne Abstracts, Add. Mss 24137; see also Brady (ed.), *Catholics in the Press*, pp. 155-7.   [57] *Parliamentary Register*, vol. 6, pp. 85-7.   [58] Kelly, 'The genesis of Protestant ascendancy', pp. 105-7.   [59] Cleaver to O'Hara, 15 Sept. 1786 (NLI O'Hara Papers, Ms 20396/12); Foster to Law, 29 Nov. 1786 (PRONI Foster Papers, D207/50/17).

erated and by the realization that any plan of commutation they proposed would be opposed 'by the episcopal part of the clergy ... as a commencement of the ruin of their establishment', the administration was obliged to rest its hopes for tithe reform on churchmen standing forth with a scheme of their own.[60] This made it improbable that tithe reform would be accomplished. Its prospects were effectively negated with the publication of a number of stirring defences of the centrality of the tithe to the Church of Ireland and of the integrity of the Protestant constitution in church and state that energized conservative Protestantism politically as well as ideologically. In their wake, it became respectable again to assert openly that Catholicism represented a threat both to Irish Protestants and to the Protestant constitution. No less significantly, it equipped conservatives with the language and arguments they needed to affirm their position in the more challenging environment of the 1790s.

The first combative defence of the Church's position on the tithe to see print was prepared by Patrick Duigenan, an alumnus of Trinity College who had previously entered the lists in opposition to parliamentary reform. In *An Address to the Nobility and Gentry of the Church of Ireland*, published towards the end of 1786, he forcefully articulated the conservative conviction that 'the constitution in church and state' was currently under threat of 'subversion' by claiming that, in contrast to the Whiteboys '18 or 20 years ago', the Rightboys were 'particularly directed against the clergy of the established Church'. This was a manifestly partisan contention given that the Rightboys also targeted the dues requested by Catholic clergy, but Duigenan preferred to interpret this as little more than a ruse to conceal the true purpose of Rightboyism; this was to reduce the Church of Ireland clergy 'to absolute beggary' and thereby to undermine 'our religious establishment' which, because it 'is the main pillar of the constitution', must herald 'the ruin of the whole structure of our government' and its replacement by 'Popery'.[61] Duigenan offered only circumstantial evidence to support his thesis. He preferred to play on Protestant anxieties by asserting that 'the insolent factious demands and pretensions' of the Rightboys were 'spirited up by agitating friars and Romish missionaries sent here for the purpose of sowing sedition'; by claiming that the actual tithe (which he emphasized had the sanction of both divine and human law) collected was significantly less than the one-tenth ordained; and by animating such traditional points of Protestant concern as the papal claim to depose heretic princes, the Catholic church's history of burning heretics and, in the Irish context, the dangers of Jacobitism, rebellion and massacre. In this respect, the repeal of the penal laws was a critical issue, and Duigenan was convinced that events in Munster proved

---

60 Kelly, 'The genesis of Protestant ascendancy', pp. 108, 111-12. **61** Theophilus [Patrick Duigenan], *An Address to the Nobility and Gentry of the Church of Ireland, as by Law Established* ... (Dublin 1786), pp. 1-4, 15-17, 94-5.

that the legislature had acted in a 'hasty and improvident' way on this subject. He identified the fact that Catholics were enabled to acquire arms through their involvement with the Volunteers as another contributory cause 'to the present disturbances',[62] but his primary message was that it was vital that Protestants stood firm and insisted that there should be no alteration to the way the tithe was administered. If there was, he forecast further Catholic demands leading incrementally to the repeal of all the penal laws, the transfer of land to Catholics, the accession of a Catholic monarch, and 'a civil war between Britain and Ireland' which would culminate in 'the exemplary punishment of restless, insidious, faithless Popish rebels or... the destruction of Great Britain, the monarchy, Protestantism and the liberties of Europe'.[63]

Despite its offensive tone, Duigenan's tract was a clarion to Protestants to rally to defend the Protestant constitution in church and state. The fact that it was reprinted in London indicated that this was a message that transcended the particular environment of Ireland, but its author's die-hard reputation ensured it had little appeal outside of conservative circles. What was needed, and what Richard Woodward, bishop of Cloyne, supplied, was a more temperate statement of the conservative case. Entitled simply *The Present State of the Church of Ireland*, Woodward's pamphlet provided a cogent and detailed case as to why the maintenance of the tithe unaltered was essential if the Church of Ireland and the Protestant constitution was to survive, and a powerful ideological argument that supplied conservative Protestants with a new language with which to defend their constitutional position against those who sought reform.

Deriving in large part from what one admirer described as his 'great but natural jealousy of the Roman Catholic religion', Woodward was convinced by the summer of 1786 that the Rightboy disturbances posed a threat to 'the whole ecclesiastical establishment and the Protestant interest on which the safety of the constitution depends'.[64] His anxieties were so heightened subsequently by the inability of the crown forces to eradicate this threat, that he undertook to prepare a detailed account of the 'precarious situation' of the Church of Ireland in order to open 'the eyes of the landed gentlemen' of Ireland to the gravity of the moment.[65] Addressed to 'the friends of the Protestant interest', seven of the pamphlet's eight sections were devoted to describing how the tithe was administered and to explaining why it was essential to the survival of the Church of

---

62 This was a conclusion he shared with the Protestant Peep O'Day boys in Co.Armagh (see James Smyth, 'The men of no-popery: the origins of the Orange Order', *History Ireland*, 1995, pp. 51-2). 63 [Duigenan], *An Address to the Nobility and Gentry*, pp. 18-20, 22, 94-107. 64 Portland to Northington, 6 July 1783 (BL Northington Letterbook, Add. Mss 38,716 ff 44-9); Woodward to Preston, 25 June 1783 (HMC, *Rutland Mss*, vol. 3, pp.315-6), 65 Woodward to Conolly, 11 July, 12 Sept. 1786 (TCD Conolly Papers, Ms 3978 ff 898, 903); Kelly, 'Religious toleration', 54.

Ireland in '*very many* parishes'. As he saw it, it was critical that the church was bulwarked by the state if the 'Protestant religion' was not 'rapidly [to] give way to Popery, till it be totally extinguished'.[66]

It is clear from this that Woodward's defence of the tithe bore close comparison with that provided by Patrick Duigenan, whom he cited approvingly. He was at one also with Duigenan, whose language he replicated at several points, in his contention in the pamphlet's preliminaries that 'the Church of Ireland is, at the present moment, in imminent danger of subversion' and that because the church 'is so essentially incorporated with the state ... the subversion of one must necessarily overthrow the other'.[67] However, whereas Duigenan focused narrowly on the subject of the tithe, Woodward abstracted from the particular, and in the key opening section to his pamphlet addressed the central constitutional question of the 'importance of the ecclesiastical to the civil constitution of this kingdom'. Little of what he had to say on this matter represented original thinking, but he presented his case with a freshness, lucidity and logic that struck a chord with 'the friends of the Protestant interest' at whom it was directed. Taking as his starting point the fact that in Europe 'almost every legislature has adopted an ecclesiastical polity', it was, he opined, a demonstrable fact that there was an identifiable link between the form of government that existed and the religious establishment it encouraged. Thus 'despotic states ... have found in the papal authority a congenial system of arbitrary dominion' while 'republics ... have adopted the levelling principle of the Presbyterian church'. By these criteria, it was logical that the religious establishment in England (and by extension in Ireland) should be the one that best conformed to the 'civil constitution' and this was an established Protestant church. Indeed, he observed, 'the best' constitution 'that ever existed' was created out of the interweaving of the civil and ecclesiastical establishments that had been accomplished in Britain and Ireland.[68]

Since, according to Woodward, the 'unrivalled' British constitution comprised a civil and ecclesiastical dimension it was essential if it was to survive that both branches were defended should either come under threat. By extension, since the opposition orchestrated by the Rightboys to the payment of tithes and to the performance by the clergy of the Church of Ireland of their duties threatened the ecclesiastical establishment, it was vital that they were brought to heel, otherwise their actions must precipitate the 'extinction' of the clergy and, by

---

[66] Richard Woodward, Bishop of Cloyne, *The Present State of the Church of Ireland Containing a Description of its Precarious Situation and the Consequent Danger to the Public Recommended to the Serious Consideration of the Friends of the Protestant Interest to which are Subjoined some Reflections on the Impracticability of a Proper Commutation for Tithes and a General Account of the Origins and Progress of the Insurrection in Munster*, 8th edn (Dublin 1787), especially p. 57. [67] Woodward, *Present State*, pp. 3, 7 and, especially, 14. [68] Ibid., pp. 17-20.

extension, the undoing of 'the established church' and the Protestant constitution. Addressing the 'Protestant proprietor of land', who he pointed out had a vested interest in ensuring this did not come about, Woodward maintained 'that the security of his title depends very much (if not entirely) on the Protestant ascendancy' and 'that the preservation of that ascendancy depends entirely on an indissoluble connexion' being maintained with Great Britain. It also, he went on, depended on his supporting the Church of Ireland over other churches because 'the members of the established church alone can be cordial friends to the entire constitution ... with perfect consistency of principle'. By implication, other religions could not be afforded equal protection under the constitution. Thus, in respect of Presbyterians, it was not possible to grant them full and equal rights because they refused to maintain an 'ecclesiastical establishment'. Woodward's observations with respect to 'Popery' were more pointed. He conceded that every Catholic should be allowed 'freedom of religion ... and every comfort as a citizen', but it was, he averred, incumbent upon a Protestant state 'to preclude him as much as possible from influence for fear of losing the power of control'. Indeed, it was not possible, he maintained, for Protestants ever to permit Catholics full rights because they adhered to tenets 'subversive of the Protestant ascendancy', and because their religion bound them 'to suppress heresy'. In support of this denial of legal toleration, he cited the presence of the phrase '*hereticos persequar et impugnabo*' in the consecration oath taken by Catholic bishops, and impugned the value of the oath of allegiance approved by the Irish parliament in 1774 whereby Catholics were enabled to profess loyalty to the state, on the grounds that the Catholic church released its members from adhering to oaths made with heretics.[69]

Woodward's powerful exposition of the case for continued 'Protestant ascendancy' elicited a series of sharply worded rebukes from spokesmen for both the Catholic and Presbyterian communions who resented his portrayal of them as undeserving of full constitutional rights.[70] Conservative Protestants, by contrast, were gratified that what one of their number deemed a 'fair' statement of their position and of the situation of their church was in print, and the eager public response suggests that their number was substantial, as the tract sold out its first four editions in four days.[71] The work's appeal derived in the first instance from the measured manner with which Woodward presented its essentially uncompromising thesis. It was helped by the author's ability to adduce apposite facts and pertinent authorities to sustain his case. However, its success

---

69 Ibid., pp. 21-31. **70** Kelly, 'Religious toleration', p. 56 ff; idem, 'Relations between the Protestant Church of Ireland and the Presbyterian church in late eighteenth-century Ireland', *Eire-Ireland*, 23 (1988), 38-56. **71** *Dublin Evening Post*, 28 Dec. 1786; Woodward to Brodrick, 7 Jan. 1787 (NLI Brodrick Papers, Ms 8870/1); W.J. McCormack, *The Dublin Paper War of 1786-88: A Bibliographical and Critical Enquiry* (Dublin 1993).

was mainly due to the fact that Woodward provided conservative Protestants with a coherent statement as to why they were justified in opposing further constitutional concessions to Catholics and a new vocabulary with which to express it. In respect of the latter point, Woodward's most significant accomplishment was to embrace and popularize the concept of 'Protestant ascendancy'. The genesis of this term has been the subject of some debate. The present author has argued that it took place in the 1780s and that the key figure was Bishop Woodward because it was he who took up a term already in the vocabulary of conservative Protestants, clarified its meaning and popularized it. W.J. McCormack, on the other hand, defines its use in the 1780s as part of the 'prehistory' of the term and maintains that its adoption by Dublin Corporation in 1792 represents its 'baptism' as a potent political 'collocation'.[72] There is, as will be seen below, no question but that both the rhetoric and ideology of 'Protestant ascendancy' was more widely articulated in 1792-3, but it is equally demonstrable that conservative Protestant thought and the language used to express opposition to Catholic relief evolved fitfully over the crises of 1778, 1782, 1786-7 and 1792-3. Significantly, the appeal to conservatives of the term 'Protestant interest' diminishes after 1778, and it gave way gradually to the more assertive 'Protestant ascendancy' from the mid-1780s. Used for the first time, as far as can be established, during the debate on Catholic relief in 1782, the latter term had its first sustained ideological application in 1786-7, when the issue of primary concern to those who appealed to it was the security of the ecclesiastical branch of the constitution.[73]

By implication, Dr McCormack's contention that the significance of the employment of the term 'Protestant ascendancy' in the 1780s was a matter for the future is only partly sustainable. It manifestly possessed a contemporary significance. As T.C. Barnard has shown, the term it displaced – 'Protestant interest' – emerged in the mid-seventeenth century.[74] It was sufficiently well established to figure in official documents during the Restoration, and by the early eighteenth century it was used widely by Protestants in a great variety of contexts – social as well as political – to define their condition as well as to describe their position.[75] Significantly, they appealed to it in the same manner that many

---

[72] This issue has generated a considerable literature, but see in particular McCormack, *The Dublin Paper War*, passim; James Kelly, 'Eighteenth-century ascendancy', *Eighteenth-Century Ireland*, 5 (1990), 173-87. [73] Kelly, 'Eighteenth-century ascendancy', 173-87. [74] T.C. Barnard, 'The Protestant interest, 1641-1660' in J.H.Ohlmeyer (ed.), *Ireland from Independence to Occupation* (Cambridge 1995). [75] *An Enquiry into Some of the Causes of the Ill Situation of the Affairs of Ireland* (Dublin 1731), p. 7; *Journals of the House of Commons (Ireland)*, vol. 1, p. 402; 'Glimpses of the penal times', *Irish Ecclesiastical Record*, 22 (1907), 76; *An Account of the Session of Parliament in Ireland* (London 1692); 9 William III, c 3; *Dublin Intelligence*, 28 Aug. 1708, 10 May 1709, 12 Sept. 1727; Brady, (ed.), *Catholics in the Press*, pp. 10, 12, 40; D. Hayton (ed.), 'An Irish parliamentary diary from the reign of Queen Anne', *Analecta*

conservatives later appealed to the term 'Protestant ascendancy'. This can be illustrated by an address of the House of Commons dating from the early 1720s against legislation to reverse outlawries on the grounds that it was 'dangerous ... to ... the Protestant interest' because those relieved would 'do all in their power to subvert our happy constitution in church and state', as well as by the routine manner by which gatherings of Protestants affirmed their commitment to uphold 'the Protestant interest' in the mid-eighteenth century.[76] The emergence of the term 'Protestant ascendancy' in the 1780s was thus a development of significant ideological import because it went to the heart of how Irish Protestants defined themselves. Instead of continuing to define and to describe themselves as an 'interest', which as the term was employed in the eighteenth century implied a 'cause' or 'party' that shared a set of broadly common principles, and which is primarily descriptive, they sought to replace it with a term whose definition implies domination, control, sway and paramountcy. Though hardly an impartial witness on this issue, Edmund Burke's contention that it signified 'pride and dominion' on the part of those who used it, and 'subserviency' on the part of those against whom it was directed, accurately captured its respective meanings for those who embraced it in the 1780s. It is, of course, significant that the term 'Protestant ascendancy' did not displace 'Protestant interest' overnight.[77] Just as the term 'Protestant interest' was used side by side with 'English interest', 'Irish interest' and 'Popish interest' in the late seventeenth and early eighteenth centuries,[78] so the term 'Protestant interest' continued to be used after the introduction of 'Protestant ascendancy' in 1786-7. This is not to say what is at issue here is a simple matter of nomenclature. The adoption by Bishop Woodward of the term 'Protestant ascendancy' in a context in which conservative Protestants feared for the ecclesiastical branch of their constitution was a development of political and conceptual as well as terminological import in the evolution of conservative Protestant thought.

Two developments bear this out. The first was the alacrity with which Dublin Castle and the Irish parliament abandoned their lingering commitment to tithe reform in 1787.[79] The second was the number of pamphlets published

---

Hibernica, 30 (1982), 140, 141. **76** PRO(L) S.P. 67/10 ff 38-9; Brady (ed.), *Catholics in the Press*, pp. 68, 90, 313; Newcastle to Devonshire, 17 Sept. 1741 (PRONI Chatsworth Papers, T3158/180); *Universal Advertizer*, 20 Dec. 1760; *Public Gazetteer*, 15 Mar. 1763; *Freeman's Journal*, 14 Dec. 1765, 22, 29 Apr. 1766; *Hibernian Journal*, 8 Nov. 1782. **77** See *Oxford English Dictionary*, citing Edmund Burke. **78** *An Enquiry into Some of the Causes of the Ill Situation of the Affairs of Ireland*, p. 7; PRO(L) P.C.2/55 f. 30; *An Account of the Session of Parliament in Ireland* (London 1692); 'Glimpses of penal times', *Irish Ecclesiastical Record*, 22 (1907), 77; Brady, *Catholics in the Press*, pp. 10, 40; Hayton, (ed.), 'An Irish parliamentary diary', 140, 141; Patrick McNally, 'Patronage and Politics in Ireland 1714-27' (unpublished Ph.D thesis, Queen's University, Belfast 1993), pp. 160, 161, 190, 233. **79** Kelly, 'Genesis of Protestant ascendancy', pp. 120-2.

by conservatives in the wake of Woodward's *Present State* that appealed to his rhetoric and to his arguments. Most display little of his finesse. Several manifest a virtually obsessive concern with the 1774 oath of allegiance, the bishops' consecration oath, which they interpreted, more unforgivingly than he had done, as a papal licence to persecute and to exterminate heretics, and other aspects of Catholic doctrine and history that they adduced to demonstrate that 'the doctrine of religious persecution was ... unquestionably the doctrine of the Romish Church'.[80] Allegations that the Rightboys sought with the help of Catholic clergy 'to overthrow our happy constitution in church and state' were also frequently made.[81] But perhaps the most significant contribution in terms of Protestant opinion are those that maintained that Woodward's arguments in favour of Protestant ascendancy represented 'the sentiments of every member of the established religion', and that recent events had demonstrated that the repeal of the penal laws was unjustified.[82] These were contestable conclusions, but the response of the alliance of churchmen and lay enthusiasts to the perception that the privileged position of their church was about to be undermined provided those opposed to any further dilution of the ascendant constitutional position of Protestants and of the Church of Ireland with a modern, clear and conceptually reinforced case for demanding that their constitution was preserved intact and 'Protestant ascendancy' sustained.

V

As well as frustrating those politicians who favoured tithe commutation, the invigoration of conservative Protestantism in the mid-1780s contributed in an

---

[80] *A Letter to the Reverend Dr James Butler, a Titular Archbishop, from a Friend* (Dublin 1787), especially pp. 9, 13-14; A clergyman [Thomas Elrington], *A Short Refutation of the Arguments Contained in Dr Butler's Letter to Lord Kenmare with a Reply to the Third Section of Mr O'Leary's Defence* (Dublin 1787); Verax, *Remarks on a Letter Lately Published Signed Arthur O'Leary ...* (Dublin 1787), pp. 11-13; William Hales, D.D., *Observations on the Political Influence of the Doctrine of the Pope's Supremacy Addressed to the Reverend Dr Butler D.D.* (Dublin 1787); *A Survey of the Modern State of the Church of Rome with Additional Observations on the Doctrine of the Pope's Supremacy addressed to Dr Butler etc.* (Dublin 1788); Kelly, 'Religious toleration', 60-4. [81] Rev. T.B. Clarke, *The Second Edition of Junius Alter's letter to Mr O'Leary with a Short Examination into the First Causes of the Present Lawless Spirit of the Irish Peasantry and a Plan of Reform* (Dublin 1787), p 4; A clergyman, *A Short Refutation of the Arguments ...*, pp. 3-6; *Remarks on a Letter lately Published signed Arthur O'Leary Stiled an Address to the Protestant Nobility and Gentry of Ireland* (Dublin 1787), pp. 8-9, 13; Detector, *Observations on the Indecent and Illiberal Strictures against the lord Bishop of Cloyne Contained in a Pamphlet lately Published under the Title of Mr O'Leary's Defence etc.* (Dublin 1787). [82] Detector, *Observations on the Indecent and Illiberal Strictures*, p. 7; T.B. Clarke, *The Second Edition of Junius Alter's Letter*, pp. 11-13.

important way to the success of churchmen in resisting separate initiatives by the marquis of Buckingham (lord lieutenant 1787-9) and Henry Grattan in 1788 and 1789 to advance plans for tithe, education and church reform.[83] The ready recourse by conservatives in these years to the argument that such changes threatened the 'subversion of the constitution in one of its branches' emphasizes their greater ideological confidence.[84] The implication was that they had won the argument with their liberal critics. However, the impact of concessions to Catholics in Britain and the stimulus provided by the outbreak of revolution in France emboldened Catholics and the proponents of parliamentary reform to seek major constitutional change in the early 1790s. The most significant consequence of this was that the conservative commitment to preserve the constitution intact in both its civil and ecclesiastical branches was to be challenged.

Though there was some earlier ideological skirmishing on the subject of events in France, the contest over the constitution did not begin in earnest until December 1791 when Henry Dundas informed the then lord lieutenant, the earl of Westmorland, of his conclusion that 'there cannot be a permanency in the frame of government and constitution of Ireland unless the Protestants will … forego their exclusive pre-eminence'.[85] Dundas's specific recommendation that Catholics should be admitted 'to a moderate and qualified participation' of 'electing' disturbed conservatives. Opposition was most ideologically vigorous at municipal level in Dublin where the corporation drafted an address to the king on 20 January 1792 in support of continued 'Protestant ascendancy':

> Sensibly impressed with the value of our excellent constitution, both in church and state, as established by the glorious revolution, we feel ourselves particularly called upon to stand forward at the present crisis to pray your majesty to preserve the Protestant ascendancy in Ireland inviolate, and to assure your majesty that we are firmly resolved to support it free from innovation, and are determined most zealously to oppose any attempt to overturn the same.[86]

The commitment, articulated in this address, to maintain the Protestant constitution contributed to the refusal of the Irish parliament in 1792 to accede to

---

[83] Oliver MacDonagh, *The Inspector General: Sir Jeremiah Fitzpatrick and Social Reform 1783-1810* (London 1981); James Kelly, 'The context and course of Thomas Orde's plan of education of 1787', *Irish Journal of Education*, 20 (1986), 236-64; Peter MacDonagh, 'The Church of Ireland and the act of union' (unpublished paper, Byrne Perry summer school, June 1999). [84] *A Vindication of the Conduct of the Clergy who Petitioned the House of Lords against two Bills relative to Tithes in the Session of Parliament held in 1788* (Dublin 1788), p. 24; *Parliamentary Register*, vol. 8, pp. 267-8. [85] Dundas to Westmorland, 26 Dec. 1791 (2) (PRO(L) H.O. 100/33 ff 205-13). [86] Lady Gilbert (ed.), *Calendar of Ancient Records of Dublin*, vol. 14 (Dublin 1909), pp. 241-2.

Dundas' instruction on the grounds that a Protestant parliament could not do otherwise without 'subverting the constitution'.[87] This was an uncharacteristic act of defiance by Irish MPs, but the support for their stand within their community was vividly illustrated by the readiness of bodies like the Guild of Smiths and Glaziers to applaud the 'determination' of their MPs

> to maintain the Protestant ascendancy in Ireland pursuant to the fundamental principles of our valuable and venerable constitution, asserted and established by the wisdom and spirit of our ancestors under the auspices of King William the Third of glorious and immortal memory.[88]

It is upon such declarations that W.J. McCormack bases his contention that the more open and explicit adoption within Protestant ranks of the language of 'Protestant ascendancy' amounts to its 'baptism' as an independent concept. It is certainly the case that the rhetoric of ascendancy was appealed to in 1792 to an extent that Bishop Woodward can hardly have anticipated six years earlier,[89] but the fact that conservatives consistently maintained that their constitution embraced the church as well as the state cautions one against affording the question of enfranchising Catholics more emphasis than a perceived challenge to the Church of Ireland. Much rests on how one interprets the definition offered by Dublin corporation in their famous declaration on this subject in September:

> we consider the Protestant ascendancy to consist in – a Protestant king of Ireland – a Protestant parliament – a Protestant hierarchy – Protestant electors and government – the benches of justice – the army and the revenue – through all their branches and details Protestant.[90]

As a statement of the structures of the state municipal conservatives in Dublin believed should be reserved exclusively to them, this is notably succinct and explicit. Its very explicitness, indeed, explains why it has been identified as a key moment in the emergence of a concept of 'Protestant ascendancy', but it did not, in practice, seek any more than Woodward had in 1786-7. Likewise, while its articulation by Dublin corporation was socially as well as politically significant, the perpetuation of 'Protestant ascendancy' as defined by the corporation, in fact as well as in expression, was the object of a wide catchment of

---

[87] Bartlett, *Fall and Rise*, ch. 8; *Sketch of the Debates in the House of Commons of Ireland, on Wednesday 9 February 1792* (Dublin 1792), p. 6. [88] F. D'Arcy and Ken Hannigan (eds), *Workers in Union* (Dublin 1988), p. 36. [89] D.A. Chart (ed.), *The Drennan Letters* (Belfast 1931), pp. 75, 90-1 158; McCormack, *The Dublin Paper War*, ch. 5; *Northern Star*, 8 Sept., 14 Oct. 1792; *Common Sense* (Dublin 1792). [90] Gilbert (ed.), *Calendar of Ancient Records*, vol. 14, p. 267

Protestants both before, as well as during, the 1790s. It was logical that middle class corporations should be as agitated by the prospect of Catholic enfranchisement in 1792 as champions of the Church of Ireland should be by a threat to the tithe of the 1780s. For this reason, the contention that one should link its emergence as a potent term with Protestants of 'mercantile and urban' origin is ultimately unconvincing.[91] Irish Protestants of all hues, be they clergymen, MPs, common councilmen or guild members, were equally committed to its defence; they just had different priorities and emphases.

The triumph conservative Protestants enjoyed in 1792 proved short-lived as the imminence of war with France and the persistence of the Catholic Committee induced ministers to instruct the Irish executive to introduce legislation enfranchising Catholics during the 1793 parliamentary session. As the most substantive threat yet posed to the exclusively Protestant character of the constitution, this left conservative Protestants aghast, but since few of their number in receipt of crown patronage were prepared to defy ministerial wishes appropriate legislation was ratified.[92] At the same time, leading conservative office holders like John Foster and John, Lord Fitzgibbon were unwilling to allow the occasion to pass without remark, and their contributions to the debates on the legislation demonstrated that, this setback notwithstanding, conservatives were determined that the struggle to defend what remained of the Protestant constitution should continue.

To John Fitzgibbon, the key question raised by the proposal to enfranchise Catholics was where the line was now to be drawn if the essential Protestantism of the constitution was to be preserved. Echoing the arguments advanced by Woodward in 1786, Fitzgibbon contended that 'religion is the great bond of society, and therefore in every civilized country there must be a religion connected with the state, and maintained by it against all attacks and encroachments'. For this reason, it was impossible *a priori* to endow Catholics with the same political rights as Protestants. Indeed, Fitzgibbon maintained that the arguments in favour of not enfranchising Catholics were compelling because it was theoretically impossible to do so while denying them

> the right to sit in parliament; ... to fill every office in the state; ... to pay tithes exclusively to their own clergy; ... to restore the ancient pomp and splendour of their religion; ... to be governed exclusively by the laws of their own church; ... to seat their bishops in [the] House [of Lords], ... to seat a Popish prince on the throne; ... to subvert the established government, and to make this a Popish country.

91 Kelly, 'The genesis of Protestant ascendancy', pp. 125-7; McCormack, *Ascendancy and Tradition*, p. 9. 92 Bartlett, *Fall and Rise*, ch. 9.

Fitzgibbon had no doubt but that this was their 'ultimate object', and the lesson of history was that it was not possible for men of different religious persuasions to agree a workable constitution. Specifically, it was not possible to allow Catholics access to political power, because they defined those who did not accept their belief as heretics whose destiny was eternal damnation in the next world and 'persecution' in this, and he supported this contention with evidence drawn from both the Lateran Council and the Council of Constance as well as the experience of Irish Protestants in 1641.[93]

John Foster was of broadly similar views. He was, he explained, prepared to allow Catholics extensive liberties in matters of religion and society, but he drew 'a line round the constitution', because enfranchisement was the first step on the road that must end inevitably in emancipation, the transfer of the payment of the tithe from the Church of Ireland to the Catholic Church, the coronation of a Catholic king and a 'total separation from Great Britain'. On a personal level, he argued that to enfranchise Catholics was incompatible with 'the trust' he received 'from Protestants, under a Protestant King, a Protestant constitution, and a Protestant ascendancy' when he was elected to parliament.[94]

Fitzgibbon's and Foster's exposition of their position highlights the permeation of the neo-conservative rhetoric most closely identified with Bishop Woodward and Dublin corporation. The appeal of this ideological rhetoric was extended in the 1790s by the recognition that the enfranchisement of Catholics would tip the constitutional balance in the direction of what Fitzgibbon termed 'complete democracy and anarchy'. In common with conservatives throughout Europe, they saw in the example of France a further illustration of the danger of constitutional innovation. Foster expressed this vividly when he opined that the effect of enfranchising Catholics would be to 'make every Catholic an advocate of the worst species of reform, where numbers and not property are to influence'. Fitzgibbon was characteristically more blunt. He forecast that if 'the right of representation' was opened 'to the mass of the people', it must produce 'a popular assembly, detached altogether from the influence of the other estates, influenced only by the people' which must culminate either in 'a state of anarchy' or in a 'pure democracy'. In support of this interpretation, he instanced mid-seventeenth century England and contemporary France where revolutionary regimes had 'murdered their king; ... subverted the church; annihilated the peerage; and under the specious name of a republic' created chaos where order should exist. Democratic reform, he averred, was a recipe for the creation of 'tyranny' or 'savage despotism', and he forecast confidently that if Ireland embarked on this road the 'country is lost'. Because

---

[93] *The Speech of the Rt Hon John, Earl of Clare ... Delivered in the Irish House of peers ... March 13, 1793* (London 1813), pp. 24-9.   [94] *An Accurate Report of the Speech of John Foster ... in the Committee on the Roman Catholic Bill February, 27, 1793* (Dublin 1798), pp. 10-12, 18, 21-2.

maintaining the 'Protestant interest' intact would ensure this did not come to pass and safeguard the British connection it was, he propounded, incumbent upon the government to ensure the Protestant constitution was 'maintain[ed] ... and support [ed]'.[95]

As Foster's and Fitzgibbon's statements emphasize, the prospect of democracy demanded a focused conservative response. Its most interesting Irish exponent was John Kells, a Dublin lawyer.[96] His most important work was the 1794 tract *The Rights of Juries* in which he advanced a strong case in support of the contention that there were few circumstances in which it was legitimate to seek actively to subvert a government in order to effect a revolutionary transfer of power. Arising out of his conclusion that 'every means will not be justified by the end', no matter how beneficial they might be in the long term, he was persuaded by the fact that since 'the progress of our [British] constitution has been rather through reformation than revolution', this was the means by which political change should ever be brought about.[97] In this context, he noted that it was 'a usual practice' of those promoting revolutionary change 'to conceal the revolutionary principles of sedition under the specious mask of reform' or 'renovation', when it was incumbent upon them to honour the 'legitimate government'.[98] If this reads like an inadequate defence of the *status quo*, it was of little concern to Kells who was content to defend the existing British constitution as superior to all other systems of government. He thus had no difficulty, for example, denying that government should be 'founded in the representation of the majority in numbers'; it was, he observed, 'fundamentally adverse to our constitution'. By extension, he concluded that it was better to endure what he termed 'abuses ... in the extreme' than to embark on revolutionary insurrection that would tip the balance of the constitution in favour of the people:

> Reassumption of the trust by an insurrection of the people enforcing their strength by the weight of numbers is an evil worse than the temporary abuse of power as it ends in a dissolution of all certain known and limited authorities, and an establishment of power manifold greater in hands unknown, unrecognized, and unqualified. It is a change of despotism circumscribed for despotism unlimited.[99]

Kells reinforced this counter-revolutionary message by presenting many of the same ideas in the more popular form of 'a dialogue on government between

---

95 *Speech of John Foster*, p. 21; *Speech of ... Clare*, pp. 35-7. **96** Edward Keane et al. (eds), *King's Inns Admission Papers 1607-1867* (Dublin 1982), p. 259. **97** Significantly he deemed it improper to describe 1688 in England as a revolution: 'it was clearly no more than a restoration or reformation of the constitution' ([John Kells], *The Rights of Juries Legal and Constitutional in Cases of Libel, Considered in a Letter to the Jurors of Ireland* (Dublin 1794), p. 34 n). **98** Ibid., pp. 13-14, 23, 33-7. **99** Ibid., pp. 46-50.

a gentleman and a farmer'. In this he excoriated the idea that government by what he tellingly termed the 'sovereign people' or the 'mob' could result in anything other than the 'reign of barbarism' that currently passed for government in revolutionary France because it, by definition, necessitated 'the subversion of all the other estates by one, the third estate or the multitude'. As this implies, as well as highlighting the savagery conservatives identified with the French Revolution and with the democracy it fostered, it was Kells' contention that the 'mixed government' that existed in Britain was that most likely to produce good law and ensure 'the happiness and security' of those who lived under its jurisdiction.[100]

Despite their inability to resist the enfranchisement of Catholics, conservatives were relieved that parallel efforts to reform the Irish representative system in the mid-1790s were rebuffed. At the same time, the rise in agrarian and politically motivated disorder in the mid-1790s ensured that their fears that a conspiracy was hatching to deprive them of their civil, political and religious liberties remained acute.[101] Their anxieties on this point, and the forecasts they made in 1793 that enfranchisement would lead inevitably to the further erosion of the legal foundations of their ascendancy seemed destined to be realized when, following his unexpected appointment as lord lieutenant, Earl Fitzwilliam gave his approval to the introduction in 1795 of legislation aimed at admitting Catholics to parliament. Fitzwilliam's controversial recall ensured that this legislation stood no chance of reaching the statute book when the House of Commons debated it on 4 May. Nevertheless, the debate is of more than passing interest.

In many respects, conservatives in 1795 were content to reiterate the arguments they had advanced in 1793 – that emancipation was incompatible with a Protestant constitution and that it must lead inevitably to a 'Popish ... church establishment'.[102] However, their tone was perceptibly sharper. This is particularly evident in the belligerent contribution of Patrick Duigenan. Significantly, Duigenan made no attempt to demonstrate the danger empowering Catholics posed to 'the civil constitution' and the 'ecclesiastical establishment' by citing the many instances of Catholic oppression of Protestants in the annals of Irish and European history. He focused instead on the evidence of Catholic 'disloyalty' he identified around him, and justified his contention that this provided ample support for his position by linking it to the doctrinal position of the Catholic church which, he contended:

100 [John Kells], *Spectacles for Sans-culottes, or Full Age or a Dialogue on Government between a Gentleman and an a Farmer* (Dublin 1794), pp. 21-3, 32-49, 56-61. 101 Deborah Jenkins, 'The correspondence of Charles Brodrick', *Irish Archives Bulletin* (1974), 46; Loftus to Loftus, 20 Feb. 1793 (NLI Autograph Letters, Ms 3009 f. 21). 102 *Report of the Debate in the House of Commons on the Bill for the Further Relief of ... Roman Catholics* (Dublin 1795), pp. 24-9.

> tends strongly to render Roman Catholics irreconcilable enemies to Protestants; how can real amity subsist between them, when the Roman Catholic believes his Protestant neighbours to be a living tabernacle for the devil, and that his spirit, immediately on its separation from the body, descends to hell and is doomed to eternal misery?

This remark, along with further comment on papal infallibility, argument adduced from Bishop Woodward's *Present State* on the consecration oath taken by Catholic bishops, as well as questionable *ad hominen* observations and unsustainable claims for the size of the Protestant population, bear witness to the fact that Duigenan's speech had more in common with an anti-Catholic tract than a traditional parliamentary statement. Like Fitzgibbon and Foster in 1793, he was convinced that, if Catholics were allowed to become MPs, parliamentary reform would soon follow, with the inevitable result that

> all aristocratic influence will be then banished from this house; it will become a mere democratic assembly, and the more Catholic the more democratic. Then adieu to all establishment; church and state will vanish before them, an immediate attempt to turn this monarchical government into a republic under the protection of France, and severed from the British empire, will be the consequence. This nation will become a field of battle for the British and the French; ... misery and desolation will overwhelm the country like a deluge ...[103]

A small number of liberal-minded MPs distanced themselves from such apocalyptic outpourings and from the discordant implications of what one termed 'the doctrines of ascendancy'.[104] But is clear from the balance of the debate and from the public and uncompromising articulation of the merits of continued 'Protestant ascendancy' that neo-conservative thinking had a firm hold of the Protestant body politic.[105]

The greater assertiveness of neo-conservatism and the increased fragility of public order as opponents of the constitutional *status quo* opted for revolutionary tactics to achieve their aims, resulted, inevitably, in intensified counter-insurgency by the state. Most conservatives had little problem with this because it represented their preferred response to disorder. Their support for such a strategy was augmented by the perception, articulated by the earl of Clare in August 1796, that, if they were allowed, the Catholic population would rise in rebel-

---

[103] *Report of the Debate ... on the Bill for the ... Relief of ... Roman Catholics*, pp. 109-23. [104] See the comments of Charles Hely-Hutchinston, Sir Thomas Osborne and Fletcher (ibid., pp. 83, 89, 97-8). [105] J.R. Hill, *From Patriots to Unionists: Dublin Civic Politics and Irish Protestant Patriotism* (Oxford 1998), p. 249; *Dublin Evening Post*, 28 Jan. 1796.

lion and 'we should see the scenes of 1641 renewed, and the country again desolated by every species of savage enormity'.[106] The attempted invasion by a French fleet in December 1796 heightened their sense of vulnerability, increased their readiness to approve extreme measures, and reinforced the conviction,[107] already well established, that the contagious example and perfidious influence of France was the main cause of the disorder gripping the country. Charles Francis Sheridan articulated this conclusion with characteristic skill in 1797. Responding to the argument of radicals that the disturbed condition of the country was attributable to the failure of government to address the grievances of the people, he maintained that the real cause was the example of France:

> the present melancholy and alarming times had not their origin either in the gross violations of our constitution, prior to the year 1782, or in the abuses of government subsequent to that year; which directly prove, that they commenced with the date of the French Revolution, grew with the growth of that revolution, and gradually attained their present formidable aspect, as French principles and doctrines became prevalent among the people. Who will assert, that if the French revolution, and its unfortunate consequence the war with France, had never taken place, we would, notwithstanding, have equally beheld the present melancholy and alarming times?[108]

The readiness of a onetime Whig such as Sheridan to defend 'the servants of government' against criticism is noteworthy. But it is even more significant that his conclusion that should the spirit of revolution triumph in Ireland, as it had in France, it would lead to 'the dreary waste of civil confusion, civil vengeance, civil bloodshed, and the unutterable horrors of every destructive ANARCHY' was shared by others of comparable backgrounds.[109] Bishop Thomas Lewis O'Beirne, who had served as Fitzwilliam's private secretary in 1794-5, was so disillusioned by what he described as Henry Grattan's reliance on 'democratic theorists' such as Samuel Thelwall and domestic radicals such as the United Irishmen, and so disturbed by the 'spirit of disaffection' he observed in the Catholic population, that he forsook the Whigs. He did not quite embrace the politics of 'Protestant ascendancy', but his confession to William Windham that he was 'full as desirous to preserve the Church of Ireland as the zealous advo-

---

[106] Clare to Camden, 28 Aug. 1796 (Kent Archives Office, Camden Papers, U840/0183/6). [107] Nancy Curtin, 'The United Irishmen in Dublin and Ulster' (unpublished Ph.D thesis, University of Wisconsin-Madison, 1988), pp. 645-52; Kevin Whelan, 'The origins of the Orange Order', *Bullán*, 2 (1996), 29-30. [108] [Charles Francis Sheridan], *Some Observations on a Late Address to the Citizens of Dublin with Thoughts on the Present Crisis*, 4th edn (Dublin 1797), pp. 14-17. [109] Ibid., pp. 17, 47-8.

cates for Protestant ascendancy' provides a significant barometer of the mounting appeal of neo-conservative thinking by the end of 1797.[110]

There were dissentients, of course, but Whigs like Henry Grattan and the duke of Leinster who openly queried the appositeness of bulwarking 'Protestant ascendancy' had little influence by this time.[111] Besides, the outbreak of rebellion in May 1798 and the conviction, embraced by large sections of the Protestant community, that the rebels aspired to their extirpation served to increase the appeal of the negative interpretation of Catholicism advanced by conservatives.[112] Anxious to ensure that this was how the rebellion was interpreted, the pages of conservative newspapers soon reverberated with accounts of rebel atrocities, while ideological die-hards like Patrick Duigenan, who had repeatedly warned of this very prospect, depicted it as the inevitable consequence of a 'Popish plot'.[113] In the short term, conservative anger was kept within bounds by the forceful suppression of the rebellion, but once the administration's priority shifted from counter-insurgency to the restoration of social harmony their determination to ensure that their interpretation of events prevailed intensified. Convinced that the lord lieutenant, Lord Cornwallis, aspired 'to gloss over our misfortunes and the massacres of Protestants', arising out of which it was claimed 'we know not the hundredth part of the dreadful scenes that have happened', conservatives perceived that a valuable service would be accomplished if 'the cruelties exercised by the Roman Catholics against the Protestants' were 'collected and given to the public'.[114] There was no consensus on the form this should take, but Sir Richard Musgrave was clear in his own mind about what should be done. A long-time advocate of 'Protestant ascendancy', he was determined that the lessons of the 'savage barbarity' of the rebellion would not be lost. So he undertook to write a history of the event which, like its exemplar Sir John Temple's history of 1641, was grounded upon real experiences in anticipation that this would serve, as Temple's history had done, to persuade Protestants to rally to the defence of their constitution.[115]

As this suggests Musgrave's primary purpose was ideological rather than historical. His goal, he confided, was 'to vindicate the Protestant church' and to

---

110 O'Beirne to Fitzwilliam, 16 Oct. 1796, 4 May, 12 Dec. 1797 (Sheffield City Library, Fitzwilliam Papers); O'Beirne to Windham, 7 Apr. 1797, [n.d] (BL Windham Papers, Add. Mss 37877 ff 16-18, 104-5). 111 James Kelly, *Henry Grattan*, pp. 35-6; Leinster to Camden, 9 May 1798 cited in R. Aylmer, 'The Duke of Leinster leaves Ireland' (unpublished paper, 1997), p.23. 112 James Kelly, '"We were all to have been massacred": Irish Protestants and the experience of rebellion' in David Dickson et al. (eds), *The 1798 Rebellion: A Bicentenary Perspective* (Dublin forthcoming). 113 Dáire Keogh, *The French Disease* (Dublin 1993), pp. 204-9. 114 Tighe to Ponsonby, 20 Oct. 1798 (NLI Wicklow Papers, Ms 4813); H.W. to Percy, 15 Mar. 1791 (NLI Musgrave Papers, Ms 4156 f. 34). 115 Bartlett, *Fall and Rise*, p. 238; Musgrave to Percy, [Oct. 1798] (NLI Musgrave Papers, Ms 4157 ff 91-2); David Dickson, 'Foreword' to Sir Richard Musgrave, *Memoirs of the Irish Rebellion of 1798*, 4th edn (Indiana 1995).

defend 'the constitution in church and state' by demonstrating that the rebellion was intrinsically sectarian and that Protestants were targeted for extirpation.[116] With this in mind, he applied to witnesses, Church of Ireland clergy, soldiers and country gentlemen for statements and information; he borrowed, made notes upon, and collected correspondence and documents; and he studied 'trial proceedings' and such 'notes' as he was given access to by military officers. The cumulative impact of 'the thousand curious anecdotes of the atrocities of the Co[unt]y Wexford' he gathered persuaded him that massacre was the intention of the rebels and 'the sanguinary' object of Roman Catholicism. It also became clear that it would take longer than he originally calculated to present this in a form that would achieve his stated purpose.[117] This was not a matter of little consequence because his contention (published under the pseudonym of Verax) that the rebellion was 'Popish' had already been challenged by James Caulfield, the Catholic bishop of Ferns. Convinced that this was too important to overlook, Musgrave set about preparing a 'rejoinder which will expose the ludicrous features of Popery and prove the guilt of not only the vulgar herd of priests but even of their bishop'. He was also eager to make 'some of the most striking features of the rebellion' and 'the abominations of Popery' public without delay. The resulting work, a pamphlet he entitled *A Concise Account of the Material Events and Atrocities which Occurred in the Present Rebellion*, was published in March 1799, and Musgrave felt vindicated by the warm reception it was accorded; his pamphlet sold out three editions and a Cork imprint over the summer of 1799 which justified, he pronounced, his decision to take time out from preparing his history to write it.[118]

The thesis of *A Concise Account* was the by now recognizable conservative argument that the 1798 rebellion was a 'popish rebellion' instigated and advanced by the Catholic clergy in order to bring about 'the extirpation of heretics' because this was the 'sanguinary' mission of Roman Catholicism. In support of this conclusion, Musgrave cited some of the evidence he had collected in the course of his research into the Wexford rebellion that attested both to the participation of Catholic clerics and to their failure to prevent atrocities. He was, expectedly, scornful of Bishop Caulfield's claim that those Protestants who suffered did so because they were Orangemen; this was, he thundered, nothing more than 'an artful attempt to hide the grim, the hideous, the gorgon

---

116 Musgrave to Percy, 22 Sept., 22 Dec. 1798 (NLI Musgrave Papers, Ms 4157 ff 89, 79). 117 Musgrave to Percy, 20 Aug., 22 Sept., [Oct.], 1, 8, 13, 26 Oct, 16, 30 Nov., 6 Dec. 1798, 2, 15 Jan., 15 Feb. 1799 (NLI Musgrave Papers, Ms 4157 ff 83, 89-90, 91-2, 93, 95, 97, 99, 101, 103, 81, 77, 7-8, 20-2). NLI Ms 4156 contains copies of materials, notes, information and correspondence to Bishop Percy that informed Musgrave's work. 118 Musgrave to Percy, 8 Oct., 22 Dec 1798, 2, 28 Jan., [early Mar.], 5 Mar., [Mar.] 1799 (NLI Musgrave Papers, Ms 4157 ff 95, 79, 77, 1, 31, 33, 39).

visage of Popery, with a political mask, while fanatical fury against Protestants in general fomented'. Indeed, Musgrave contended, citing Archbishop Troy of Dublin on the unchanging nature of Catholic tenets, this was how Catholicism was and how it had always been:

> we find them equally destructive against the Albigenses and Waldenses in the 13th century, against the Protestants of Paris in the 16th, in the expulsion of the Moors from Spain, in the Irish rebellion in 1641, against the Protestants of France in 1791, in the massacre on Vinegar Hill, in the barn of Scullabogue, on the bridge of Wexford, and in the general carnage of Protestants which took place in that once-peaceful and happy country.

Musgrave's explicit linkage of the Wexford rebellion with previous Catholic 'massacres' amounted to the modernization of classic Protestant massacre theory to embrace the events of 1798. As such, it offered little that was conceptually new. But then this was not what he sought to achieve or what his Protestant readers sought. What was new, and what the pamphlet provided, was a reasoned argument as to why 1798 belonged in this familiar gallery of testaments to bigotry and why conservative Protestants were justified in urging the preservation intact of their constitution in church and state. The fact that the extensive evidence he supplied to sustain the rebellion's inclusion was presented in a text that traced the policy of disposing of heretics from the Lateran Council, and that he documented his contention 'that many doctrines of the Popish church, not only encouraged but even recommended persecution and bloodshed', gave his tract authority. It provided Protestants with a rationale for the conclusion they had already arrived at emotionally, that the 1798 rising was 'a Popish rebellion against Protestantism', and that the Protestants who were killed died for the same reason that their forebears had died in 1641 – because 'the spirit of Popery, as ravenous as the grave, and as relentless as death, dictated their destruction'.[119]

This was an interpretation Musgrave sought to reinforce with his history of the rebellion, which he continued to research through most of 1799. During that time, he collected much additional information on events in 1798. But of greater consequence, he increased his knowledge of 'the factions and insurrections' that had dominated much of the Irish rural landscape since the early 1760s.[120] This allowed him to incorporate that disorder, which had so agitated

---

[119] Veridicus [Sir Richard Musgrave], *A Concise Account of the Material Events and Atrocities which Occurred in the Present Rebellion with the Causes which Produced them, and an Answer to Veritas's Vindication of the Roman Catholic Clergy of the Town of Wexford*, 3rd edn (Dublin 1799), especially pp. 2, 16, 19, 33, 41-2, 48.   [120] Musgrave to Pery, 25 June 1799 (NLI Musgrave Papers, Ms 4157 f. 54).

many Protestants since its commencement, into his narrative to show that the warnings they had articulated about the Whiteboys and Rightboys were correct, and to present the rebellion of 1798 as the culmination of a phase of rural disorder dating back over four decades. Such retrospective validation was important for conservatives who had frequently been dismissed as alarmist for their observations on agrarian disorder. Musgrave was so intent that this allegation should not be levelled at his history of the rebellion that he determined it should present a detailed account of the background to as well as of the course of the rebellion, and not resort to the overtly polemical style of *A Concise Account*.

This is not how Musgrave's history, which he entitled *Memoirs of the Irish Rebellion of 1798*, the first edition of which was published in the spring of 1801, is perceived today. But the lengths to which the author went to gather and to collate testimonies 'in order to avoid the smallest aberration from truth' deserves acknowledgement. As this implies, *Memoirs of the Irish Rebellion* offers an elaborately detailed, vigorous statement of the conservative Protestant thesis that the rebellion was prompted by the sectarian ambitions of Irish Catholics that still resonates because of the detail of the narrative and the high emotion with which the 'sanguinary' intent of those in rebellion and the bloody fate of their Protestant victims is related. Interpretively, it offers little not available in *A Concise Account*. But it dwarfs the earlier work in scope and in scale, in accordance with Musgrave's wish to provide a full and expansive chronicle of the brutality experienced by Protestants during the rebellion, of the excesses of the rebels, and of the complicity of the Catholic clergy.[121]

Because it provided the account many believed the authorities were intent on occluding, and because it 'proved' they had been targeted for decimation, Musgrave's *Irish Rebellion* was warmly received by the growing constituency of conservative Protestants. Its acceptance was aided by continuing disorder that reinforced their conclusion that Catholics remained as determined as ever 'to cut off all the Protestants'.[122] In view of this, it is hardly surprising that Musgrave enthusiastically endorsed an act of union as the means most likely to perpetuate the constitutional and religious liberties of Irish Protestants. Indeed, he delayed publishing his history, on the duke of Portland's request, 'till the union question was finally decided'. Once the book was in print, however, he took the necessary steps to ensure it sold well in Britain; he was no less eager to make it clear to Protestant opinion there as well as in Ireland that 'the Protestant religion' was 'the only bond of union' binding Ireland to Britain.[123] The reception

---

121. Musgrave, *Memoirs of the Irish Rebellion*, passim. 122 See, inter alia, P. Power, 'A Carrickman's diary 1787-1809', *Journal of the Waterford and South-East of Ireland Archaeological Society*, 17 (1914), 14; Garde to Heaton, Apr. 1800 (PRONI Chatsworth Papers, T3158/1801); Musgrave to Loftus, 16 May 1801 (NLI Autograph letters, Ms 3009 f. 51). 123 Ibid.; Musgrave to Devonshire, 24 Apr. 1800 (PRONI Chatsworth Papers, T3158/1802);

it was afforded exceeded his expectations. Musgrave's *Irish Rebellion* was widely reviewed in British conservative periodicals and the virtually unanimous conclusion was that he had proven conclusively that the object of the 1798 rising was to exterminate Irish Protestants and that Catholics remained as committed as ever to this policy. Arising out of this, Musgrave's *Rebellion* became one of the defining texts of the new British right and of conservative Irish Protestantism in the early nineteenth century. It proved so influential, indeed, that William Bennett, afterwards bishop of Cloyne, claimed it was of 'the utmost service' in prompting a palpable shift in political attitude in Britain from favouring Catholic relief in the late eighteenth to upholding the Protestant constitution in the early nineteenth century.[124]

VI

This was a satisfactory outcome for conservative Protestants. Over a period of nearly half a century, Protestants of a variety of intellectual hues had sought to defend their constitution against incursion by Catholics. Until the late 1770s, the broad consensus that exclusion was the best policy had ensured that such sorties and sallies as were made to breach the protective legal fortifications Irish Protestants had erected were repulsed. This reflected agreement within the Protestant body politic that their security demanded that they accord Catholics no additional legal, political or economic rights because *any* weakening of the protection the Protestant interest was accorded by law was likely to hasten the destruction of their liberties, the subversion of the Protestant constitution in church and state and, possibly, their wholesale massacre. However, during the late 1770s and early 1780s, the wish of the British government to conciliate Catholics and the emergence of a strand of opinion within Protestantism disposed to favour legal toleration contributed to the fracturing of that sectional consensus, and a host of economic and religious restrictions affecting Catholics were repealed. Matters looked distinctly gloomy for those committed to uphold the Protestant constitution at that point, but they regrouped in the mid-1780s to rally to the defence of the ecclesiastical branch of their constitution. This was a key moment because the emergence then of a strong neo-conservative strand emboldened many Protestants to affirm their continuing commitment to the defence of what they now termed 'Protestant ascendancy'. In rhetorical and conceptual terms, this was perhaps the greatest achievement of conservative Protestant thought in the late eighteenth century because it provided its adher-

---

Musgrave to Stockdale, 11 June 1801 in HMC *Laing Mss*, vol. 2, pp. 685-6. **124** Sack, *From Jacobite to Conservative*, pp. 96-7, 240-2; Bennett's notes on Musgrave's History (NLI Ms 637).

ents with a name, a slogan and a definition, which was significantly more potent than the term 'Protestant interest' they had used up to this.

The absorption into general political discourse of the term 'Protestant ascendancy' increased in the early 1790s when the exclusive political dominion exercised by Protestants in Ireland faced its most serious threat in over a century. Enfranchisement could not be resisted, but conservative Protestant thought was reinforced by linkage with the opponents of democracy and other radical ideas emanating from revolutionary France. This and growing popular disorder increased the resolve of Protestants to hold the line, but while neo-conservative arguments became increasingly attractive to those of their communion as political disorder intensified in the 1790s, they remained vulnerable. This was underlined by the outbreak of rebellion in May 1798. However, as had happened in 1786-7, this crisis resulted in the further energizing of conservative Protestant thinking. Publications by Richard Musgrave in 1799 and 1801 convinced Protestants across the British Isles of the rectitude of the contention that Catholic empowerment was incompatible with the survival of Protestant civil and ecclesiastical liberties. Since from 1 January 1801 Protestants in Britain and Ireland were joined together in a new constitutional entity known as the United Kingdom, political developments assured them of a more sympathetic context in which to articulate their reinforced conservative thinking on law, government and religion. It was a development of enormous consequence, without which the invigoration of conservative Protestant thought that took place in the aftermath of the 1798 rebellion could not have so decisively influenced the course of Irish history during the first three decades of the nineteenth century.

Protestant Ireland:
the view from a distance

J.G.A. POCOCK

The Centre for the History of British Political Thought, which has played a part in the production of this volume, has promoted a number of related enterprises. After the six seminars which led to the writing of *The Varieties of British Political Thought, 1500-1800*,[1] we confronted the fact that the subject matter of that volume was overwhelmingly English – at least until its eighteenth-century chapters, when David Hume, Adam Smith, John Adams, Thomas Jefferson and Edmund Burke made their appearance. We had not yet escaped the inherited incubus of saying 'British' and meaning 'English', but in order to begin throwing it off we promoted two seminars on the mainly Scottish debates attending the Anglo-Scottish Unions of 1603 and 1707,[2] and a third exploring the conceptual links between the latter event and its antithesis, the revolution that accompanied the American Declaration of Independence of 1776. In these debates, Scots were to be seen constructing a 'Britain' and asking whether it could have any meaning beyond that the English were prepared to accord it; while 'Americans' – the majority of them who did not end as 'Canadians' – were finding that in order to fulfil their self–image as 'English' they must cease being English altogether and engage in a discourse of federalism which had never been employed in the construction of 'Britain'.[3]

The present volume is the latest of three[4] arising from seminars in which the Centre for the History of British Political Thought has enquired into political debate, literature and theory in Ireland between the Nine Years' War ending in 1601 and the act of union exactly two centuries later. There are obvious tensions here; much Irish thought is neither British nor English, and much Irish history is that of resistance to being conquered and included in either an English kingdom or a British multi-national (but English-dominated) union. A Centre named as this one is must excuse its inclusion of Irish (or American) political

---

1 Edited by J.G.A. Pocock with the assistance of Gordon J. Schochet and Lois G. Schwoerer (Cambridge 1993). 2 Roger A. Mason (ed.), *Scots and Britons: Scottish Political Thought and the Union of 1603* (Cambridge 1994); John Robertson (ed.), *A Union for Empire: Political Thought and the Union of 1707* (Cambridge 1995). 3 J.G.A. Pocock, *La Ricostruzione di un Impero: Sovranità Britannica e Federalismo Americano*, trans. Sergio Luzzatto (Macerata 1996). 4 Hiram Morgan (ed.), *Political Ideology in Ireland, 1541-1641* (Dublin 1999); Jane H. Ohlmeyer (ed.), *Political Thought in Seventeenth-Century Ireland* (Cambridge 2000).

thought within its purview by stressing that inclusion does not mean annexation. A phenomenon in history cannot be understood without understanding of its opposite, and therefore British and Irish political thought, even when most deeply opposed, cannot be understood without an understanding of each other. The Other – to use language now in fashion – is part of the Self to which it is opposed, and relations between self and anti–self are often surprisingly complex. They do not go away even when a dissolution of the self is attempted.

There are two methodological settings in which this volume, and those belonging with it, may be situated. The first is that provided by the new history of political thought, which aims at reconstructing the languages of discourse used in political societies in the past, and enquiring who performed discursive acts with them and what were the acts performed.[5] This approach tends to emphasize the authors rather than the audiences of these acts, those who did them rather than those to whom they were done; but this is not altogether misleading, since discourses tend to be self-enclosing and addressed to those who already accept and employ them. The most hegemonic of discourses are commonly intended more to encourage rulers to maintain their hegemony than to encourage the ruled to submit to it; and since the life of ruling communities is seldom free from uncertainty and insecurity, their discourses may contain quite explicit discussions of the ambiguities and problems they discover in maintaining their position. The present volume is largely, though not wholly, about the problems which the Protestant Irish of the eighteenth century debated among themselves.

The second setting is that provided by the 'new British history', a field of study which has taken shape without ceasing to be inherently problematic.[6] It aims at presenting the interacting histories of the peoples inhabiting the islands of northwest Europe, an archipelago to which the term 'British Isles' has been applied by some while being rejected by others; a circumstance which is enough to render the use of the adjective 'British' problematic and questionable. 'British history', furthermore, is very largely the history of the rise, extension and modification of that Anglo–British state, empire and union known as the 'Kingdom of Great Britain'. Ireland both has been included in this entity and has rejected that inclusion, with the result that relations between the two are inherently part of the history of each. The case for including Irish in 'British' history in the former sense is, paradoxically, the strength with which it has rejected inclusion in the latter.

---

[5] For a detailed enquiry into the methodology of this history, see James Tully and Quentin Skinner (eds), *Meaning and Context: Quentin Skinner and his Critics* (Cambridge 1989); also J.G.A. Pocock, *Virtue, Commerce and History* (Cambridge 1985), ch. 1.   [6] Glenn Burgess (ed.), *The New British History: Founding a Modern State, 1603-1715* (London 1999); Tony Claydon and Ian McBride (eds), *Protestantism and National Identity: Britain and Ireland, c.1650-c.1850* (Cambridge 1998).

Protestant Ireland: the view from a distance

The several histories – Irish, English, Scottish, possible British, and so forth – of which 'British' history consists are, as we have seen, discourses, and discourses are constructs; though it can scarcely be necessary to remind Irish readers that history may be experienced as well as invented. The 'history' an 'imagined community' constructs of itself will in the first place be addressed to itself; it will be a history of how the community has come to exist and be invented, and a set of reasons for continuing the existence of this entity. This formula is equally true of communities whose existence has consisted in the maintenance of hegemony and of those whose existence has consisted in rebellion against it; each will see its history as, in a certain sense, the exercise of sovereignty. But if each history is a discourse addressed to a collective 'self', it is also a history of interactions with 'others' outside that self and will be, at times almost inadvertently, addressed to those others. These, furthermore, may have engaged in the construction of historical discourses of their own, addressed to their 'selves' as collective entities; and the several histories will be uttered concurrently, all too often in denial of one another but capable of interaction and possibly dialogue. The 'new British history', therefore, consists of a number of histories which peoples tell to and of themselves, but can hear being told to and by others; and it is possible to induce them to re–tell their own histories as they may have appeared to, and been experienced by, one another. Each history, it will follow, can be told from more than one point of view: e.g. that of self and that of other.

The political discourse most prominently presented in this volume is a special case, since it consists in the self-fashionings and self-questionings of a people on the whole no longer existing: the Irish Protestants of the eighteenth-century 'ascendancy' (though they did not begin to use the term until the supremacy it described was under new kinds of threat). The dominant themes in the recorded and printed 'political thought' of the seventeenth century are provided by the Catholic Old English;[7] as that people is broken up and leaves the apparent scene – surviving in whatever forms wherever they did – it is replaced by another, the Protestants formerly known to us as the New English. These continue for some time to think of themselves as 'English' (rather than 'British') and to employ modes of discourse ancient-constitutionalist, whiggish and recognizably English; it would be a temptation to describe them as 'west Britons' had they known the term or thought of themselves (they evidently did not) as involved in that Anglo–Scottish union out of which the term 'Britain' must emerge. Here the non–Irish reader needs to be reminded that 'Protestant' is a term of art denoting members of the Church of Ireland closely modelled on the Church of England. Presbyterians and others were known by the English term 'Dissenters', though as the Scots they largely were

[7] Ohlmeyer (ed.), *Political Thought*.

in the northern counties they were either members of the established Church of Scotland or Secessionists from it; English hegemony came in many linguistic forms.

The 'political thought' left on record by the 'Protestant' community is Irish in the sense that it is produced in Ireland, about living in Ireland, by authors increasingly disposed to regard themselves as 'Irish' in some sense which they are concerned to define. If it has a connecting theme leading to a climax – it would be whiggish to assume that it has one, but not necessarily whiggish to suggest that perhaps it has[8] – this is the shaping of what may be defined by terms as various as 'colonial nationalism' and 'settler patriotism'.[9] The latter may be preferable: the word 'colonial' risks confusing the experience of those who colonize with that of those who are colonized, while 'nationalism' invokes both the unmanageable body of theory surrounding that word and one of the major and now most disputed themes of Irish history. Communities of settlers, it may be suggested, face the problem of establishing the cultural and political identity they have brought with them in a new environment; they claim both to have remained what they were, and to have taken root where they are and derive identity from it. Tensions with their community of origin may equal or exceed tensions with the indigenous community among whom they have settled; they may find themselves claiming both to continue part of the original community and to assert themselves against it. In both Protestant Ireland and the American colonies, eighteenth-century British history is rich in phenomena of this kind. The enterprise is not necessarily doomed, as language now fashionable likes to suggest, but it is complex and may have many outcomes.

Those of the 'Protestant ascendancy' considered themselves 'English', and were often angry with the English for calling them 'Irish' in ways that seemed to confound them with either or both the 'Catholic' and the 'native' Irish. (The inability of communities of origin to understand or comprehend their communities of settlement is a theme more important than explored.) They came, over time, grudgingly to call themselves 'Irish' and to attempt their own constructions of that term. Their initial need, however, was for political language in which they could declare themselves English and oblige the English to hear their voice, as both 'English' and 'English' in a distinctive way; language both oppositional and historical. Of such languages there were several available. One – a distinctive language of Irish Protestantism – may perhaps (but not certainly) be dismissed; the 'Protestant' confession may have been too small, and

---

8 I write as a sometime pupil of Herbert Butterfield, whose *The Whig Interpretation of History* was not intended as the indictment of all narrative structure it has occasionally been allowed to become.   9 A thoughtful analysis of these terms and their attendant phenomena will be found in D. George Boyce, *Nationalism in Ireland*, 3rd edn (London 1995), pp. 99-101, 106-8.

too beleaguered in its ascendancy, to redefine itself in terms as original as those of James Ussher in the previous century.[10] Among languages of secular self-definition, the first to hand was that of ancient-constitutionalism: the assertion of medieval liberties still necessary to vindicate the Revolution of 1688. Here the problem arose that the liberties of England – which entailed denial that the Normans had conquered England in 1066 – had been brought to Ireland, a hundred years later, by Norman conquerors from whom the Catholic Old English had claimed descent. The solution was to argue that these settlers had enlarged the English kingdom by compacting with the English crown to retain their liberties under its protection; an argument which implied a certain aboriginality of title. Here the Protestant Molyneux can be seen annexing or at least echoing the discourse of the Catholic Patrick Darcy,[11] and suggesting that the Irish parliament was subject to the English king but not the English king-in-parliament; it was to be long, however, before Irish Whigs needed to carry his argument to such lengths.

American colonists, drawing on Molyneux where they knew of him, evolved their own version of this argument. Their claim to aboriginality of settler title, however, could rest on an image of settlers occupying a wilderness and acquiring title by simple appropriation; the Lockeian model became relevant once that author had attained (as he soon did) a sufficient authority.[12] Once it was asserted that pre-settlement aborigines had not occupied the soil and possessed no title to it, conquest over them ceased to be important to the argument. In the Anglocentric history being constructed of Ireland, however, this was not the case. However scornfully the 'mere Irish' had been dismissed as a people of pre-civilized cattle herders, they remained – for whatever reasons – a necessary feature of the argument. The claim that the Norman invaders had made compacts with the English crown was enhanced rather than diminished by the claim that they had entered into compacts with Gaelic kings and chiefs; conquest and compact were two faces of the same medal, and there was no need of an equivalent for the English myth that William the Norman had been no conqueror in the first place. It was necessary, however, and had been since the times of Edmund Spenser and Sir John Davies, to construct relatively complex histories of the medieval English 'conquest' of Ireland, culminating in surrender and regrant.[13]

---

10 Alan Ford, 'James Ussher and the creation of an Irish Protestant identity' in Brendan Bradshaw and Peter Roberts (eds), *British Consciousness and Identity: The Making of Britain, 1533-1707* (Cambridge 1998), pp. 185-212. 11 See above, p. 134, note 15, for different views on Molyneux's seventeenth-century sources. 12 James Tully, *An Approach to Political Philosophy: Locke in Contexts* (Cambridge 1993). 13 Morgan (ed.), *Political Ideology*, especially the editor's introduction and the essays by Nicholas Canny, David Edwards and Eugene Flanagan.

The history of Protestant Irish ancient-constitutionalism thus leads towards a recurrent feature of settler patriotism/nationalism, the reconstruction of pre-settlement legitimacy in order to lend authority to settler claims to aboriginal title. There are many specimens of this strategy; one from thirteenth-century England might be the baronial affirmation of the laws and charters of Edward the Confessor in the construction of Magna Carta.[14] In eighteenth-century Ireland, antiquarian scholars who were often Whigs and Protestants engaged in the reconstruction of Gaelic history, while in Peru the memory of the Inca became part of the creole case against the Spanish crown.[15] The former is a significant move in the construction of a pan-Irish nationalism, with hindsight on which we are bound to read the history of political thought in the Ireland of Protestant ascendancy. But if Peruvian nationalists have needed the Inca and Mexican the Aztec, United States nationalists have not until very recently (and very questionably) needed the Iroquois. They have notoriously preferred to ground the national myth in a Lockeian universalism of natural right which seems at times indifferent to history altogether, and does not have the effect of involving settlers in an aboriginal and pre-settlement history of their own country. Argument of both kinds can be found in Ireland as the eighteenth-century scene moves into crisis in the 1790s; there is a radical republicanism which offers all rights to all men. It is the contention of this paragraph, however, that the language of natural right and that of historicist nationalism may arise at the same time and from the same needs.

A second 'English' language available to Protestants was that of 'patriotism', in which a parliament composed and representative of virtuous citizens confronted an executive which might be their partner and equal in a constitution of balance, or – in a negation of the same – might be bent on corrupting them. This idiom – whose Protestant Irish authors include Molesworth and Trenchard – may be detected at one level in the language of Charles Lucas; it occurs at quite another in that of Wolfe Tone, whose conviction that the connection with England was the root of all evil might be reduced to the proposition that an executive responsible only to an English crown must invariably corrupt a parliament representative of Ireland. This would indeed be a reduction; there was a good deal more on Tone's mind, and before he reached the point of rebellion there had been a whole corpus of patriot thought, seeking to formulate the notion that the crown enjoyed two kingdoms, one in Britain and the other in Ireland, and was in fact a double crown, standing in the relation of two heads to two bodies.[16] George III liked this division of his royal substance no

---

[14] Janelle Greenberg, *The Radical Face of the Ancient Constitution* (Cambridge forthcoming).
[15] Anthony Pagden, *Spanish Imperialism and the Political Imagination* (New Haven 1990), chs. 4 and 5. [16] For seventeenth-century formulations of this concept, see David L. Smith, *A History of the Modern British Isles, 1603-1707: The Double Crown* (Oxford 1998).

better than James VI and I had, and the reasons why the double crown must fail were as much English (rather than British) as they were Irish. In Irish history, however, the failure of the Volunteers and Grattan's Parliament is a climax (not the last) in the history of the 'Protestant nation', and an aspect of this complex story is the ambiguity inherent in the term 'patriotism'. A 'patriot' might mean simply one who practised ancient virtue, but he might be one who loved his country even more than his king; and once the term was applied to a parliamentary opposition upholding virtue against the king's ministers, the question might arise whether parliament was the *patria's* sole representative and had an exclusive claim on the patriot citizen's loyalty. This had become the ultimate question in the English Civil War, and especially after the patriots of 1782 had appeared in arms as the Irish Volunteers, they had to decide whether they were raising it again. Given that the war of the American revolution was a Civil as well as a Social war,[17] there was the possibility that a dissolution of government in the empire was occurring; and the convention at Dungannon might be the assembly in arms of a people, or a *patria*, to whom power had reverted according to the Lockeian formula, and who were free to choose whether to lodge it in old hands or in new. Charlemont might find himself in the role of Washington; but this possibility was unthinkable, and the Volunteers appeared – in the setting of a war now more French than American – in the role of loyalists, offering as loyalists do (and the Confederation had done 140 years earlier) loyalty on terms defined by themselves. Instantly, however, the 'patriots' reverted to the status of loyal opposition, seeking their proper place in a balanced constitution, and must decide whether to accept or reject the executive offered them by the king. There were reasons of practice as well as of theory – the two are not opposed – why the parliamentary patriots failed to solve this problem. Those who went on to positions of rebellion had drawn the conclusion that loyalty proffered must logically be converted into loyalty withheld and refused; but they found further reasons of principle for making this refusal irreversible. These were intended to convert an Irish rebellion, as an American rebellion had been converted, from a civil war into a war of independence.

Looking ahead to this point, to the United Irishmen and the later 1790s, we reach a moment when English patterns of discourse, taken up and used by the Protestant Irish, develop into an ideology of rebellion in the name of universal rights, capable as it had been in 1776 of becoming an argument for the separation of one people from another. Like the language of American independence, that used in Ireland is distinct from that of romantic nationalism in the following century; it proposed to constitute a nation, or rather a *patria*, on the basis of

[17] For this distinction, see J.G.A. Pocock, 'The Atlantic archipelago and the war of the three kingdoms' in Brendan Bradshaw and John Morrill (eds), *The British Problem, c.1534-1707: State Formation in the Atlantic Archipelago* (London 1996), pp. 172-91.

rights common to all; but the special character of Irish history meant that it must at the same time seek to effect a union of three confessions and three ethnic groups. Here we must look beyond the Anglo-Irish thinking of 'Protestants' in the restricted ascendancy sense, and in considering other ethnic histories consider the importance of religion. We have to take account of Presbyterian participation in the rebellious process, and recognize that the Presbyterians of Ulster were a people of Scottish settlers, displaying settler characteristics in a context formed by the extension of Scottish history. The work of Ian McBride in particular[18] has made it clear that in this Scottish colony we have a case of Scotland without the Moderate ascendancy to which the term 'Scottish Enlightenment' has become peculiarly attached;[19] capable indeed of Enlightenment, but in a different and more radical sense. Without the liberalizing yet deadening hand of Moderatism – no doubt present in Ulster but not exercising ascendancy – Presbyterians inclusive of Covenanters and Secessionists tended to separate into New Light and Old Light. The former, like Rational Dissenters in England and the 'dissidence of dissent' detected by Burke in America, were capable of equating religion with the freedom of the spirit and drawing anti-trinitarian conclusions pointing to the separation of church and state. Linked to the American revolution by the massive emigration of Scots-Irish to the New World, they could see it as a war of religion[20] and at the same time advance into that radically Enlightened democracy that looked sympathetically on all religions and all revolutions. This state of mind accounts for many of the Presbyterians who came out in 1798, and so helps provide the foundation of that undenominational democratic nationalism which has remained part of the republican myth.

Old as well as New Light Presbyterians may be found taking part in both the American and the Irish rebellions, and it is a possible explanation that the Old Light continued to think in terms of a covenanted people which must be on its guard against prelacy, and so against the church's inclusion in an uncovenanted state; this would be enough to align it with some uncongenially liberal allies. It would not be a long step, however, from designating prelacy to designating Popery as the enemy; and here we have an obvious clue to the turn of mainstream Irish Presbyterianism – it is beyond the competence of this essay to determine when this turn was completed – from Protestant republicanism to Protestant loyalism. That is a nineteenth-century story, central to the history of

---

[18] Ian McBride, *Scripture Politics: Ulster Presbyterianism and Irish Rebellion in the Late Eighteenth Century* (Oxford 1998); see also his essays in Claydon and McBride (eds), *Protestantism and National Identity*, and in the present volume. [19] Richard B. Sher, *Church and University in the Scottish Enlightenment: The Moderate Literati of Edinburgh* (Princeton 1985). [20] J.C.D. Clark, *The Language of Liberty, 1660-1832: Political Discourse and Social Dynamics in the Anglo-American World* (Cambridge 1994).

the union of 1800-1; the view of the present volume seems to culminate with the United Irishmen and their attempt to construct a secular republicanism. That enterprise, and the Catholic, Presbyterian and Jacobin rebellion to which it gave rise, became part of the foundation myth of later Irish nationalism, republican and Catholic, violent and parliamentary. This essay, written from the stand-point of the 'new British history' and the 'new history of political thought', has not based itself on a nationalist foundation; it has not presupposed a shared Irish patriotism in the several strands of ethnic discourse — English and Scottish, settler and indigenous — which it has briefly explored, and if there came a time when they converged on such a nationalism, it would still tend to present nationality as a convergence, a construct rather than a primordial given. A possibility it has not considered is that there may have been a peasant nationalism that had something primordial about it; such would not be likely to surface in the rhetorical and reflective tracts and treatises making up the printed record of 'the history of political thought', though this does not mean that it did not exist.

The climactic point of this volume is reached when a 'patriot' and ancient-constitutionalist language, employed to assert (sometimes to criticize) the practice of a quasi–independent Protestant parliament, gives rise to, and is challenged by, the radical language of the United Irishmen, erecting the image of a republic founded on natural rights common to all three confessions. This language looked beyond tolerance to equality; the latter is a secular concept, and it must never be forgotten that the project of liberalization is a project of secularization. The supernatural claims of no religion are to be allowed authority in the political field, and must operate only in privacy and subjectivity; almost all liberals aim to reduce the religions they tolerate to something less than those who profess them may affirm them to be. There were tensions, accordingly, between the liberal, covenanting and (in due course) evangelical components of Irish Presbyterianism, and between the first and third of these in the texture of Church of Ireland Protestantism. A further, and in Irish history all-important, set of tensions occurred when governmental, patriot and United thinking severally confronted the problem of the Catholic majority. Side by side with the Protestant resolution to maintain 'ascendancy' — meaning here those penal structures which emancipation would mitigate or dissolve — the last third of the eighteenth century, the period roughly defined by the dissolution of the Jesuits and the French Revolution, saw strong tendencies for Enlightenment and Catholicism to approach an accommodation. It was believed that the church had accepted its place within civil society, and the Catholic hierarchy was disposed to accept the authority of civil government even when exercised by non-Catholics. In these circumstances arose the questions of what the British and Irish regimes might do to tolerate and even support the Catholic confession, and what the hierarchy and the laity of that confession might feel able to accept by way of support, authority and even dependence. A sustained intolerance might seem a sin against both Enlightenment and the regime which practised the latter, and here the views of that restless and unmanageable man Edmund Burke might be brought into the story. His indictments of Protestant ascendancy, which have been thought residually crypto-Catholic, may in fact be whiggishly Enlightened and at the same time proto-evangelical.

The executive, the ascendancy and the radical republicans all had their own attitudes towards the place of Catholics under civil government, and Enlightened elements are not absent even from thinking under the second heading. As for the third, the more radical and the more republican it became, the more it resembled the revolutionary generosity of France; Catholics were seen as emancipating themselves from papalism and priestcraft, ready to assume their station under the Civil Constitution of the Clergy. Wolfe Tone, one feels, was a good deal closer to the Abbé Gregoire than he ever was to Archbishop Troy. It was not clear that the generous sentiments of Enlightenment were acceptable to Catholics or that they did not imply drastic changes in their ecclesiology and even theology; and the higher and lower clergy, the clergy and laity among Catholics, were by no means of one mind on these matters. The present volume has been a study of Irish Protestant thought, and has not explored in depth the responses, or the independent pursuits, of Catholic thinking about church and state in the eighteenth century. It may be added that the 'new British history', so many of whose departure points lie in the sixteenth century, is under a temptation to define itself in terms that exclude or marginalize the history of Catholicism. That history may be treated as one of response to Protestant or Enlightened or British history, or it may be treated as autonomous, perceiving, setting and resolving its own problems. A 'Catholic history' and an 'Irish history', it is further apparent, may come into being and contextualize one another. If the 'patriotism' of eighteenth-century Irish Protestants faded away, or was transformed into parliamentary nationalism, under the union; if Presbyterian radicalism resisted the romantic nationalism of Davis and Mitchel, and took a course of its own; there is a history of how Catholicism, nationalism and republicanism interacted with one another in and beyond the history of Ireland. The 'new British history', furnishing the standpoint from which this essay has been written, is inherently self-questioning, self-problematizing and self-enlarging; it need not hesitate before providing itself with this new agenda.

Notes on contributors

S.J. CONNOLLY is Professor of Irish History at Queen's University, Belfast.

JACQUELINE HILL is Senior Lecturer in the department of Modern History at NUI Maynooth.

ROBERT MAHONY is Associate Professor of English at the Catholic University of America.

PATRICK KELLY is Fellow and Senior Lecturer in Modern History at Trinity College, Dublin

IAN McBRIDE is a Lecturer in Early Modern History at the University of Durham.

JAMES KELLY is head of the History department at St Patrick's College, Drumcondra, Dublin.

J.G.A. POCOCK is Professor emeritus of History at the Johns Hopkins University, Baltimore.

Index

Agar, Charles, abp of Cashel (C of I) 193
American Revolution 15, 21, 78, 144, 146, 159
ancien régime 18, 66, 160
ancient constitution 15, 25, 188, 225-6
Arbuckle, James 22
Archdall, Nicholas 57
aristocracy 70-1
army 19-20, 152

Belfast Harp Festival 169
Berkeley, George 19; on Catholics 189-90; economic thought 105, 107, 112, 114, 115, 120, 121, 128-9; 'Passive Obedience' 43-5, 49, 52; *Querist* 123-6, 127
Bindon, David 105, 107, 108, 115, 116, 118, 121
Birch, Thomas Ledlie 163
Blackstone, Sir William 144, 157, 162
'body politic' 65, 141
Bolton, Theophilus, abp of Cashel (C of I) 59, 108
Bonnell, James 37
Boulter, Hugh, abp of Armagh (C of I), 116, 118, 119
Brooke, Henry 14, 15, 58, 146
Browne, Sir John 106, 108, 113, 114, 115, 116-17, 118, 122
Burke, Edmund 11, 81, 161, 205, 230
Burlamaqui, Jean-Jacques 13
Burnet, Gilbert 34
Butler, Edmund 194

Catholics: threat posed by 90-5, 189-92; Catholic Relief Acts 80, 194-5, 200-1, 209-10; condition of 84-6; political disabilities of 71, 81, 92-4, 191-2; political thought of 22-5; toleration for 159, 166-7, 178, 193, 229-30
Caulfield, James, bp of Ferns (RC) 216
Charlemont, James Caulfield, 1st earl of 145, 157, 164, 195, 227
Charles I, commemoration of 42, 48, 59
'Children's Catechism' 177
Church of Ireland 132; attacks on and defence of 186, 198-204; and corporatism 67-9;
Convocation 66, 69-70, 93; and Revolution of 1688 29-38, 51, 69
civic humanism: *see* republicanism
Clayton, Robert, bp of Killala, later Cork (C of I) 59, 108
Cleaver, Euseby, abp of Dublin (C of I), 199
colonies 88-9
commonwealthmen: *see* Whigs
Conolly, William 119
'constitution of 1782' 130, 145, 152-3, 157-8, 166
Cooper, Austin 197
Coppinger, William, bp Cloyne and Ross (RC) 24
corporatism 18, 65 and chap. 3 passim
Cox, Sir Richard [jr] 147, 149, 152, 153, 154, 156, 188
Cox, Sir Richard 40-2, 49, 148
Cromwell, Oliver 19, 45, 52, 54, 91
Curry, John 24

Davey, Samuel 60
Declaratory Act 96, 157
Denmark 14, 58

Dickson, William Steel 14, 163
Dobbs, Arthur 105, 107, 108, 113, 114-15, 119, 129
Dodwell, Henry 38
Domville, Sir William 134
Dopping, Anthony, bp of Meath (C of I) 133
double crown 155-8, 159, 226-7
Drennan, Thomas 22
Drennan, William 56, 61, 144-6, 161-2, 168, 181
Dublin, corporation of 56, 72-8, 207-9
Duigenan, Revd Patrick 200-1, 212-13, 215
Dundas, Henry 207
Dungannon, Convention at 163, 168

Emmet, Thomas Addis 173, 174, 176, 183
Enlightenment 21, 22, 24, 68, 106
Essex, Arthur Capel, earl of 75
Exclusion Crisis 37-8, 60

Fitzgibbon, John, earl of Clare 196, 209-10, 213-14
Flood, Henry 61, 139, 195-7
Foster, John 199, 210
French Revolution 21, 159, 163, 166, 168

Gaelic revival 20, 169-71
Gothic constitution 14, 58, 137, 140
Grattan, Henry 15, 20, 79, 145, 148, 157, 164, 214-15; on Catholic question 196, 197, 207; on Irish rights 130, 139-40, 143-4, 155; on Revolution of 1688 60-1
Grattan, Henry jr. 148
Grotius, Hugo 13
guilds 72-4, 208

Harrington, James 19
Harris, Walter 192

Henry II 17, 76, 87, 135, 138, 139, 149, 150, 155, 188
Higgins, Revd Francis 55-6
Hottman, François 14
Hutcheson, Francis 11, 12, 13, 22
Hutchinson, Francis, bp of Down (C of I), 108

Jackson, Richard 148
Jacobite Parliament (1689) 134-5, 166
jacobitism 23, 44, 51, 54, 56, 95, 148
James II 27-8, 30-3, 35, 53
Jebb, Frederick 148, 151, 152-3, 154
John, Prince, as Lord of Ireland 87, 135-6, 139, 149
Jones, William Todd 166-7

Kells, John 211-12
Kelly, Patrick 15-16, 28, 60
Keogh, John 177-8
Kildare, William Fitzgerald, marquis of 12
King, William, archbp of Dublin (C of I) 13, 33, 44, 48, 93, 107, 121
Knox, George 176
Knox, William 149-51, 154

landlords and land system 85, 90, 101-2, 120, 128
Lawrence, Richard 83-4
Leerssen, Joep 18, 169
legislative independence: *see* 'constitution of 1782'
Leighton, Sir Ellis 74
Leslie, Charles 34
Leslie, John 61-2
Locke, John 14, 16, 35, 45, 47, 60, 61, 68, 77, 117, 127, 136-7, 162, 167
Lucas, Charles 15, 16, 56, 57, 68, 130, 135, 147; on Catholic question 18, 73, 143, 193; on Irish rights 76, 138, 141-3

Index

Macartney, George 148, 152, 153
McCormack, W.J. 204-6, 208
McDowell, R.B. 11, 169, 173
MacGeoghegan, James 23
MacLaine, Alexander 57
McNally, Patrick 17, 131-2
MacNeven, William James 173, 183
McTier, Martha 168, 176
Machiavelli, Nicolò 19
Maculla, James 107
Madden, Samuel 105, 107, 120, 121, 127, 128, 129
magna carta 76, 139, 149
Maple, William 107
Mason, John Monck 154
Maurice, Revd Edward 191
Maxwell, Henry 19, 88-9
Miller, David 21
Modus Tenendi Parliamentum 133-4, 136, 138, 139
Molesworth, Robert, 1st viscount 13, 14, 18, 20, 58-9, 146
Molyneux, William 12, 13, 17, 130, 131, 149, 155, 187-8, 225; *Case of Ireland ... Stated* 71-2, 135-7, 140, 143; debt to seventeenth-century predecessors 134; and Locke 47, 136
money and currency 110-12, 115-19, 124-5
money bills 19, 56, 132, 147, 148, 149, 152
Montesquieu, Charles de Secondat, baron de 13
Musgrave, Sir Richard 215-19

Nary, Revd Cornelius 23-4
National Bank controversy 111, 123, 125-6
nationalism and national identity 16-17, 20, 98, 224-5, 230
New Rules 75-6, 77, 193
Newton, Isaac 116
non-jurors 34, 38, 51, 69
Northern Star 163, 167, 171, 172, 174

oaths: of allegiance 30-1; of abjuration 23, 45-6; of supremacy 67
O'Beirne, Thomas Lewis, bp of Ossory (C of I) 214
O'Brien, Gerard 130-2
O'Connor, Arthur 168, 183
O'Conor, Charles 24
O'Doherty, Charles, bp of Derry (RC) 62
Ogle, George 195, 196, 197, 199
O'Gorman, Nicholas Purcell 62-3
O'Leary, Revd Arthur 196
O'More, Rory 130-1
O'Mullan, Cornelius 62-3
Orange order 82, 180

Paddy's Resource 170, 177, 182
Paine, Thomas 162, 165, 167, 174, 176, 178-9
parliament 53-4, 66, 70-2, 76, 79-80, 132, 142-3, 160
passive obedience 30-2, 33-4, 43-5, 52, 55, 56, 59
patriotism 18, 130-58, 171-2, 224, 226-7, 230
penal laws: see Catholics
Perceval, John, earl of Egmont 108
Peterborough, Charles Mordaunt, 3rd earl 87, 89, 90
Petty, Sir William 83, 113, 115, 121
Plunkett, Nicholas 116, 120
Plunkett, William 108
political thought, study of 25-6, 159-61, 222
Porter, James 163, 175, 177, 179
Pownall, Thomas 156
Poynings' Law 73, 134, 138, 157
Presbyterians 223-4, 228-9; and Catholics 166; legal position 67, 80, 94-5, 203; and radicalism 21-2, 57, 163, 168, 176, 177-8, 181, 184
Prior, Thomas 105, 107, 108, 113, 114, 115, 116, 118, 120, 129

'Protestant ascendancy' 204-6, 207-8
'Protestant interest' 187, 204-5
Pufendorf, Samuel von 13

quarterage 72-3, 193
real Whigs: *see* Whigs
 rebellion of 1641 59, 90, 101, 214;
  commemoration of 91-2, 190
Regency crisis 157-8
republicanism 18-20, 76, 81-2, 159-84
Revolution of 1688 15-16, 27-8 and
 chap. 2 passim, 142, 144, 149, 188,
 211, n. 97
'Revolution Principles' 16, 46, 52, 53-4, 168
Richardson, Revd John 93
Rightboys 198-9, 206
Robertson, John 106
Rowan, Archbald Hamilton 161
Russell, Thomas 174, 181

Sacheverell, Henry 53, 54, 57
Sampson, William 179-80
Sheridan, Charles Francis 151-2, 152-3, 154, 154-5, 157, 214
Sidney, Algernon 19, 61
Skelton, Philip 15
Smith, John 22
Smyth, James 17, 174
sole right 132, 138-9, 148, 153
Stokes, Whitley 182
Stoughton, William 48-9, 53
Swift, Jonathan 11, 14, 19, 20, 105, 106, 107, 113, 117, 118, 119, 130, 131; on Catholics 85-6, 94; on consumption and dependence, chap 4; on Presbyterians 94-5; on the Revolution 45-7; *Drapier's Letters* 96-8, 137-8, 142-3; *Proposal for the Universal Use of Irish Manufacture* 84-5, 96, 106; *Modest Proposal* 99-103, 122
Synge, Edward, abp of Tuam (C of I), 93, 108, 189
Synge, Edward, bp of Clonfert (C of I) 93-4
Synge, Samuel, dean of Kildare (C of I) 42, 48, 50

Tandy, James Napper 161
Temple, Sir John 90, 190-1, 215
test act 67, 80, 95
Thucydides 88
Thuente, Mary Helen 169-70, 180-1
Tisdall, William 52
tithes 69, 198-203
Toland, John 11, 19
Tone, T.W. 130-1, 161, 163, 165, 166, 172, 230
Tory politics 16, 48-9, 51-6
Townshend, George, 1st marquis 132, 148
Trinity College, Dublin 53-4, 67, 81, 107, 109, 120
Troy, John Thomas, archbp of Dublin (RC) 24-5, 217

union, act of 157-8
United Irishmen 21-2, 80, 82, 159-84, esp 164-6, 227

Vesey, John 39-40, 49-50
Volunteers 20, 22, 80, 144, 198

Walpole, Sir Robert 97, 99, 118
Webb, Daniel 108, 115
Wetenhall, Edward, bp of Cork and Ross (C of I), 29-33, 42, 92
Whig politics 16, 48-9, 51-6, 61-2, 103; real Whigs/commonwealthmen 18, 59, 168, 183, 188; Whig Club 162, 164-5
William III 17-8, 35, 61-3, 185-6
Winder, John 51, 53
Wood's Halfpence 107, 113, 116, 97-9, 140
Woodward, Richard, bp of Cloyne (C of I) 25, 70, 78-9, 201-4

Young, Revd Edward 190